The Peoples of Bali

The Peoples of South-East Asia and the Pacific

General Editors
Peter Bellwood and Ian Glover

Each book in this series will be devoted to a people (or group of associated peoples) from the vast area of the world extending from Hawaii in the north to Tasmania in the south and from Fiji in the east to Cambodia in the west. The books, written by historians, anthropologists and archaeologists from all over the world, will be both scholarly and accessible. In many cases the volumes will be the only available account of their subject.

Already published
The People of Bali
Angela Hobart, Urs Ramseyer and Albert Leemann

The Khmers
Ian Mabbett and David Chandler

The Peoples of Borneo
Victor T. King

The Bugis
Christian Pelras

In preparation

The Maoris
Atholl Anderson

The Lapita People
Patrick Kirch

The Melanesians
Matthew Spriggs

The Peoples of the Lesser Sundas
James L. Fox

The Malays
A. C. Milner and Jane Drakard

The Fijians
Nicholas Thomas and Victoria Luker

The Peoples of Bali

Angela Hobart, Urs Ramseyer and
Albert Leemann

Copyright © Angela Hobart, Urs Ramseyer and Albert Leemann 1996

The right of Angela Hobart, Urs Ramseyer and Albert Leemann to be identified as authors of this work has been asserted in accordance with the Copyright, Designs and Patents Act 1988.

First published 1996

2 4 6 8 10 9 7 5 3 1

Blackwell Publishers Ltd
108 Cowley Road
Oxford OX4 1JF
UK

Blackwell Publishers Inc.
238 Main Street
Cambridge, Massachusetts 02142
USA

British Library Cataloguing in Publication Data

A CIP catalogue record for this book is available from the British Library.

Library of Congress Cataloging-in-Publication Data

Hobart, Angela.
The people of Bali / Angela Hobart, Urs Ramseyer, Albert Leemann.
p. cm. — (Peoples of South-East Asia and the Pacific)
Includes bibliographical references and index.
ISBN 0–631–17687–X
1. Bali Island (Indonesia) I. Ramseyer, Urs. II. Leemann, Albert.
III. Title. IV. Series.
DS647.B2H58 1996   95–51998
959.8′6—dc20   CIP

Typeset in 11 on 12½ pt Sabon by
Pure Tech India Ltd, Pondicherry

Printed in Great Britain by Hartnolls Limited, Bodmin, Cornwall
This book is printed on acid-free paper

Contents

Plates

Figures

Maps

Acknowledgements

The authors wish to thank Mrs Eileen Walliser-Schwarzbart and Dr Cheri Ragaz-Wastell for translating the chapters by Urs Ramseyer and Albert Leemann.

They also wish to thank the following for permission to reproduce several maps and figures: S. Wälty for figure 1.1 and map 5; N. Backhaus for map 2; and Professor C. Geertz, for figure 4.2.

Note about the Authors

Angela Hobart lectures at University of London Goldsmiths' College on Anthropology of Art and Intercultural Therapy. Her PhD from the School of Oriental and African Studies was on the performing arts of Bali, with special reference to shadow theatre. She is also Honorary Research Fellow in the Anthropology Department at University College, London. She has travelled widely in south-east Asia and has made frequent study trips to Bali. Her present research, which is under the auspices of the Indonesian Academy of Science, is on healing and ritual performances in Bali that are considered beneficial and protective in their effect. She has written *Dancing Shadows of Bali: Theatre and Myth* (1987).

Albert Leemann is Emeritus Professor at the University of Zurich where he taught human geography. His post-doctoral work was on the cosmology of the Balinese in relation to their culture and geography (1976). Since 1966 he has visited Indonesia regularly, in particular Bali. His research, which is in co-operation with the Indonesian Academy of Science, focuses on the socio-cultural and socio-economic dynamics of Bali and Lombok. He was granted the Charter of Merit by the Department of Social Affairs of the Republic of Indonesia for his work on the poor farmers in the province of Nusa Tenggara Barat. He was also commissioned by the Ministry of Public Works for the assessment of the water association which is part of the integrated irrigation project in south-east Sulawesi. He has written *Bali: Insel der Gotter* (1979).

Urs Ramseyer is Curator of the Indonesian Department at the Museum of Ethnology in Basel, Switzerland. His post-doctoral work focused on the ethno-musicology and sociology of Tenganan Pegeringsingan, Bali. He has made frequent trips to Indonesia. His studies from 1972 onwards have been concerned with Balinese art and culture, with special reference to their historical and religious background. He has arranged exhibitions at the Museum, accompanied by catalogues, on rice cultivation, dance, music, textiles and traditional as well as contemporary paintings of Bali. His main publications are *The Art and Culture of Bali* (1977) and, together with two other scholars, *Balinese Textiles* (1991).

1

The Land and its People

The life-world of the Indonesian comprises the land *and* the sea. Nothing could express this better than the Indonesian conception of 'native country': *tanah air kita* ('Our Land and Water'). A British scholar, James Richardson Logan (at that time resident in Singapore), coined the word 'Indonesia' in 1850. The term derived from the Greek words '*nesoi*' (islands) and '*indos*' (the Indian),[1] as a designation for the immense chain of islands which, over an east–west extension of a good eighth of the circumference of the equator, joins the Eurasian land mass with the Australian continent. As the successor state of the Netherlands East Indies colonial empire, the Republic of Indonesia comprises 13,677 islands, of which scarcely a quarter are populated. Their dimensions extend from tiny coral reefs and cliffs to the major portions of the second and third largest islands of the world: New Guinea (785,000 km²) and Borneo (736,500 km²). Even Sumatra (473,660 km²) possesses twice the area of Great Britain.[2] Measured in terms of number of inhabitants, Indonesia is, after China, India and the USA, the fourth most highly populated country in the world.

In every respect, Indonesia's dimensions exceed those of its neighbouring states, as 42 per cent of the land area of South-East Asia is taken up by Indonesia and 43 per cent of all its inhabitants live there (1992: 195 million people on a land area of 2,027 million km²). In addition, Indonesia claims 3,166 million km² of territorial waters.[3] The insular position on both sides of the equator (6° 08′ N to 11° 15′ S) determines to a great extent the maritime-influenced tropical cli-

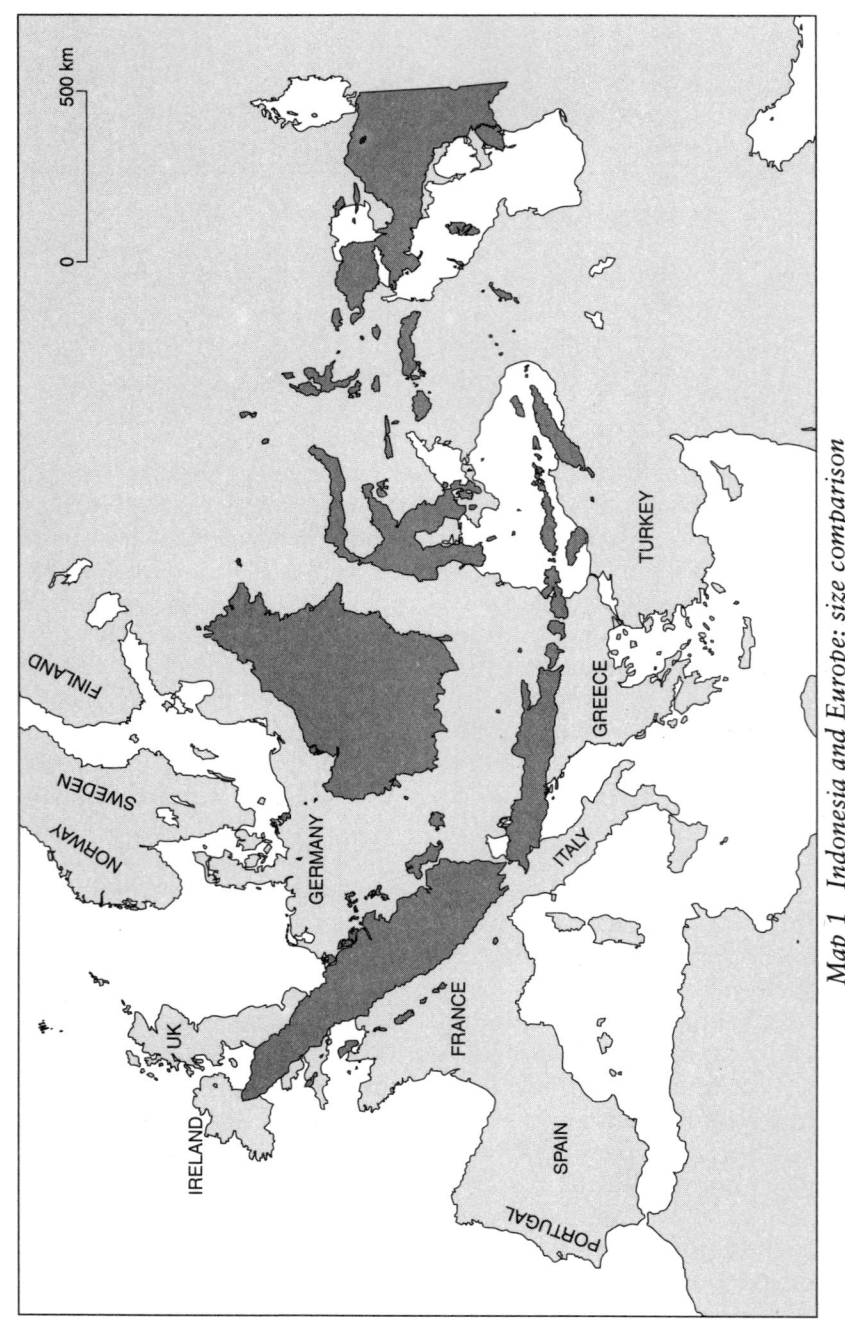

Map 1 Indonesia and Europe: size comparison

mate of the island arc, which is surrounded by the Indian and Pacific oceans and their adjacent seas.

As the distances between islands are relatively small (many isles being within sight of others), the sea functions as a binding rather than a separating factor. How much more laborious it is to negotiate landlocked areas with tropical rain forests, swamps and mountains![4] History furnishes evidence of Indonesia's openness to foreign influence, but also of Indonesia's role as a source of influence on mainland Asia and the islands lying outside the contemporary state territory. Since the dawn of history, members of foreign populations have settled in Indonesia (see chapter 2, pp. 16–18). On the other hand, Indonesians settled in Madagascar, for example, set up trading posts in Sri Lanka and Hadramaut and cultivated good relations with south Thailand and the Khmer empire of Angkor.

Geographically, the Indonesian Archipelago is grouped into four regions:

- the Greater Sunda Islands, comprising Sumatra, Java, Madura, Borneo and Sulawesi;
- the Lesser Sunda Islands, including the islands from Bali to Timor (Bali, Lombok, Sumbawa, Sumba, Flores, Alor, Sawu, Roti, Timor et al.);
- the Moluccas, comprising all those islands between Irian Jaya and Sulawesi (Halmahera, Ternate, Tidore, Buru, Seram, Ambon, Banda et al.);
- the western part of New Guinea with its surrounding islands.

It is not the location but the extreme differences in population density that is the criterion for the dichotomous principle of classification of C. Geertz. He differentiates between the so-called Inner Islands and Outer Islands. The Inner Islands (Java with the exception of the south-west, Madura, south Bali and west Lombok) are marked by high population densities and therefore scarcity of land, whilst low population densities and large land resources are characteristic of the Outer Islands.[5] The great differences in population density are partly reflections of great variations in soil fertility (volcanic versus acid and leached non-volcanic soils) and the consequent agricultural systems (wet-rice versus shifting cultivation). Since the Dutch colonial period attempts have been made to reduce these disparities through government-led and private transmigration programmes.

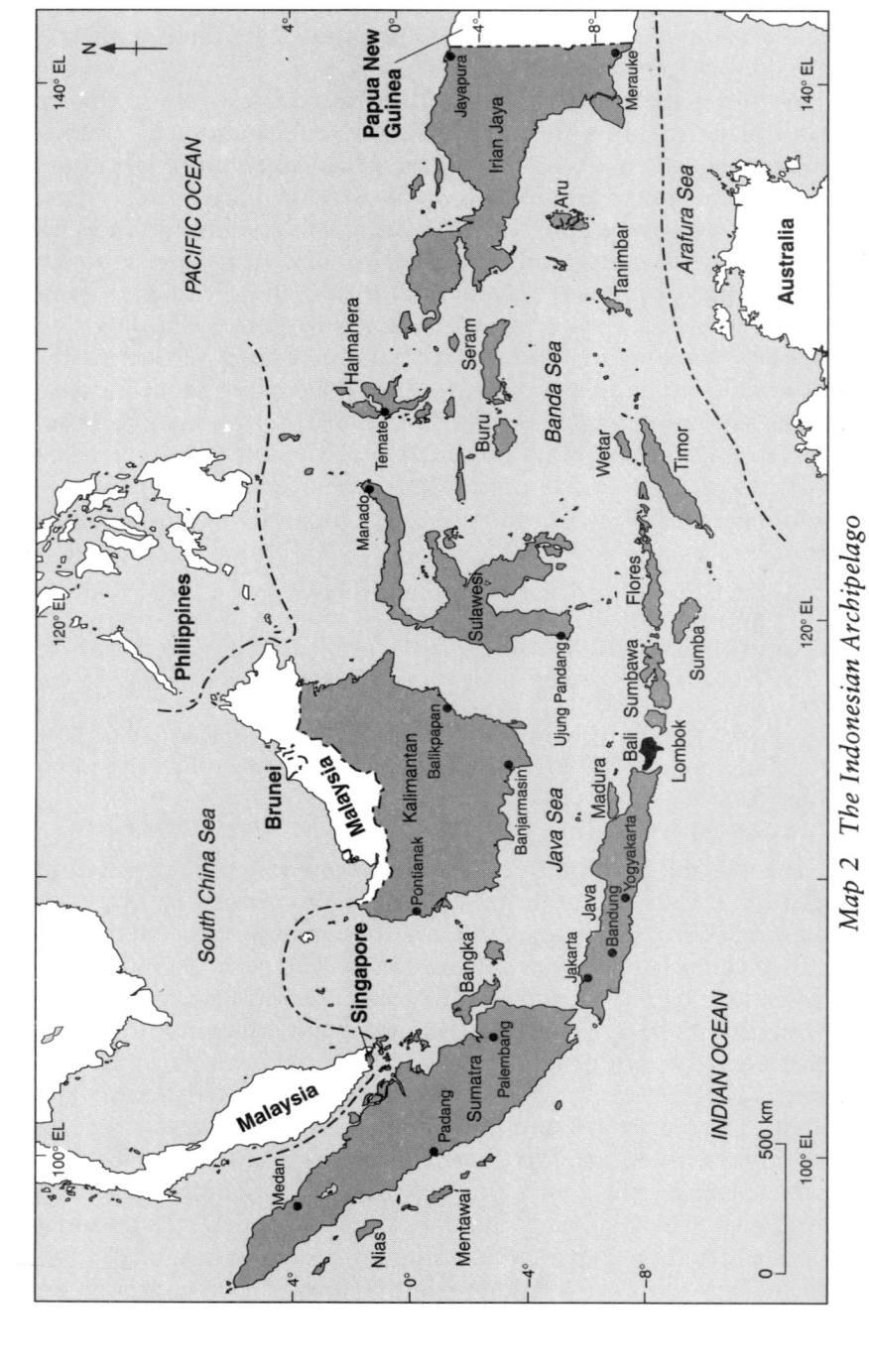

Map 2 *The Indonesian Archipelago*

Even though the last census to include ethnic factors (1930) lists only 61 ethnic groups, anthropologists distinguish between over 360 groups, not including the peoples of Irian Jaya who represent an extremely diversified ethnic-cultural spectrum. Insular dispersal and the clearly marked isolation of various regions is expressed through the approximately 250 regional languages, all of which (west of Halmahera, Timor and Pantar) belong to the Austronesian language group. Non-Austronesian languages are spoken only in Halmahera, Timor, Alor, Pantar and in most of New Guinea (where Austronesian languages are spoken only in coastal pockets). The most widely spread Indonesian regional languages (which are not simply dialects) include Javanese (spoken by 60 million people), Sundanese (15 million) and Madurese (eight million). Balinese is spoken by about three million.[6] Balinese (like Javanese) belongs to the group of Indonesian regional languages with various language levels. According to the social stratum to which one belongs, the person spoken to or about can provoke 'vulgar' (*kasar*), 'ordinary' (*lumbrah*), 'modestly respectful' (*alus madia*) or 'respectful' (*alus singgih*) modes of expression from one and the same speaker.[7]

In the last few years, however, a relaxation of the once-binding language rules has been observed. For inter-Balinese communication, an 'average Balinese' is increasingly being used. The national language, Bahasa Indonesia (which is first learnt in primary school), is occasionally spoken by Balinese amongst themselves. On the one hand, this is due to the government-backed process of unification; on the other hand, younger Balinese in particular find it liberating to use the largely status-neutral Bahasa Indonesia in certain social situations. Based on the Malayan spoken in the Malay Peninsula, the Riau Archipelago and Central Sumatra, Bahasa Indonesia contains additional elements from other languages, above all Javanese and Sundanese. Indian influence from the period of the earliest centuries AD is manifest in Sanskrit words. Arabic expressions have been included as a result of Islamization from the late thirteenth century onwards and Arab trade activities in coastal cities. In the colonial era (from the sixteenth century) Portuguese and later Dutch loan-words were incorporated, whilst in contemporary times the worldwide trend to take on Anglicisms has also been noticeable in Indonesian.[8]

Administrative Structure

Administratively, the Republic of Indonesia is subdivided into 27 provinces whose area and number of inhabitants vary greatly. The province with the largest area, Irian Jaya (421,981 km²), was populated by only 1.5 million people in 1990 (average population density: four inhabitants per km²). Accordingly, only 1.4 per cent of all the inhabitants of Indonesia live on this fifth of the total land area. Apart from two special regions with administrative province character

Plate 1   Balinese mother and infant, after ritual purification

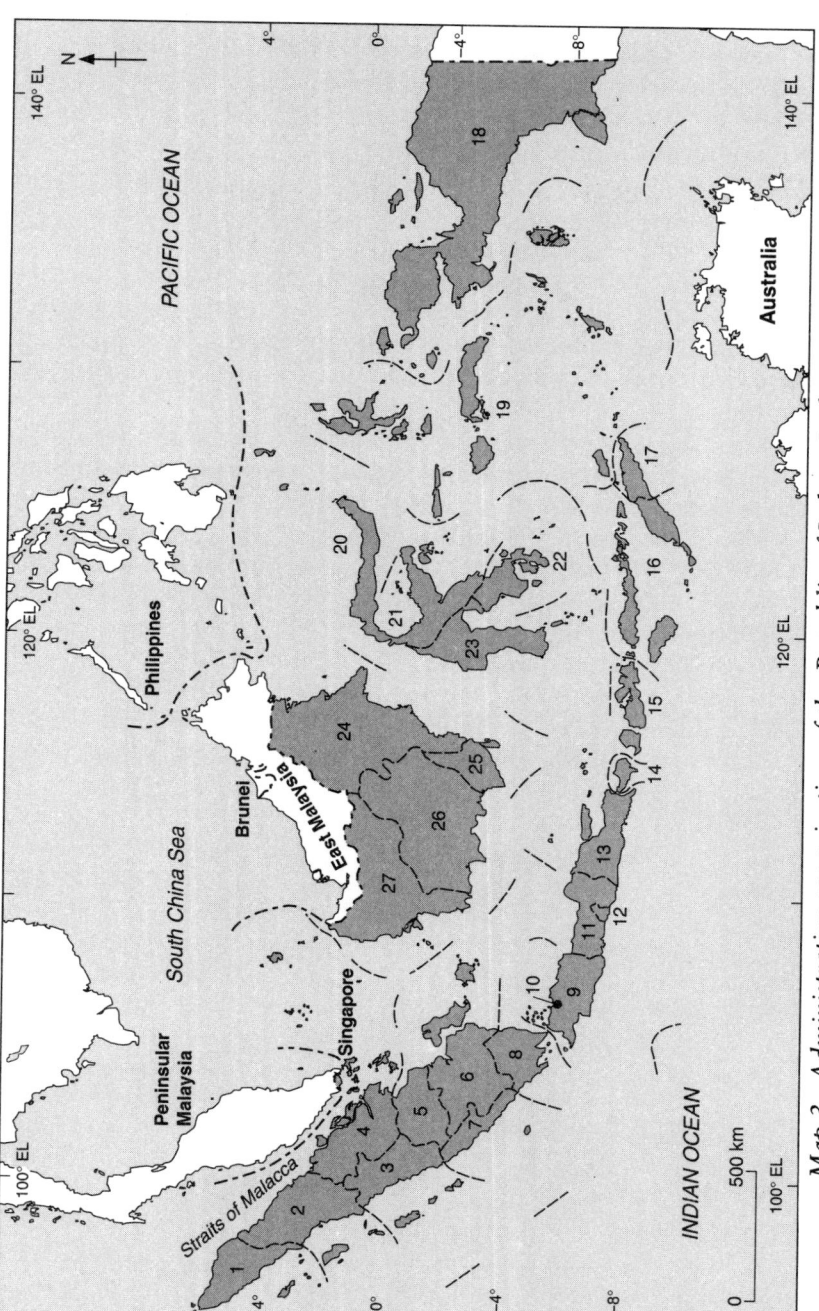

Map 3 Administrative organization of the Republic of Indonesia, by provinces

(Daerah Khusus Ibukota Jakarta: 590 km², into which eight million people are crowded, and Daerah Istimewa Yogyakarta: 3,169 km²), Bali is (in area) the smallest 'real' province of the Republic of Indonesia. It encompasses 5,633 km² and at the end of 1990 had a population of 2,656,649 million people (average density: 469 inhabitants per km²). This means that 1.44 per cent of the total population of Indonesia lives on less than 0.3 per cent of the area of the country. Nevertheless, the small island of Bali was and is, according to surveys in western countries, better known than Indonesia. One goal of this book is to explain why the name of Bali has attained this worldwide reputation.

Of all the Lesser Sunda Islands Bali lies furthest to the west. It is separated from the neighbouring island of Java by the shallow, 2.5 km-wide Straits of Bali and from the island of Lombok by the 33 km-wide Lombok Straits. The island stretches from 114° 25′ 53″ E to 115° 42′ 40″ E (maximum east–west extent: 142 km) and from 8° 03′ 40″ S to 8° 50′ 48″ S (maximum north–south extent: 87 km).

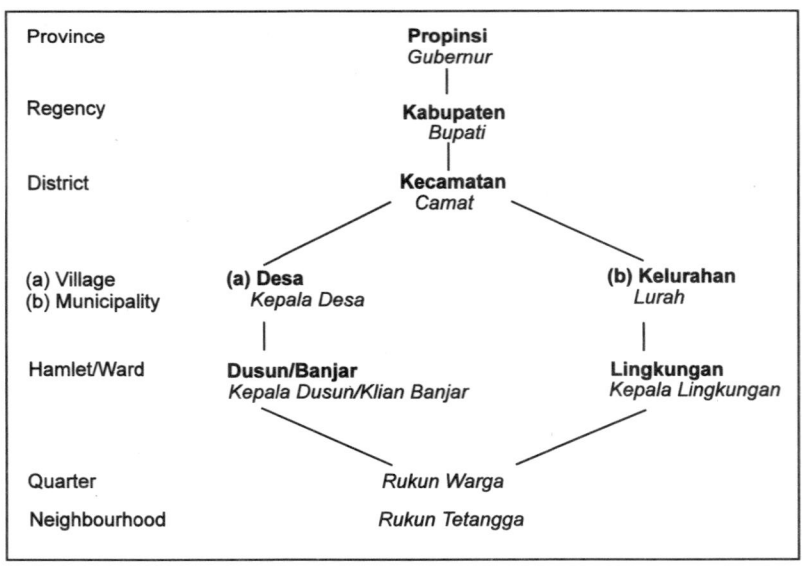

Figure 1.1   Administrative hierarchy of an Indonesian province[9]

Table 1.1   Administrative organization of the Province of Bali, 1990

Kabupaten	Area (km²)	Inhabitants	Capital city of Kabupaten	No. of Kecamatan
Jembrana	841.80	207,234	Negara	4
Tabanan	839.33	349,115	Tabanan	8
Badung	542.50	586,888	Denpasar[a]	7
Gianyar	368.00	321,578	Gianyar	7
Klungkung	315.00	154,563	Klungkung[b]	4
Bangli	520.81	173,065	Bangli	4
Karangasem	839.54	339,545	Amlapura	8
Buleleng	1,365.88	524,661	Singaraja	9
Total	5,632.86	2,656,649		51

Notes

[a] Also serves as capital city of the Province.

[b] A few years ago, the name of the town of Klungkung was officially changed to Asmarapura.

Sources: Kantor Statistik Propinsi Bali, *Statistik Bali–Statistical Year Book of Bali, 1989* (Denpasar, 1990), pp. 2–4, 20, 31; Kantor Statistik Propinsi Bali, *Statistik Bali–Statistical Year Book of Bali, 1990* (Denpasar, 1991), p. 31; Kantor Statistik Bali, *Buku Saku, Statistik Bali–Statistical Pocketbook of Bali, 1988* (Denpasar, 1989), p. 12.

The borders of the contemporary regencies correspond largely with those of the earlier small Balinese kingdoms. One exception is Mengwi, which was divided amongst the three kingdoms of Gianyar, Tabanan and Badung in 1891 as a result of armed conflicts. In terms of the natural topography, the rivers have cut deep gorges into the soft sediments of the mountain slopes. They form the natural borders of the former kingdoms. Communication and transport were easier to effectuate from the coast to the mountains than parallel to the main mountain range. Therefore the natural hinterland of the lowland centres lies upstream.

Physical Geography

'Where volcanoes rise up and rivers run down their flanks, where sun and moon shine, there is also God, who blesses man.' This introduction to the classical text Tantu Pagelaran

expresses not only the bond and contentment of the Balinese
with their religion and their environment, but also refers to the
volcanic character of the mountainous island. The chain of
mountains which runs from west to east as a part of the
Sunda-Banda Arc forms the watershed. The scarp is asymme-
trical. On the steep north flank, short rivers run in deep gorges
towards the coast and, with the exception of the only two big
alluvial plains of Singaraja and Seririt, discharge directly into
the sea. Extensive areas of the north coast are sparsely populated in comparison and can only be cultivated by dry-land
agriculture. Accordingly, the harvests here are small, as is the
income of the population dependent on agriculture. The case
is different for the central-south part of the island, where the
rivers in their upper and middle course have cut deep canyons
in the soft volcanic ash and sandstone but in their lower
course have deposited large alluvial plains. The terraced,
lower-slope zones with their ingenious irrigation systems for
wet-rice agriculture and the coastal fringe with its coconut
palm groves make up not only the densely populated econ-

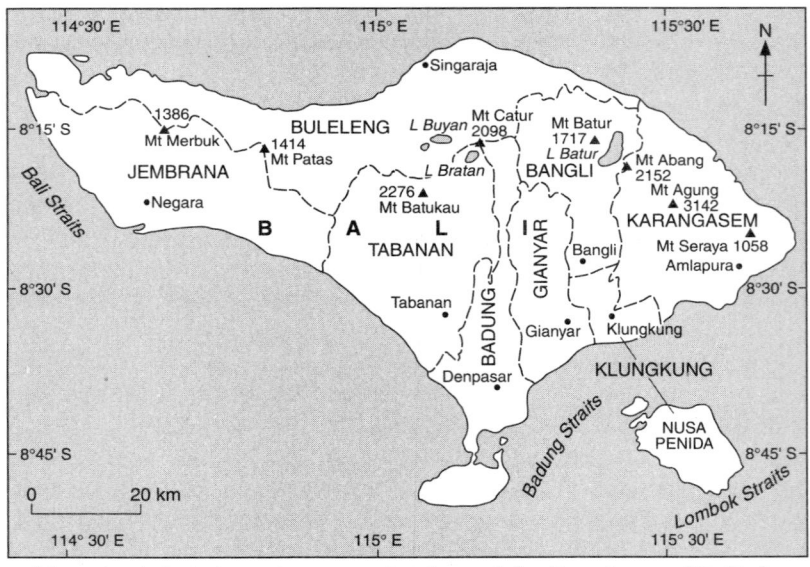

*Map 4   Administrative organization of the Province of Bali, by
regencies*

omic core zone of Bali but also the 'centre of Balinese civilization'. The Bukit Pecatu Peninsula is joined to the main island
in the south by a narrow landbridge. As with the island of
Penida, situated to the east and also part of the province of
Bali, Bukit Pecatu is a raised limestone tableland which in the
tropical monsoon climate is intensively weathered by chemical
erosion and, despite generous rainfall during the summer
rainy season, shows no surface run-off. On the south coast of
the peninsula, dominated by the Uluwatu Temple, an 80-
metre-high cliff falls vertically to the sea.

In west Bali, where the mountains are older than in the
eastern part of the island, fluvial erosion has worn down the
relief more extensively. West Bali stands out from the edaphi-
cally more favourable zones of central south Bali because of
its desolate appearance and lower population density. Decidu-
ous bushes and shrubs extend over a wide hilly area which is
the habitat of wild pigs and game. The volcanic character
expresses itself here in numerous warm-water springs,
amongst other things. The chain of hills runs toward the east
into the central mountainous country where the highest peak,
the Gunung Batukau, reaches 2,276 m. Three shallow mountain lakes without outlets – Danau Bratan (3.70 km²), Danau
Buyan (3.60 km²) and Danau Tamblingan (1.10 km²) – are set
in the volcanic landscape which is covered with tropical rain
forest. In years of heavy monsoon rainfall, they overflow and
flood settlements and cultivated areas close by. Thus in 1990,
for example, the platform of the temple of Ulun Danu on Lake
Bratan lay deep under water, so that the temple festival had to
be cancelled and in its place an *upacara matur piuning* – a
ritual proclamation to God that the great temple feast could
not take place – had to be performed.[10]

A pass divides the mountainous central country from the
eastern mountain region, where the Gunung Agung ('big
mountain') rises to 3,142 m – the highest peak on the island of
Bali. On the eastern end of the island, the flanks of the
Gunung Seraya (1,058 m) fall steeply to the sea. The impressive beauty of the double caldera of the Gunung Batur is
well known to the island's many visitors. Measuring
10 km × 13.8 km, it is one of the biggest calderas in the world.
Within the basin-like depression a second subsidence has oc-

curred which has begun to cut into the older, higher floor of the caldera and the Abang volcano (2,152 m) on the rim. In the deepest area of subsidence, water has accumulated in Lake Batur (17.19 km²). The younger stratovolcano, Gunung Batur (1,717 m), on whose flanks there are active secondary craters, dominates the centre of the depression. Numerous eruptions confirm that the volcanoes Batur and Abang are active. Twice this century, the village of Batur, which was originally on the west side of Lake Batur, has been buried under streams of lava, forcing the people who managed to escape this natural catastrophe to give up their endangered habitation and move their village to the safer, higher rim.

As the point of highest elevation, Gunung Agung (3,142 m) was marked 'Piek van Bali' on Dutch maps. In the conceptual world of the island inhabitants, God lives on, or rather just above, the tip of the volcano. The Mother Temple of Bali – the temple complex of Besakih – lies on its southern flanks. The

Plate 2   Gunung Agung, lofty abode of deities and ancestors, focal point of the Balinese world

volcano was inactive for 120 years, so that many Balinese thought it to be extinct. But in the rainy season of 1963, massive eruptions occurred. Over 2,000 people perished in this terrible natural disaster. Many Balinese lost all their belongings, and the regencies of Klungkung and Karangasem suffered immeasurable damage. A molten mass, combined with water and mud, flowed towards the coast and created broad patches of burnt land. Sand and ashes were tossed into the air and ultimately fell on the east Javanese port of Surabaya – 220 km away. Hot gases and glowing dust burned the casuarina forests on the flanks of the volcano. The settlements in the path of the lava were destroyed. Erupted stone blocks, sand and ash rendered large sections of land useless for agriculture. About 100 km^2 of former wet-rice fields were deprived of irrigation for two years. A further 25 km^2 cannot be cultivated for decades. The destruction of the wet-rice fields can be attributed mainly to the fact that streams of lava disrupted the water ducts, depriving certain agricultural complexes of water, while others were destroyed by uncontrolled penetrating water and silt. In addition, numerous bridges in east Bali were destroyed and main as well as secondary roads damaged.[11]

Tectonic earthquakes are a further source of danger. In the most recent, in 1976, inhabitants of the western area of the north coast and around the mountain village of Pupuan were severely hit. Brick buildings – some of which were schoolhouses – collapsed. Falling bricks and tiles killed over 550 people and wounded thousands. Ironically, the poor, who could only afford bamboo wickerwork shelters, were the lucky ones. Their flexible houses were capable of withstanding the shocks undamaged.

Bali is subject to a tropical monsoon climate. Refreshing sea breezes during the day and cool winds from the mountains during the night alleviate the heat. The average daily maximum temperature of the hottest month reaches a mere 32–3°C in the capital city of the province, Denpasar. The average daily minimum there in the coolest months is 22°C. Temperatures are slightly higher on the north coast. Even though the mean annual temperature varies only slightly, the daily amplitudes are marked. In coastal east Bali, the temperature can sink to

20° just before sunrise – in the area around the mountain and pass villages even down to 10°. Thick morning fog is characteristic of pass regions. Just as noticeable is the drop in temperature after heavy cloudbursts.

A (winter) dry season and a (summer) rainy season can be differentiated by the seasonally variable rain. The half of the year receiving less rain and average sunshine of over 90 per cent, falls in the period from May to October. Only on the islands further to the east do we find a totally rainless dry season. Especially on the south flank of the Balinese mountain range, the air masses of the south-east trade winds bank up and cause some precipitation (which is important for irrigation agriculture) even during the period of poor rainfall. In Denpasar, there is a yearly average of 1,800 mm of rainfall, but with large annual variations. For example, during 1986 an annual total of 1,500 mm was registered, whilst in 1984 the precipitation amounted to 2,700 mm.[12] In mountainous areas, the annual amount of precipitation rises to over 3,000 mm, whilst in the dry north and in west Bali less than 1,500 mm is usually registered. The annual mean values do not fall below 1,000 mm anywhere.

Climatically, the seasons can be divided up in the following way: the south-east trades blow from May until the end of September (winter monsoon). They flow from the subtropical anticyclone over Central Australia towards the equatorial low-pressure area. On its short passage over the warm sea, the air mass can absorb only a small quantity of moisture, making this a low-rainfall period for Bali. In October and November, the south-east trade winds abate. In the so-called inter-monsoon period, heavy thunderstorms are caused by thermally determined, vertical air movements.

The Javanese west monsoon (summer monsoon) blows from November until March. It causes heavy wind squalls and high rainfall. The average duration of sunshine sinks to 50 per cent. On the north coast, which has few inlets, the west monsoon causes such high waves that the unprotected port of Buleleng is often inoperable. The transition period between the Javanese west monsoon and the south-east trades can be considered a second inter-monsoon period. It lasts from April into the month of May. Irregular winds which flare up and quickly subside again and heavy stormy showers are characteristic of this time of the year.

The notion that it always rains and that the sky is cloudy during the humid period does not correspond with reality. The sky is never so blue nor the air so fresh as after a heavy downpour. In coastal areas most rain falls during the night, especially just before dawn. The sky then becomes clearer. Towards midday the summits of the volcanoes are usually hidden again under cloud cover. Rain also falls during the day, but this is mostly restricted to certain localities. First, huge cumulonimbus clouds move upwards, then black stratus clouds begin to cover the sky. The first heavy drops begin to fall and everyone runs for cover. Consecutive forks of lightning strike trees and sometimes electric wires. Heavy downpours transform paths into torrents. Sewage systems cannot cope with the water, and traffic is brought to a stop. Strong wind squalls uproot old trees. Streams carrying debris are flooded and fords are impassable. Communications and work come to a standstill for some time in the areas affected by the heavy downpours. Women put out large clay vessels and plastic buckets to catch the rainwater that drips from the roof in order to lay in a supply of drinking water. In this way they can avoid the difficult walk to the stream in the evening. If the sun shines through the clouds after heavy rainfall, then the warm earth steams. Barefoot, the Balinese wade up to their ankles through the water which has collected on the hard-packed loamy soil of the family yard. The relative humidity in the rainy season reaches a monthly average of 80 per cent, and even in the dry season it is over 70 per cent. The high humidity causes people to perceive temperature as being higher than they really are.[13]

2

Pre-colonial Bali

The First Balinese (Bali Mula)

There has been a legend abroad in Bali for several decades according to which Rsi Markandeya, a great saint in Hindu tradition, was the first person to set foot on Bali. He and a retinue of 8,000 had come over from Mount Raung in eastern Java to turn the densely wooded land into arable. But the gods and demons did not look favourably upon the enterprise and forced the pioneers to turn back. Many years later Rsi Markandeya set out once again, this time with a smaller group of pious followers, and quickly obtained the grace and protection of the supernatural powers. The areas alleged to have been the first to be cleared and settled by the Bali Mula, the original Balinese, are the present temple district of Besakih and the territory around the villages of Taro and Payangan, where several holy places still commemorate Markandeya and the settlers from Mount Raung.[1]

The traditional Balinese view of history traces the historical beginnings of Balinese culture to two sources, India and the Indo-Javanese courts of central and eastern Java. This perspective on the subject precludes any exploration of pre-Indian prehistory. But slowly the curtain is beginning to rise on prehistorical events, and the first act of the story of the settlement of Indonesia and Bali provokes amazement and interest even among the Balinese themselves. We must bid farewell to earlier theories of settlement, and with that to one of the hobby-horses of ethnological diffusionism. According to this latter view, the ancestors of the present-day Austronesian-speaking inhabitants of Indonesia – certainly not the first

Balinese, but the first for whom we have linguistic and archaeological identification, recognizable by the rectangular-sec-
tioned, polished and unshouldered stone adze as their guiding
archaeological fossil – all migrated to the archipelago from the
South-East Asian mainland, via the Malay Peninsula.[2] The
present state of research in the field of South-East Asian
archaeology requires some modification of this line of reason-
ing. It is now widely agreed by linguists and archaeologists
that the first Austronesian settlers moved south from southern
China via Taiwan and the Philippines (not via the Malay
Peninsula) into Indonesia between 4,000 and 5,000 years
ago.[3]

The history of the initial, pre-Austronesian, settlement of
Indonesia extends far back into the Pleistocene. Whether Bali
had any part in it is uncertain, for no early Stone Age finds
have as yet been made in the densely settled areas of Central
Bali, with their thick layers of volcanic soil, or in the comparatively inaccessible wooded mountains in the west. Consequently there is no way to determine whether early forms of
humanity walked Bali in the era of the *Homo erectus* hominid,
now widely believed to be an extinct sideline of human evol-
ution and found in the sites of Sangiran, Trinil, Sambungma-
can and Ngandong in the Solo river basin of central Java.[4] And
there is little trace in Bali of the pre-Austronesian hunters and
gatherers, claimed by some biologists to have been similar in
physical appearance to the ancestral New Guineans and Abo-
rigines of Australia. These people had migrated to Australia
by at least 50,000 years ago so they must have had relatives in
Bali as well by this time.

In terms of clear archaeological evidence, the first provable
inhabitants of Bali lived in coastal settlements, of which two
dating to about 2,000 years ago are now known: Gilimanuk
in the north-west, Sembiran in the north-centre. The finds at
Gilimanuk[5, 6] that have been made indicate a population of
fishermen, hunters and farmers already in possession of
bronze and iron objects. This means that their culture must be
ascribed to the South-East Asian Bronze and Iron Ages, which
Bali had presumably entered a little over 2,000 years ago. The
skeletons found near Gilimanuk bear clear typological indica-
tions of belonging to the southern Mongoloid, Austronesian-

speaking populations numerically dominant in western Indonesia today.

Having acquired the skill to construct and navigate seaworthy outriggers, the Austronesian-speaking ancestors of the first Balinese left the coastal regions of present-day southern China some 7,000 years ago and set off in the direction of Taiwan and the Philippines. The development of rice cultivation[7] and resultant demographic growth led to continuous population expansion southwards into Indonesia, resulting eventually in the immense dispersal of the 270 million people who today speak Austronesian languages, from Madagascar to the New Zealand Maoris.

The chronology of this migration has been reconstructed with the help of archaeological and linguistic data.[8] Between five and six millenia ago (around 4000–3000BC), the Austronesian emigrants reached Taiwan. Perhaps during the third millenium BC they moved further south in their outriggers and reached Luzon.[9] It was there that the Malayo-Polynesian languages, to whose western grouping Balinese belongs, separated from the other major subgroup of Austronesian, Formosan. The Malayo-Polynesian rice farmers and fisherfolk gradually spread throughout the Philippines and some of them then moved east towards Oceania, while others moved west towards Java, Sumatra and the Malay Peninsula. The groups that ultimately settled in the Moluccas went over to cultivating crops better adapted to their equatorial environment: tubers (taro, yams), starch-rich fruit-bearing plants and palms (banana, sago).

The ancestors of the first-known (Austronesian-speaking) Balinese, who had travelled south-west, probably remained faithful to rice cultivation, given recent dates for cultivated rice as early as 2500BC from Sarawak in Borneo. Starting in the Philippines, they had first reached Sulawesi and then, some 2,500–3,000 years ago, West Indonesia and with that Bali.

Coastal and Inland Dwellers

The finds at Gilimanuk indicate a form of life adapted to coastal conditions. The first Balinese did not restrict themselves to rice farming and small cattle breeding; they also gathered, fished and hunted what they needed along the coast. During the rainy season they cultivated their fields and gardens. They used stone adzes and a range of bronze and iron tools.

The excavation of over a hundred buried children and adults of both sexes also reveals a good deal about the society and the beliefs of the people of this time (*c*.2,000 years ago). Most of the finds derive either from inhumation burials in pits or from secondary burials of defleshed bones, sometimes placed in large earthenware jars. Two unique double-urn burials are of particular interest to cultural anthropology.[10] Archaeologists found the secondarily transferred bones of a single individual in a large urn placed in the ground. A second, smaller urn was placed upside-down over the top as a lid. Beneath one of these urn burials lay another burial, claimed by the excavators to be a human sacrifice perhaps killed to escort the deceased person, who was of high social standing, into the hereafter.

Grave furniture also conveys the impression that the dead were granted the opportunity to continue their earthly lives in the hereafter: the conceptual principles of the first Balinese evidently ascribed considerable significance to the belief – still alive today – that there is an unbroken link between the society of the living and the spiritual world of the dead. Not only did the layer of soil covering the skeletons contain the remains of dwellings, plain and decorated pots, pearls and bronze jewellery; it also concealed iron spearheads and daggers and bronze ceremonial axes with heart- and half-moon-shaped blades – artefacts which may have been used as cult objects and status symbols rather than as actual tools.

A different burial tradition was probably developing in Bali's mountainous interior during the period of the coastal dwellers of Gilimanuk. There the dead were placed in two-piece sarcophagi, with separate coffins and lids, made of volcanic tuff. Sarcophagi with stone covers were carved in various sizes for different forms of burial and are a speciality of Bali.[11] Similar but less elaborately carved stone slab graves also occur in Java, southern Sumatra and the Malay Peninsula. The grave furniture in the Balinese stone coffins is comparable to that found in Gilimanuk – where recently two sarcophagi have been discovered – and suggests that the first inland Balinese, too, had already developed comparatively complex social structures and an elaborate death cult for the leading members of their society.

International Trade Relations and Early Metallurgy

The similarity of the grave furniture on the coast and in the mountainous interior of the island gives evidence of a brisk trade in metal objects and in glass and cornelian beads. These items will have reached Bali via an extensive network of trade links and been acquired as status symbols by members of the island's ruling families.

Copper, bronze and, later, iron were perhaps first imported from the South-East Asian mainland as finished goods, but the technologies necessary to produce them did not accompany them. Some time between 500BC and AD300 a lively metal-working culture, which was to exert a significant influence on early Indonesian cultural history, flourished in a wide area of present-day north-eastern Vietnam. It has been named after the Dong Son excavation site in Thanh Hoa Province. Some of the most striking and most professionally executed artefacts of Dong Son culture in the Metal Age are deep-rimmed bronze kettledrums.[12] These richly decorated gong-like instruments, produced in the Dong Son area from approx. 500BC until AD300, were obviously appreciated by the ruling families of the Indonesian archipelago at about the time when evidence for Indian contact and trade was first beginning to appear.

The island of Bali was thus already involved in inter-regional South-East Asian trade at the start of the Christian era, maintaining links both to the rest of the archipelago and to the mainland. There are several pieces of evidence to prove that with the import of bronze objects to the archipelago, the Balinese ultimately became acquainted with technologies that enabled them to cast or smelt copper, bronze and iron. Various stone and earthenware casting moulds for axes found in the Philippines and Indonesia (but not yet in Bali) provide information about the growth of local metalworking centres in the first centuries of the Christian era.[13]

The assumption that specialized bronze-casters and -smiths were at work in late prehistoric Bali is confirmed by the discovery of stamps of volcanic tuff used to press patterns into wax for casting. The stamp fragments found in Manuaba (Gianyar) in 1932 and more recently a datable specimen for stamping a pattern on a drum from Sembiran in North Bali[14] lend credibility to the idea that, beginning in the first century AD, kettle drums of the so-called Pejeng type were produced in Bali itself.

One of the most spectacular specimens of the South-East Asian Bronze Age, and a model of local metallurgy, is the so-called 'moon' of Pejeng. A massive, hourglass-shaped kettle drum, it is 186.5 cm in length and has a projecting sounding surface measuring 160 cm in diameter.

Plate 3   The famous 'moon' of Pejeng

Concentric triangle patterns and f-shaped marks run round
the kettle. Between the four handles there are pairs of powerful human faces. The sounding surface has a central, eight-
pointed star surrounded by the wavy, double-spiral bands
characteristic of the Dong Son designs so influential in Old
Indonesian art.[15]

To sum up, we may conclude that cultural relations began to
develop in South-East Asia even before contact was made with
Indian religion and writing systems – cultural relations rooted
in the prehistory of South-East Asia itself. And it was above all
the coastal populations, as trading partners and seafarers,
who gradually learned about well-organized state systems,
ultimately creating the conditions for establishing small Indianized states in Indonesia as well.

Contact with India and China

In the course of his 1987 and 1989 excavations in the vicinity
of the north-east Balinese villages of Sembiran, Pacung and
Julah, Balinese archaeologist Wayan Ardika[16] discovered not
only Metal Age artefacts but Indian pottery sherds as well.
The type of ceramic and a short scratched line of Brahmi or
Kharoshthi characters on one sherd indicate that they origin-
ate from various stylistic areas of the eastern coast of India
and reached Bali in the first century AD. This means that the
island must already have been a port for Indian traders 2,000
years ago: it cannot have been an untouched, isolated Austronesian outpost until well into the first millennium, as had
previously been assumed.

The Balinese may have played a more peripheral role in international trade than other coastal populations of Indonesia, and
the first discoverable traces of Indian influence may be correspondingly later than elsewhere in the archipelago. None the
less, the island was at the edge of an important trade route plied
by Indonesian and Indian ships carrying spices and aromatic
woods to India and as far afield as the Mediterranean. For
several centuries, North Bali must have been a port of call for
some of these ships, for it can be no coincidence that the old
ports and commercial centres of Julah and Sembiran played a

special role in the edicts of the Old Balinese kings of the ninth and tenth centuries (see chapter 4, pp. 73–5).[17]

Between the first and fifth centuries AD, a series of small, local commercial states developed on the South-East Asian mainland and the Malay Archipelago, and later in the Indonesian archipelago. The first signs of the local potentates of these new commercial states orientating themselves towards the style of Indian kings appear in East Borneo and West Java between AD400 and 500 in the form of inscriptions in an early southern Indian Pallava writing. So Indianization in any real sense cannot be said to have set in until several centuries after the trade routes sailed by both Indonesian and Indian ships had been established. According to the account of a Chinese monk, China joined the network of trade relations around AD400,[18] at which point Buddhist pilgrims began to make increased use of merchant vessels to travel from India to Indonesia and then back to China.

In 1924 small clay *stupa* were discovered in Pejeng, testifying to the presence of Buddhists in the eighth century AD. Miniature *stupa* of this kind were sold to pilgrims in many Buddhist countries as amulets and religious souvenirs; they may also have been sacrificed as offerings at sacred spots. All of them had clay seals imprinted with the Mahayana creed or Tantric charms. Though not typical of Bali, the Pejeng finds shed significant light on local cultural history: they attest to contact between sectors of the Balinese population and Buddhist – particularly Tantric – groups from Nalanda (northern Indian) and other international centres of Buddhism, foremost among them Srivijaya and Central Java, where the Sailendra dynasty built the great Borobudur stupa in the eighth century.

Stories of mighty Indian and Indianized Indonesian *raja* and their supernaturally gifted priests must have reached Bali through pilgrims, merchants and seafarers. Reports of Indian forms of administrative organization began to kindle the imaginations of the ruling families. Brahman priests and legal counsellors were summoned to the island to help ambitious local rulers achieve glory, authority and organizational skill as they gained power. At no time in the history of Indonesia, including Bali, was there an Indian migration or conquest during which military or economic colonies could have been established.[19] Thus the Indianized Old Balinese kingdom to which we shall now turn was never an institution imposed from outside. In Bali it was domestic political needs and demands that enabled religious and political ideas from India to take hold.

The Rule of the Old Balinese Kings

Seven bronze edicts (*prasasti*) in Old Balinese (both language and writing) dating from AD882–914 have been found.[20] They suggest that political power in Bali at the time was monopolized by one of the leading regional clans and transferred to a central authority – a prince or king. Though the names of individual rulers during this first phase of the kingdom are not mentioned, the Indianized name of a royal household – Singamandawa – is. A further sign of the incipient Indianization of the courtly domain is the fact that from this time on, all royal decrees published on sheets of bronze were dated according to the Indian *saka* calendar.[21] The use of Old Balinese as the official and court language, on the other hand, shows that the early rulers were evidently autonomous enough to decide how much Indianization was good for them.

The first Balinese king to record his name in writing designated himself Sri Kesari Warmadewa. He is considered the founder of the Warmadewa Dynasty, which ruled Bali for several generations. Its most famous representative, King Udayana, was to go down in Balinese history a century later. The name of the founder of the dynasty can be found on a high stone pillar in Belanjong (Sanur); the carved inscription, dated 836 *saka* (AD914), is partly in the Old Balinese language and partly in Sanskrit. Moreover, two different types of characters have been used: Old Balinese and Pre- or Early Nagari.

The nine subsequent bronze edicts, dating from AD915–942, all bear Indianized forms of kings' names: five relate to the reign of Sang Ratu Ugrasana; the other four show various names, among them Candra-bhaya-singha-Warmadewa, who founded the famed bathing-place of Tirtha Empul in 962. These edicts are once again written completely in Old Balinese and are entirely free of Javanisms.

An analysis of the royal edicts does not yield a clear picture of the personalities of the early kings or the social conditions that prevailed during the first six decades of their rule. And yet the incomplete textual mosaic does afford a number of interesting insights into the organization, structure and instruments of royal rule and into the channels of communication available between court and village, which were vital to the viability of the system.

In the absence of written evidence, the location of the first Balinese court and capital of the kingdom can be identified only with reference to the location of historical finds. These sites occur in striking concentration near the Pakerisan river, in the vicinity of the present-day villages of Intaran/Pejeng and Bedaulu – the presumed centre of Old Balinese royal power – and on the axis connecting the region with the mountain temples, particularly the mountain sanctuary of Panulisan near Kintamani. Monastic cells, rock tombs, hermitages and sculptural groups showing deities associating with kings establish that both royal rulers and Buddhist and Siwaist priests and monks once lived here, the religious figures serving as counsellors and members of the royal law court and thus exercising distinctly worldly power alongside the ministers and officials of the lower hierarchy.

But the role of educated priests and monks was not restricted to the court; they also formed a key element in the wide-ranging, decentralized system of government. On the one hand, they functioned as religious and ritual representatives of the ruling ideology; but as legal authorities they also had to impose the concrete, worldly claims of the ruler and his administration on whole village communities.

The first edicts already prove that where kings wanted to control the administrative, religious and ritual affairs of a village, they built fortified monastic settlements nearby to oversee and implement their claims to power. Both Buddhist and Siwaist priests and monks resided there with their families, servants and slaves. Several of these monastic settlements were established in the Lake Batur region of the Kintamani Mountains, which served as a royal hunting-ground and contained a number of important temples for the fire cult. Significantly, a second focus of royal attention was in north

Bali, near the old maritime commercial centres of Sembiran and Julah (see chapter 4, pp. 73–5).

The king, his court and officials in the villages, and the spiritual and legal counsellors and supervisory organs in the monastic settlements were expressly required to offer protection and mediation in village quarrels; in return the villages had a variety of services to provide, tasks to fulfil and taxes to pay. The lines of communication evidently ran between, at one end, the council of village elders and the village scribes and, at the other, the administrative, legal and ritual authorities of the state – some of whom resided in the monastic settlements and some in the villages themselves. Occasionally the kings travelled personally to the territories they held or granted village delegations audiences at court.

Conditions must often have been unsafe and there are repeated accounts of raids, plundering and wanton destruction. Royal and priestly concern for the safety of the monastic settlements led to village citizens being pressed into service as armed guards and protectors. They could also be obliged to perform collective forced labour in addition to having to pay taxes to the king and his administration, to contribute to the maintenance of temples and to participate in sacrificial rituals and ceremonies for the dead.

The edicts make repeated reference to a number of specific professional groups, which we may surmise were particularly dependent on the king and of great importance to the public welfare and the system of government. These specialists included the blue and red dyers; weavers; iron- and goldsmiths; tunnel builders for irrigation; carpenters; masons and shipbuilders; and musicians, singers and dancers. This high level of specialization plus the complexity of the social hierarchy presuppose a healthy, surplus-producing economy. Of commercial importance beyond the framework of family and village subsistence were wet- and dry-rice cultivation, vegetables, cotton and kapok, but also horse-, cattle-, goat- and pig-breeding.

It is striking that these royal edicts were often addressed to village communities that are generally classified as 'original' Balinese (Bali Aga or Bali Mula). In other words, even in the era of the early kingdom they were already highly dependent on the court and the monasteries, and entertained lively commercial relations with the outside world. Consequently it would be wrong to equate Bali Aga or Bali Mula with an original population that had retained its Austronesian identity. They would be more aptly described as genealogical and territorial groups which, in early Balinese history, were situated amid the Indianized royal administration network and later were for the most part able to evade the grip of Majapahit and Brahman reforms. For many of these groups, the term Bali Aga is a term used by others; the inhabitants of Trunyan, on Lake Batur, even consider it degrading and humiliating.[22] In contrast, the initiated members of the village community of Tenganan Pegeringsingan are filled with pride at the knowledge that they are Bali Aga. At the climax of the annual ritual cycle each year, the village bachelors go to their clubs to hear the names of the Aga deities to whom they owe their existence as Bali Aga.

Any attempt to interpret the Indian influence on Bali or to disengage it analytically from the Old Balinese, Austronesian substratum is futile. In the melting-pot of their history, the Balinese have created an independent, unmistakable, syncretistic culture of their own. The existence there of an Austronesian element completely free from Indian influence is unlikely; but the notion of an Indian element unaffected by the Old Balinese, Austronesian substratum is equally improbable.

Bali and the East Javanese Claim to Sovereignty

With the marriage of the Balinese prince Udayana, of the Warmadewa Dynasty, and the great-granddaughter of Sindok, King of East Java, the two leading royal houses established close bonds that would leave revealing archaeological and epigraphic traces. A clearly recognizable Javanization of the Balinese court suggests that this alliance may have been the intended result of a Java-inspired, imperialistic policy of marital alliances – a phenomenon repeatedly encountered in the later political development of the kingdoms of East Java and Bali.

Written documents mention the title of Java's queen – Gunapriya Dharmapatni – before that of her husband, probably because of her noble descent and her influence on shaping the court. After AD989 (*saka* 911), royal decrees were written in the Old Javanese rather than in the Old Balinese language. Having gained precedence as the official administrative language and court idiom, Old Javanese increasingly began to dominate formal communication between court and village representatives as well. Several edicts suggest that masked dances and shadow plays had acquainted villagers with the contents and ideology of Javano-Balinese courtly culture.[23]

The seat of the royal couple and their court remained in the vicinity of present-day Bedaulu and Intaran/Pejeng. If there is any truth in the popular Calon Arang drama,[24] the queen, better known among her people by her maiden name,

Plate 4   Sculpture of a standing king and queen, Gunung Panulisan (AD1011)

Mahendradatta, must have been a great mistress of black magic. Her reign is thought to have seen the birth of Tantric rites and sorcery, still perceptible today in the belief in witches (*leak*) and witchcraft.

Although Queen Gunapriya's name ceased to appear in edicts after the year AD1001, her husband signed a further decree ten years later. Near Kutri (Gianyar), on a hilltop – Bukit Dharma – shaded by massive *bingin* trees (*Ficus benjamina*), stands the badly weathered funeral monument alleged to be that of the prematurely deceased royal sorceress. As befits her demonic nature, she has been immortalized as Durga Mahisasuramardini, dancing on a bull; the fluttering streamers and leaping flames around her emphasize her superhuman energies.

The year of Udayana's last recorded sign of life, AD1011, is also the date of a sculpture of a standing royal couple. It was erected in the Pura Tegeh Koripan of Sukawana, Bali's highest mountain temple built on an elevation on the rim of the Batur crater. Whether this work from the year marking the end of the king's reign is a joint monument to Gunapriya and Udayana cannot be established conclusively, but the very possibility is fascinating enough.

Udayana was succeeded by his eldest son, Dharmawangsa, a somewhat nebulous figure. He was, in turn, succeeded by Anak Wungsu, his youngest brother, in 1049. The new king established a high profile by promulgating numerous decrees. Airlangga, one of Gunapriya and Udayana's other sons, had entered the service of his East Javanese grandfather at an early age. After spending long years reuniting the small, inimical principalities of East Java, he became one of the most powerful kings in Javanese history. But he ultimately failed in his attempt to annex Bali for the empire, thwarted by the iron will and power of another Javanese: the Senapati and priestly reformer Mpu Kuturan.[25]

The most impressive proof of the Javanization of courtly society, as well as evidence of the growing importance of royal funeral cults, is provided by nine massive, stupa-shaped royal tombs by the upper course of the Pakerisan river near Tampaksiring. Five of these funerary monuments are carved in relief into the wall of rock east of the river; four corresponding structures are on the opposite bank. According to an inscription, the so-called 'Mountain of Poetry' (Gunung Kawi) was completed around AD1080 and is supposed to be covering the ashes of King Anak Wungsu and his wives, who followed him into death.

Two sacred places are of prime importance in interpreting the relationship between the pre-Majapahit kingdom in Bedaulu/Pejeng and the Old Balinese clans and villages. One of them has already been mentioned: the temple grounds of Pura Tegeh Koripan, an Old Balinese mountain sanctuary near the village of Sukawana on the Gunung Panulisan. The other is at its opposite pole, the Pura Panataran Sasih, state temple of the Pejeng Dynasty, in the valley of the Pakerisan River. That both temples contain whole groups of statues of deities and kings indicates the existence of a god-king cult of the type known in other parts of South-East Asia and particularly in Java. The

Plate 5   Wooden funeral figure: portrait statue of a king (thirteenth or fourteenth century)

fact that statues of kings, often with individual, portrait-like features, appear in conscious association with female figures leads us to assume that the statues of dead kings were escorted by their wives, priests and advisers. The statues and symbols of gods dating from this period were created in connection with a royal ancestral cult, not a Hinduistic divine cult: they symbolize the character traits and deeds of a dead king in the form of the god whose incarnation he was considered to be during his lifetime.

Important Old Balinese clans and the villages near the temples evidently also participated in this royal ancestral cult. The temple complex of Pura Tegeh Koripan, on an elevation of the vast rim of the Batur caldera, has been an important sanctuary for neighbouring Bali Aga villages since time immemorial. It was to these villages that the edicts of the rulers from Bedaulu/Pejeng were repeatedly addressed, for the mountain and its temple were of essential sacred significance to both parties. In his monograph on the Old Balinese Pande clans,[26] the French ethnologist Jean-François Guermonprez shows that the Pande Besi, the ironsmiths' clan of Pejeng, also traced their origin back to the Gunung Panulisan and believed that their ancestors resided in the temple.

In other words, the Hinduized Old Balinese clans and villages took an active part in the ancestral cult of kings and queens, which was sited on sacred ground long used for sacrifices to Old Balinese nature deities and ancestors. The style of the royal portrait statues is visible proof that no simple imitation of Indian culture is at issue here. The anthropomorphic gods of Central Java and the Indian-influenced portraits of god-kings of East Java have been transformed in a specifically Balinese way and adapted to the local religion, with its Siwaist, Buddhist and Old Indonesian influences.

In the Bali of the pre-Majapahit era, Indian and Indo-Javanese conceptions, practices, titles and terms moved beyond the court to pervade many spheres of Old Balinese life and popular religion. And yet the Old Indonesian, Austronesian spirit survived, and it remains alive today, lending modern Balinese culture its unique, incomparable quality.

Royal documents reveal that rulers descended from dominant local clans considered themselves ritual leaders in the broadest sense. This extended even to popular ritual, to which they are bound to have been more sympathetic than the later East Javanese colonizers from Singasari and Majapahit. On the other hand, adjudication in matters of inheritance and the control of religious affairs was decentralized: it was delegated to a staff of officials and religious advisers with worldly authority, compliance being ensured by a network of monastic settlements and fortresses. Ritual authority was of prime importance to the ruler's status, perhaps even more so than law and order, which were regulated and upheld by virtue of perennial relations between the tributary villages and clans on the one hand, and the court, its officials and the monasteries on the other.

Javanese Rule

The year 1284 turned the page on a new chapter in relations between Java and Bali: for the first time, Bali was subject to the foreign rule of an imperialistic East Javanese ruler. Kertanegara, king of the Singasari Empire founded by Ken Angrok in 1222, had launched a military campaign and had conquered Bali.

The Singasari rulers employed religion and ritual as ideological instruments of leadership, locating the ritual centre in the midst of their radius of power. As a result, the Old Balinese ritual polarity between state and mountain temples temporarily waned in importance. Now court and state temples became the focus of magic and politics in the empire and the cosmos at large, with the king himself embodying divine cosmic power.

As the rituals of the Singasari court possessed a strong Tantric component, the 'left path', black magic and sorcery were major factors in confronting and combating the disturbing and disastrous sides of life. King Kertanegara is known to have sought deliverance in magic cults of the Tantric Kalacakra sect and to have given the court religion a Bhairawa orientation, with a mixed Siwaist–Buddhist pantheon featuring gods such as Bhairawa; that is to say, Siwa in his manifestation as 'the Terrible'.

Demonic figures and a statue more than 3 m high of Bhairawa in the Kebo Edan Temple at the southern exit of the village of Intaran signal that this formerly Singasari magic temple contains important requisites for a Tantric redirection of the Balinese system of belief and ritual. Introduced in the era of Gunapriya (Mahendradatta), the sorceress-queen, these concepts are still manifest in present-day trance cults, occult practices, the belief in witches and goblins, and the active role of demonic figures in fending off evil. The distinctive spiritual climate of Tantric Buddhism and Siwaism is more perceptible in Singasari-influenced southern and south-western parts of Bali, particularly in Badung (Sanur, Kesiman), Tabanan and Gianyar, than in the rest of Bali, where the 'right path' prohibits extreme practices, and devotion and worship provide the impulse for ritual.

From Chaos to Order in the World

The death of Singasari ruler Kertanagara granted Bali half a century of renewed independence, which came to a violent end with the military defeat inflicted by the East Javanese Majapahit Empire. But it was half a century clouded by the culture-bearer myth with which the new rulers transfigured and legitimated their dominion. Thus until not too long ago, anything predating Majapahit was either ignored or relegated to a chaotic prehistory of demonic, irreligious kings. In this early age, order prevailed only under Javanese influence, particularly under Udayana, Gunapriya, Mpu Kuturan and Anak Wungsu in the eleventh century.

This Javanocentric myth of the Majapahit origins of culture has gained so much credibility in the course of time that the preponderant majority of Balinese believe in the historical truth of this ideological artefact and trace themselves back to Majapahit (Maospait). Thus, despite the new knowledge imparted by archaeology and cultural history, the Old Balinese world continues even today to possess an aura of unreality and mystery – even among the Balinese themselves. Gunung Kawi, Goa Gajah and other monuments of Old Balinese history tower over a remote, misunderstood time like alien erratic blocks casting their shadows over the present. Whispered stories circulate about the small territorial and genealogical groups known as Bali Aga; and though these stories may have more to do with rumour than history, they help to cement the prevailing order and its underlying ideology.[27]

But even the history of the conquest by the vassal rulers from Majapahit is animated by the power with which chroniclers throughout history have legitimated ruling systems and shown them in a flattering light. Finding sources for an accurate historical reconstruction is problematic, and from the fourteenth century there cease to be royal edicts comparable to those from the Old Balinese era. Where traditional datings exist, they are often difficult, if not impossible, to set into a chronological context. To exacerbate the situation, the majority of 'historical' texts were not edited until the seventeenth century or later.

And yet, anyone who wishes to study present-day social conditions in Bali cannot simply set aside this 'history' because of its chronological inaccuracies and methodological flaws. For the momentum of this 'history' – permeated though it may be by a combination of ideology, myth and fact – has made history; and it sparked off the social processes that have allowed Balinese society to become and remain unique, even in the face of social and cultural change.

Majapahit and its Consequences

Once minister of state Gajah Mada had brought the Majapahit dynasty to the height of its power, he decided to launch a military campaign to break the power of the Old Balinese *raja*. In his panegyric on King Hayam Wuruk (1350–89), court chronicler Prapanca reports that the 'vile, long-haired princes of Bali' were beaten and wiped out by the Javanese in 1265 *saka* (AD1343) and that 'all customs [in Bali] are now consistent with Java'.[28]

The court chronicler's last remark betrays imperialistic over confidence and underestimation of the opponent. But it glosses over the fact that the Balinese did not capitulate across the board; on the contrary, they continually resisted the occupying power. Opposition to the new rulers and their programme of cultural Javanization was particularly strong in the Old Balinese villages near the crater lakes, which were very much in sympathy with the Old Balinese kings. There could be no question of cultural conformity with Java, not even in the defeated and colonized lowlands of Central Bali, for here, too, numerous Old Balinese elements have survived up to the present day.

In any case, Bali was now treated as a Javanese colony and divided up among the descendants of the *raja* of the east Javanese Kediri Kingdom: the Arya Kanuruhan, for example, were responsible for Tangkas; the Arya Kutha Waringin for Gelgel; the Arya Senteng for Canang Sari; and the Arya Belog for Kaba-Kaba.[29] As the country lacked strong central leadership, a Balinese thrust for independence soon gained momentum; opposition mounted and the Javanese imperial administrators were incapable of breaking it. Alarmed, Gajah Mada sought ways of countering this new urge for autonomy and securing Majapahit's long-range influence. A vassal king and colony of occupiers under the direct control of Majapahit and its new ruler Hayam Wuruk would serve as the instrument of leadership, imposing the East Javanese Empire's claim to sovereignty.

The man chosen to become vassal king was Ketut Kresna Kapakisan, youngest son of Danghyang Kapakisan, a Brahman priest and wise man valued by Gajah Mada. Preparations for his new administrative duties included a change in status, from *brahmana* to *satria*. When Ketut Kresna Kapakisan shouldered a worldly burden, he became progenitor of the Javano-Balinese Satria Dalem and founder of the dynasty that would determine Bali's destiny until well into the first decade of the twentieth century (see chapter 4, pp. 76–8).[30]

In 1352, two years after the coronation of King Hayam Wuruk, Dalem Ketut Kresna Kapakisan established his court and palace in Samprangan, near the present-day city of Gianyar. His model in matters of both architecture and the symbolic structure of the *kraton* was, of course, the court of Majapahit. From it the young ruler had received all the paraphernalia (*pusaka*) and insignia necessary to create and maintain an ordered empire orientated towards the centre of the world. The sacred Ganja Dungkul *keris* dagger was one of the most important trappings, for it was a symbol of power and embodied the strength of the ruling house, which, in conjunction with the war lord from Kediri (Satria Jawa), was now preparing to organize and develop the new vassal state.

Little is known about the reign of Dalem Ketut and his *kraton* in Samprangan. What the various versions of the history of the Dalem Dynasty (Babad Dalem) make clear,[31] however, is that the first *dalem* and his successors over the centuries derived their authority and claim to power from Gajah Mada and Hayam Wuruk's original installation of Dalem Ketut Kresna Kapakisan. Decrees from 1394 and 1398 also reveal that more than fifty years after the conquest, Bali was still considered a Majapahit dependency.

In the fulfilment of his administrative duties, the first Balinese ruler by the grace of Majapahit could count on the support of his loyal Javanese imperial administrators, who were located in such strategically important places as Nyuhaya, Tabanan, Kapal and Tangkas. A further factor of inestimable importance in imposing power and propagating the ideology behind the Majapahit claim to it was the collaboration of the Bandesa and Pasek. These leading local clans traced their origins back to holy Javanese *mpu* (high priests) and had been entrusted with leadership tasks in Balinese society since the time of King Airlangga and Mpu Kuturan. Dalem Kresna Kapakisan had assigned them special tasks pertaining to the regulation of the temple system and the village order, the latter organized and overseen in the assembly long house of married male villagers (*krama desa*) in the centrally sited *pura desa* village temple. As the social spectrum of modern-day Bali changes under the influence of economic development and democratization processes, the descendants of these Pasek families have become a major power factor, challenging the traditional hierarchical structure and striving to modify it.

The Magic Centre is Lost

When Dalem Ketut Kresna Kapakisan died, his eldest son, Ida I Dewa Samprangan, assumed the duties of vassal king in

Majapahit's name. The demands on a ruler were enormous, for he was expected to do more than deal with worldly power; he also bore what might be termed universal, cosmic responsibility for the welfare of his secular and sacred dominion, known as Nagara. Dalem Samprangan, who should have carried on the process of unifying the empire created out of Chaos and Nothingness, was not equal to the task. He was described in local history as a fop and a cuckold, a man more interested in amorous strategies than in the political art of statesmanship. In consequence, he and his court increasingly lost magical power (*kesaktian*) and grew ever more vulnerable.

The worrisome power vacuum and loss of the magic centre in Samprangan ultimately impelled Krian Kubon Tubuh, a powerful figure in the empire and apanage holder of Gelgel, to request Ida I Dewa Ketut Ngulesir, the Dalem's younger brother, to come to Gelgel and establish a new court there. As a line of the Bandesa clan, the Kubon Tubuh were leading representatives of the Old Balinese society so vital to the survival of the new lords and masters.

Though preceded by a dubious reputation as an inveterate gambler, Ida I Dewa Ketut Ngulesir went to Gelgel to be crowned Dalem Ketut Semara Kapakisan. He built the new *kraton* of Sweca Lingarsa Pura there and founded the Gelgel Dynasty, which was to be so crucial to the cultural and social development of Bali. Under the wise and skilful leadership of the new Dalem and the divine protection of Mahadewa, god of the sacred mountain of To-Langkir (Gunung Agung) – with whom the ruler was compared – social, political and cultural foundations were laid and reinforced. And it was upon these foundations that Waturrenggong, his son and successor, would build, leading Bali into a golden age.

The Golden Age

Little is known about Bali in the fifteenth century. Majapahit had succeeded in retaining its imperial thrust unopposed until, in the late fifteenth century, disputes over revenues from maritime trade sparked off civil wars which sorely weakened the empire and initiated its gradual decline. Islam had already gained a foothold in Sumatra in the thirteenth century and was now, at the beginning of the sixteenth century, making headway on the coasts of Java. As Majapahit became eroded, Islamic coastal regents pressed forward into the interior of the country, dealing the empire its final blow between 1515 and 1528.

All those who were unwilling to accept Islamization now moved to the easternmost parts of Java (Blambangan) and to Bali, among them the aristocracy, the priests and jurists, and whole groups of artists and artisans who had been in the service of the court. Specialized artists and artisans had already served the Central Javanese court; and in the Majapahit Empire, groups of artists and guilds of artisans were established in the vicinity of the court. It thus comes as no surprise that in Gelgel, too, people engaged in the same craft congregated in a village or village district near the court. The gold- and silversmiths (Pande Mas) lived in Banjar Pande Mas, the painters and draughtsmen (Sangging) in Banjar Sangging in the village of Kamasan, near Gelgel. Their descendants continue to practise their traditional crafts there today. The ironsmiths had settled in Klungkung and Kusamba, the coppersmiths in Banjar Budaga and the gongsmiths in nearby Tihingan. Only the sculptors and architects appear not to have lived and worked in occupational organizations and territorial communities. This can probably be explained by their backgrounds, for, like the producers of *songket* and *endek* textiles[32] for the nobility, they were themselves aristocrats, and later *brahmana*, who had learnt about and mastered the esoteric sides of building.

In the first half of the sixteenth century, under the rule of King Waturrenggong, Bali developed into a major imperial force and a bulwark against the advance of Islam. Waturrenggong's empire extended from Blambangan and Pasuruan in East Java to the islands of Lombok and Sumbawa, bordering on other great powers of the archipelago: the Islamic kingdoms of Surabaya and Mataram in Java and Macassar in Sulawesi. The chroniclers had spirited words of praise for his lion-hearted courage, incomparable daring and magical powers in battle. Thanks to his charisma and ability to galvanize political opinion, he succeeded in integrating and uniting the aristocracy and the people to forge a unified empire whose centre was in Gelgel. Although Waturrenggong was regarded as omnipotent, the incarnation of Wisnu, the divine sustainer, the divine kingdom had gradually become sufficiently secularized for its rulers to cease to be worshipped and immortalized as stone statues, as had been the case in pre-Majapahit times. The divine kingdom had now been superseded by a more abstract cosmic order, expressed in complex systems of classification and in numerological and colour symbolism.

And yet in Bali the king remained the vehicle of cosmic responsibility for the empire, and this in turn enabled religion and religious practices to remain integral components of sovereignty and politics. In the state temple Pura Dasar in Gelgel, the power of the king became an expression of the will of the gods. He represented the magical-political centre of the empire and the cosmos. The king himself was directly associated with the divine power of the centre, thereby gaining sacred and ritual authority. This authority was reinforced when the mother temple of all Balinese, the old mountain sanctuary of Besakih, was designated the second focus of royal ritual policies.

Drawing Closer to the Common People

Ritual politics, organized and structured by the aristocracy and the priests, ultimately became an important instrument in the process of strengthening ties to the ordinary populace as well. Under King Waturrenggong and his prime minister Kiai Batan Jeruk, relations with the leading Old Balinese clans, already cultivated by earlier vassal rulers, were intensified and expanded. Members of the Pasek and Bandesa were trained 'in the centre of the world', the spectacular palace of Swecapura which symbolically embraced the whole world. Later the Pasek Gelgel were entrusted with leadership tasks in the village, the Pura Dasar state temple and the palace itself. The Bandesa were made responsible for the administration of temple property (*laba pura*) (see chapter 3, p. 55).

The palace acquainted members of the ordinary population with courtly pomp. Painting, literature, music and theatre so thoroughly imbued them with courtly culture that they became ideal propaganda vehicles for the royal policy of drawing closer to the people. But Waturrenggong also maintained direct contact to his subjects, who numbered some 300,000, by travelling out into the country, attending temple rituals, granting public audiences at court and mounting theatrical performances in an open, rectangular square just outside the walled palace grounds.

A major role in the reform and consolidation of government, caste and religion was played by Danghyang Nirartha, Waturrenggong's priestly teacher and advisor, who, according to documentary sources, came to Mas in Bali from East Java in 1537 (see chapter 4, p. 79). News of the Padanda Sakti Wau Rauh, the 'Just Arrived Magic-Powerful High Priest', soon spread from there to the court at Gelgel. The king dispatched the poet-prince of his empire, Kiai Dawuh Bale Agung, to Mas to bring the holy man to the palace. Once there, he concerned himself primarily with questions of ritual connected with death, soul purification, weddings, pregnancy, birth and maturity. It is owing to his influence that the Siwa cult and its Brahman priests attained the most important role in Hindu-Balinese religion.

Nirartha is worshipped as the father of the Balinese Brahmans, and his sons are the forefathers of the *brahmana* families scattered throughout Bali today (see chapter 4, pp. 79f). Danghyang Nirartha's position in Balinese cultural history does not derive solely from his part in religious and ritual reforms; together with the court poet Dawuh Bale Agung, who gave him a daughter in marriage, the royal adviser became a prime force in the literary world. Nirartha himself wrote songs and literary works; the Usana Bali, a combination of myth, legend and history, is ascribed to him. The people around him studied Old Javanese works and created new works in Old Javanese or in a later variety of the language, known among philologists as 'Middle Javanese'. Historical, epic, moralistic and didactic pieces plus speculative religious texts relating to the worship of the gods combine to form a stock of literature still read, studied and copied today.

Signs of Decay

With King Waturrenggong's death, the Golden Age of Bali soon went into decline and the unity of the centralistic empire began to falter. Two sons figured as possible successors: Ida I Dewa Pamayun and Ida I Dewa Dimade. As both were still too young to rule, I Dewa Anggungan, one of five paternal uncles, was appointed regent and entrusted with raising and educating the boys. Anggungan appears to have quickly taken on the traits of a *wayang* servant figure in the hands of powerful *dalang* Batan Jeruk, who, as prime minister and court counsellor, was weaving a web of palace intrigue and fomenting rivalries between the various noble houses. As a Satria Jawa and descendant of the Javanese Kediri rulers, Batan Jeruk had trained his sights on shifting the balance of power away from the Gelgel Dynasty, the Satria Dalem. The armed conflict that ensued saw the usurpers beaten by the legitimate *raja* in 1556. While the Arya Kubon Tubuh made a substantial contribution to the victory by supporting the future Dalem, the role of the Arya Nginte, who came from Kapal to help and were instrumental in persuading several disloyal ministers to return to the fold, should not be underestimated. Batan Jeruk was killed in Bungaya (Karangasem) by Nginte warriors, his family escaping to Watuaya. They would later become the dominant dynasty of Karangasem.

In 1560 the elder of Waturrenggong's two sons was crowned Dalem Pamayun Bekung. He was an inept, luckless *raja*, and once again imperilled the magic, cosmic powers of the palace. As suspicion, jealousy, private feuds and murderous treachery threatened to challenge the equilibrium of the whole empire – Lombok, Sumbawa, Pasuruan and Blambangan – the court council decided to depose the Dalem and replace him with his younger brother, who succeeded to the throne as Dalem Seganing in 1580. Dalem Bekung moved first to a neighbouring palace in Gelgel and from there eastward to Purasi, known today as Prasi.

Dalem Seganing attempted to carry on the policies initiated by Waturrenggong and did, in fact, succeed in strengthening and unifying the empire, granting Gelgel a renewed surge of power. In laying the groundwork for unity and welfare, Seganing first reunited his own family by marrying his niece, daughter of his elder brother Bekung. The former *dalem* ultimately returned to Gelgel as well, once the birth of two grandchildren had made reconciliation easier.

The Collapse and Disintegration of the Empire

Dalem Seganing remained a wise, pious, courageous ruler of enormous authority until well into advanced age. Upon his death, his eldest son, I Dewa Anom Pamayun, succeeded him. Taking a relentless course from the outset, he ousted all Batan Jeruk's allies who had remained in office and appointed a completely new cabinet to help him impose his drastic plans for political reform. The most important ministerial posts went to the *dalem*-faithful clans Kubon Tubuh and Tangkas, the Brangsinga becoming secretaries of state. Rancour and a desire for revenge seethed in the hearts of those who had fallen from grace and lost their fortunes and sinecures.

It was a situation tailor-made for Kiai Agung Maruti, an ambitious, power-hungry member of the Arya Nyuhaya clan who, like Batan Jeruk himself, traced their origins to the Arya Kediri and disputed the *dalem*'s right to rule. Maruti became leader of a group of conspirators whose goal was to put I Dewa Dimade, the *dalem*'s more susceptible and weaker-willed brother, on the throne. The dissension systematically sown between the two brothers gradually spread to the court and society at large. Had this conflict led to civil war, the floodgates would have been opened for the advance of Islam, and that might easily have meant the end of Balinese culture.

Recognizing the danger, Dalem Anom Pamayun consulted his ministers and officials and his priestly adviser, Padanda Sakti Peling, and then abdicated. He had decided to put the unity of empire and society before his own interests. The unbeaten Dalem Pamayun took his family and loyal followers and retired to Purasi (Prasi), the former residence of his father's brother, Bekung. His reign had lasted only six months. The hour of the sixth Gelgel king, Dalem Dimade, had come. But in the wings stood prime minister Maruti, pulling the strings of power, particularly now that the new *dalem* could no longer count on the support of the Pasek and Kubon Tubuh.

Thirteen years after Dalem Anom Pamayun's withdrawal from Gelgel and seven years after he and his retinue had moved on to Temega in Karangasem, Maruti placed Dalem Dimade under house arrest and declared a state of siege. The elder brother died in Temega that year. He did not live to see the usurper come to power in Gelgel in 1687 or his own younger brother Dimade and his family forced to flee to Gulyang near Bangli.

The Satria Dalem remained divided until 1694, when the court in Singharsa (Sidemen) undertook the first steps towards reconciliation and alliance against the common enemy in Gelgel. By this time Dalem Anom Pamayun's son, Ida I Dewa Anom Pamayun Dimade, resided and ruled in Singharsa, with support from the influential Anglurah Sidemen clan. Negotiations between representatives from Sidemen, on the one side, and Dalem Dimade's son Ida I Dewa Agung Jambe, on the other, led to the development of a common strategy for reconciliation and the retaking of power in Gelgel. Upon Anom Pamayun Dimade's premature death in 1694, his cousin Dewa Agung Jambe moved into the palace in Sidemen, assuming the mantle of leadership and responsibility for raising the children of the deceased.

With the co-operation of the Anglurah Sidemen, Jambe and his legal adviser Padanda Wayan Telabah – who began chronicling events in a kind of diary in 1687 – could now undertake direct consultations and seek allies. And they were ultimately found: in Badung and Buleleng. The Brahman priest established Anggara Paing Bala Isaka 1626 (AD 1704) to be a propitious date for the assault on Gelgel, and the army from Singharsa began its march towards the palace of Gelgel in the north, with Buleleng attacking from the north-west and Badung from the coast in the south-west. Maruti was taken by surprise and defeated, but succeeded in fleeing to Jimbaran. His subsequent petition for mercy was granted and he re-

ceived the right to live in Kramas and Mengwi, where his sons
would later rule as *raja*.

Asmarapura: the New Royal City

As Gelgel had forfeited its cosmic power as the centre of the
empire, the new king, Ida I Dewa Agung Jambe, established
his court in neighbouring Asmarapura, home for the next 200
years to the Dewa Agung, the supreme, if only nominal, kings
of Bali. Bali's disintegration into various kingdoms and principalities could no longer be stopped. As early as 1687, powerful *satria* who had denied Maruti their allegiance had
withdrawn from Gelgel and created their own tiny, autonomous states, which they ruled as kings or princes. A time of
social and cultural change had begun, a time marked by political struggles, wars and enmities, by envy, resentment, revenge
and lust for glory.[33]

An empire that in its golden age had extended from East
Java to Sumbawa was, in the eighteenth century, developing
into a mosaic of small, belligerent kingdoms (Karangasem,
Badung, Mengwi, Gianyar, Tabanan, Buleleng, Bangli, Negara and Klungkung). Rivalry was unabating, and with the
passage of time each became an independent cultural centre
with a court intent on outshining the others by expanding and
giving new stylistic impulse to its own rituals and courtly
pomp. This, in turn, resulted in a dramatic increase in artistic,
dramatic and musical variety. Close scrutiny reveals that this
cultural and artistic competitiveness, whether spurred by en-
vious admiration or wholehearted contempt for one's rival, is
still perceptible today, both in its positive and negative aspects.

It was in this Bali of tiny, warlike states that the Dutch,
driven by economic and geopolitical interests, began to assert
themselves (see chapter 8, pp. 201–3). They fought from 1846
until 1908 before achieving their goal and gaining control
over the whole of Bali. It took no less than seven military
expeditions to subjugate the Balinese kings, to turn
their 'theatre states'[34] into showcases for exemplary cultural
colonialism and open the door to tourism. Now Bali was
ready to approximate the image of paradise on earth – an

image created by new rulers and foreign guests (*wong jaba*). An image so successful that, in the meantime, many Balinese have begun to believe in that 'paradise' themselves.[35]

3

Agriculture, Crafts and Spheres of Exchange

Regardless of the degree of controversy about the impact of external influences on endogenous culture, researchers agree that agriculture, the dominant form of livelihood on Bali, comprises numerous autochthonous elements – even up to the present day. These are confirmed in the literature on the subject, above all for wet-rice cultivation and the organizational and technical matters associated with irrigation (cf. chapter 4, pp. 93–7). What will be shown below is that there are also many craft activities embedded in the socio-religious context. Economic activities must not, therefore, be considered exclusively from the point of view of the individual and material satisfaction of needs. Economic action underlies specific socio-cultural rules which set down what is fitting or what is inappropriate. As these maxims are laid down in the *adat*, which is in turn inseparable from religion (cf. chapter 4, pp. 65–8), many aspects of gainful activity which in western tradition are regarded as being in the sphere of the profane are in Bali bound to religious elements. In the Balinese all-embracing thought world, man does not stand apart from the environment but is an equal part of the '*Mitwelt*' or total world. Animals, plants, the soil and 'material things' are considered spiritually animated, especially if they fulfil real or imaginary functions for man. This striving for 'partnership-like' behaviour is expressed, for example, by the *tumpek uduh* holiday, when coconut palms are given gifts in gratitude for their harvests. *Tumpek landep* is the commemoration day for all metals, which are of use to man in many forms. Their radiation is reactivated on this day and directed towards the good of man. A new building constructed out of 'dead' material is consecrated during the *mapakuh (malaspas)* ceremony; only then do the inhabitants feel sheltered and protected within its walls.

The connection of agricultural matters with religious ideas will first be considered with reference to an outline of various tenure systems. It will then be shown that western principles of law cannot be automatically transferred to foreign cultures. At the end of the chapter, it will be argued that by pre-colonial times, external influences entered into conflict with autochthonous systems of values. Using the example of trade, it will be shown that Bali never played the role of a 'last paradise' (as many western romantics saw it) or of an 'exotic reservation', still glorified by tourism in the twentieth century, where those tired of western civilization hope to recuperate in a pure, intact world.

By the nineteenth century, visitors from the west were impressed by the quality of Balinese wet-rice agriculture. On the occasion of his visit to Buleleng (1815), the Englishman Thomas Stamford Raffles wrote:

The inhabitants of Báli like those of Java, are principally employed in agriculture. The fertility of the island may be inferred from the number of people maintained on so limited a spot. Rice is the chief produce of the soil, and of course the chief article of subsistence. From the mountainous nature of the country, advantage cannot so easily be taken of the periodical rains for the purpose of rice irrigation, but the lands are irrigated by an abundant supply of water from streams and rivers. In some places, as in Karang Asem, two crops of rice are obtained in one year; but over the greatest part of the island only one.[1]

Thirty-four years later, Heinrich Zollinger, a Swiss naturalist in the Netherlands colonial service, reported:

The whole area right up to Kassiman [that is, between the present capital of Denpasar and Kesiman] . . . is a well-cultivated, fertile plain . . . We did not see any uncultivated land the length of our route . . . We observed fine rice-fields as far as the eye could see . . .[2] The *sawah* [irrigated fields] are more beautiful and better kept than in Java. The rice harvest of Balie must be extremely large. There is a regular trade in rice with China, and during the last price-rise many shiploads were brought to Madura, Surabaya and other places from the eastern part of Balie.[3]

Among further agricultural products, Zollinger mentions 'millions of coconut palms' in Karangasem, rice under dry cultivation and corn (1845: 28). He noted that, in contrast to wet-rice agriculture, coffee groves in mountainous areas were not well cared for. On the contrary, he praised the quality of Balinese cattle and mentioned the export of oxen to Java. There was no shortage of pigs and dogs (ibid.: 45f).

Plate 6   Rice is life: the divine rice plant is considered a female being

Concepts of Land Ownership and Land-tenure Systems

Who does the land belong to? If we judge land ownership analogously to the crops which grow there, the answer given by Dutch scholars of the nineteenth and early twentieth centuries is obvious: the land belongs to the gods:

The land, with everything that grows on it, the water that flows through it, the air that envelops it, the rock it holds in its womb, belongs without exception or limitation to the invisible gods and spirits who inhabit it . . . Also completely in keeping with this notion of overriding rights of the deity is the fact that land is never farmed before permission has been requested from the local deity and that as soon as cultivation has begun nothing is considered more essential than to erect an altar to the deity as an expression of gratitude. A part of the crops harvested from the lands should be presented to the deity as an offering, and whenever wood and other materials for the repair of temples or altars are needed they are taken where they are best to be found, regardless of whatever rights

Plate 7　Cili: symbol of the goddess of wet-rice production, Dewi Sri

persons may exercise on the lands where they occur . . . All in all, the above removes every doubt that, in the view of the Balinese, the land is owned by the gods who inhabit the country.[4]

Another pronouncement stands in opposition to this fictious awarding of the soil to the gods, namely that the ruler is master of the land (regardless of whether it is put to agricultural use or remains uncultivated), the forests, the water, the air – that is, of all resources (including people) in his realm. The *raja*, who commanded almost godly respect, was raised to the status of Sang Amawa Bumi[5] and his kingdom, and therewith its soil, was by extension regarded as his 'property' (*druwe Anak Agung*). But not only gods and kings 'owned' land. Villages, temple associations and other population groups, families and individuals also referred to their landed 'property'.[6] This is a reference to the fact that earlier Balinese land-ownership rights have no claim to exclusiveness, as is the case in the western understanding of law, but that the 'possession' of resources is rather to be understood symbolically. Geertz demonstrates that the term *druwe* ('property') reflects a hierarchy of patterns, in which every step is a version of the next higher (and finer), each higher step representing an image of the one below it (being a coarser version) – a graded symbolism which expresses itself in numerous other Balinese cultural matters. Balinese property rights are therefore not 'either/or' matters with only one legal claim to property; there can be several such 'ownerships' existing at the same time.[7]

To what extent did nobles and commoners, villages and *banjar*, temple associations and other specific groups of the population possess land? This question cannot be answered in a way which is generally valid for the whole of Bali. Before the introduction of colonial agrarian legislation, diverse property rights existed not only regionally side-by-side, but were also subject to differences over time. Law must be understood as a process, not as something static. In the case of Bali, the implementation of binding legal principles was hindered by the absence of a centre with absolute power. It is more appropriate to accept the evident legal pluralism than to speak of a 'Balinese legal system'. Therefore, it is almost impossible to map the different land-tenure systems.

The disintegration that was obvious from the seventeenth century onwards, the intrigues between rival rulers or between rulers and their governors with regard to access to resources, led to permanent instability, which permitted subjects a certain freedom in the choice of their lords. The fragmentation of supra-village authority, the binding of households to various lords within one and the same village, within one and the same *subak*, weakened the institutional authority. After his visit to the ruler of Buleleng in 1815, Thomas Stamford Raffles, the British lieutenant-governor of Java and its dependencies at the time, gained the impression that the King was not to be considered as the universal landlord, but that the land was, almost without exception, privately owned by the subjects and was freely sold, leased, mortgaged[8] or bequeathed according to the wishes of the owner.[9] Data collected by Liefrinck in Buleleng and Jembrana in 1871 revealed that irrigated land was almost exclusively under private ownership and that village communities could exercise only certain rights over uncultivated land within the borders of their village territory.[10] It will be verified later that right up to the 1980s villages in these regencies were authorized to award their citizens plots for dry agriculture in usufruct according to *adat* rules.

The plurality of Balinese land-tenure systems reflects the complex structure of the society which was, in turn, more or less strongly influenced by the high nobility, who were mainly resident on the plain. At the top of the hierarchy were the kings (*raja*), whose lords, being governors (*punggawa*), were responsible for the implementation of royal edicts within their circle of subjects. To fulfil their duties, the governors had *perbekel* (one step down on the ladder) at hand to help them. These *perbekel* in turn saw to it that the services which peasants and craftsmen were, as subjects (*kaula*), required to render to the palace were duly performed. The bondsmen of the lords (*sepangan, parekan*) were at a lower level than the *kaula* (which included the large mass of the commoners). The former were those without resources and, while serfs of a lord, had to carry out all tasks required of them in exchange for board, keep and clothing, which were awarded to them by their owner.[11] Finally, slaves (*panjak*) were families or persons who, being personal possessions of the lord, could be sold.

What was decisive for the political structure of Bali was that the '*kaula*-property' of the *perbekel* or the '*perbekel*-property' of the *punggawa* was not territorially defined, but almost arbitrarily scattered over hamlets and villages. Lords used people rather than territories as a political resource.[12]

The characteristics of the land-tenure system of certain so-called 'Mountain Balinese' villages are mentioned in chapter 4, pp. 68–75, where attention is drawn to the distribution of plots (belonging to the village) for usufruct to resident families in the area. Core citizens who could trace their origins to a common ancestor – the village founder – were in a privileged position. Extensions of this system sometimes developed by way of granting newcomers the right of domicile at the margins of established settlements, thus allowing these pioneers to constitute a satellite community within the village territory. Villages were, in this epoch, not only responsible for political-juridical matters within their borders, but also for their economic milieu. Therefore the land, as the most substantial element of wealth, was often subject to the right of disposal by the village (*hak purba*). As land was viewed at its highest as the property of the gods, the attachment of the people to the land and soil went far beyond their function as a factor of production, and also encompassed religious values and social norms. The *hak purba* conceded to family heads the right of usufruct over land within the village boundaries, whereby the individual granting of plots from communal land was subject to various restrictions. For example, newcomers received the right of usufruct only upon formal request and sometimes only against payment, the applicant having to pledge observance of the village *adat*. Land transfers to non-residents were often forbidden. Likewise, the right to clear woodland for cultivation was vested only in members of the village community involved.

How rights of disposal or rights of usufruct change into rights of ownership has not been entirely explained. The gradual structuring of the village society could have contributed to the dismantling of communal rights of disposal. Perhaps the prescriptive rights of certain families crystallized out of the practice of transferring the right of usufruct over specific plots to (male) heirs. It would be worth investigating the extent to which bearers of inheritable official positions in the village and the corresponding award of 'fields associated with office', as compensation for assiduity, were at first granted rights over larger areas under cultivation than ordinary commoners received, a difference which becomes even more pronounced under Hindu-Javanese influence. Further, the question remains open as to whether (along with villages with land in communal possession) *desa*, in which individual ownership of land according to the *adat* had been the rule since early times, existed.

How then can the tenure systems in the small kingdoms of Bali be explained, when the source material from Raffles (researched in 1815 and published in 1817) and Liefrinck (researched in 1871) point to the fact that neither the ruler nor the village communities exercised absolute rights over land, but that land in the area mentioned by them was *de facto* under individual ownership? What emerges from the mentioned social structure is that, with the exception of serfs and slaves, all other Balinese were potential landowners. The *raja* owned estates which he (the king) as an individual arranged to have managed and cultivated for him. Estates inherited from his ancestors were parts of the king's landed property. Extensions to these possessions resulted from conquests of foreign areas, land purchases, land which was brought to the marriage as dowries by wives of the king, and confiscated plots. Even though the accumulation of royal landed property was not excluded, a characteristic feature was the strong fragmentation of his lands. These could be distributed over various villages and *subak*, located amid other properties owned by the nobility or by commoners. The royal right of confiscation (*hak camput*),[13] which allowed the *raja* to transfer the estate of a deceased person without male heirs into his own possession, contributed to this fragmentation. Immovables (such as landed property) and mobile goods (which included widows and daughters who became serfs of the ruler) alike could be confiscated. The cultivation of royal private land was entrusted either to serfs or to share-croppers (*panyakap*) – more often the latter, especially for scattered plots of land: they were known to be honest and hard-working peasants living close to the fields concerned.[14] As the term 'share-cropper' suggests, a *panyakap* had to give the landowner a fixed (absolute or relative) portion of the harvest in return for the right of cultivation. He in turn received the rest as compensation for his work. If the employer was (and is) pleased with the work furnished, such rights for share-cropping could (and can even today) be transferred to male successors of a deceased *pa-nyakap*, so that sometimes this work contract can *de facto* seem like permanent tenancy.[15] In this connection, it must be mentioned that the production factor 'labour' was rare right up to the nineteenth century, thus share-croppers had a stronger position than is the case today in view of the scarcity of land. Share-cropping contracts with several landowners were (and are) permitted. Village, *banjar* or *subak* associations had a say in deciding whom the working contracts were given to and also in influencing the cultivation according to the *adat* of the place concerned.[16]

Analogous to private royal land, all families other than serfs and slaves could own land, which they could either work themselves or let share-croppers do it; in the case of the nobility, servant workers would do the work. Where the village *adat* (see chapter 4, pp. 65–8) was already weakened (or perhaps individual restrictions over disposal did not exist), land could be (as both the above-mentioned informants suggest) sold, bequeathed or mortgaged according to the will of the owner. However, these peasants (*kaula*) were obliged to carry out certain services for the king and the village. In case of war, nobles as well as commoners were liable to do military service. In addition, *kaula* had to perform ritual duties at palace ceremonies, for which they were also urged to supply certain goods.

Ties with the lord were strengthened in that the latter ceded land to specific groups of the population (*pauman*) as compensation for their work and their services to the palace; for example, to smiths for the production of weapons with magic power as well as metal instruments and bronze gongs for orchestras; to weavers for the fabrication of sacral textiles; to weapon carriers and so on. Members of the royal family of Karangasem stress that royal land was also granted to other groups, such as clans (*dadia*) and *banjar*, to ensure their loyalty. These were tactical calculations which arose from numerous battles in the course of power struggles between nobles. *Pauman* land may be inherited but may not be sold.

The harvests from such land are divided equally amongst the families which make up the group, after the deduction of any quantities resulting from share-cropping.[17]

Laba pura is land bound to a temple, which, according to interpretations of the east Balinese nobility, was ceded to the temple as a royal gift. Temple land is tax-free but is subject to severe restrictions. It may be neither sold nor mortgaged. The profits of the harvest are for the benefit of the *pura*, for example, the upkeep of the temple, and for ceremonies. Parts of the *laba pura* can be transferred for share-cropping or given in usufruct to the temple priest (*pamangku*). In the latter case, the profits of the harvest serve as a kind of pay-off for the assiduity of the *pamangku*, whose task it is, among other things, to take care of the temple.[18]

As mentioned for the early kingdoms of Mengwi and Gianyar as well as for parts of south Bangli and Klungkung, interpretations concerning the so-called *pacatu* fields are contradictory. According to Korn, *pacatu* in principle originates from village land. *Pacatu* holders were obligated to do royal services, including the upkeep of the *puri* and the delivery of necessary materials.[19] Peasants on *pacatu* land als had to pay taxes to their lord or his substitute in the form of rice and money.[20] Geertz attaches importance to establishing the fact that such fields were neither royal lands, leased by the king as indemnity to commoners for their services, nor 'owned' by the village collectivity as compensation for fulfilling collective *desa* obligations to the palace. *Pacatu* lands rather belonged to persons who either tilled the fields themselves or allowed share-croppers to do it. Crop yields from *pacatu* can be considered as productive support which enabled *pangayah* to fulfil their political-religious duties. Geertz argues that *pacatu* cannot, therefore, be regarded as a system of land law but rather as a method of classifying the kinds of labour obligations to which villagers were subject: that is, to a lord, a village or a temple.[21]

The stress on *de facto* individual ownership may be justified in many cases. But other examples indicate that communal land ownership actually existed in which cultivators were in no way landowners but can only be considered to be usufructaries. Such village communities were careful to ensure that the idea of individual ownership did not arise. Julah, in the contemporary regency of Buleleng, is a case in point. In this village on the northern piedmont, the land was in the possession of the *desa* (*tanah milik desa*) until 1982; plots were given to the villagers in usufruct and in a manner that allocated to the benefiting families a different field every year. The yearly rotation of plots – originally thought to prevent the establishment of common law over a certain field – concealed obvious ecological disadvantages. As the village possessed land which was exclusively suitable for dry-field cultivation, the plots could only be planted with crops in the rainy season and therefore had a short growth-period. The peasants, aware of the rotation of plots, were thus tempted to maximize their harvests on a short-term basis, thereby impoverishing of the soil, the consequences of which the next usufructary had to bear. The results were obvious. Soil erosion devastated the unprotected slopes. Through a motion passed by the village council, the village land was transferred to individual ownership in 1982, enabling the peasants henceforth to grow perennial plants (for example, orange-trees), a type of cultivation that is not only economically profitable but offers ecological advantages in that soil is stabilized by the tree growth.[22]

Division of Labour and Exchange of Goods and Services

In a rural society whose economy is marked by a limited division of labour, domestic trade plays a modest role and traders enjoy only relatively low-status prestige. The aim of families mainly engaged in agriculture is to ensure their food supply by means of subsistence-oriented production. This is also the case in Bali. The peasants did not deal on the retail market in order to fill their barns. The harvests of traditional rice varieties were stored in the form of sheaves brought in through the granary roof (granaries are part of the family compound). Daily portions were taken from a little door underneath. The unused surplus was reduced from time to time by conspicuous expenditure[23] for mass ceremonies or was exchanged for essential commodities which could not be made by the peasants. There is, in fact, no subsistence economy in

Plate 8   Traditional way of salt-making at Kusamba

Plate 9   Weaving a traditional hip cloth (kamben) *on a backstrap tension loom*

which everything that is produced is also consumed and no entity of reproduction makes everything that is required. Consequently, a brief description follows of how barter took place, how goods were bought and sold in a modest way in the village markets, and then (in addition to these local exchanges) how interinsular and international exchange was established in which the different systems were not at first connected.

Certain *banjar* and kinship groups traditionally specialized in the production of certain essential commodities and luxury goods. They could not always produce enough food for themselves to cover their requirements. There were more or less stable relationships between craftsmen – that is, smiths, weavers, brickmakers, stonemasons, potters, woodcarvers, roofmakers and those plaiting bamboo mats, and so on – and peasants, whereby craft products were exchanged for rice and other foodstuffs. Valuable works of arts and crafts were commissioned by princes from specialists, who enjoyed the patronage of the nobility which brought with it special privileges. In the same way, products from the primary sector, such as palm sugar, rice- and palm-wine, coconut oil, fish, cattle and that vital commodity salt, were demanded and exchanged for other products or sometimes for money.[24] There was no actual labour market for at the courts serfs were given the work to do, if necessary supported by subjects liable for service, whilst family and neighbourhood associations helped each other out, not only in a material way but also with work (*saling tulung*). In larger groups, such as the *banjar* association, mutual assistance manifests itself in the *rites de passage* and by unremunerated work for the community (*gotong royong*).[25]

The reciprocal exchange referred to does not exclude the fact that a small, locally restricted retail trade in daily necessities developed, with in particular women[26] offering small quantities of food and luxuries, wood and other fuels as well as craft products for cash. In fact, the sale or exchange of gathered goods such as wood and corallime has enabled those with little or no land to better their economic situation up to the present day. From Zollinger's description a clear picture emerges of the modest scale of supply and demand in the market places (in 1845). Thus: 'The market in Kutta [i.e. Kuta] lies in the middle of the kampung. It is, in fact, a rather wide square in a street whose sides are lined with a few *warung* [i.e. stalls] where fruit, rice and fish are sold. I didn't see anything else for sale.' The cock-fighting square is adjacent to the market place: 'An especially large group of people was assembled in the market [i.e. in Kesiman]. We watched the cock-fights for a while. On the right and left there were hundreds of "fighters" in their cages. We could hardly get through the crowds, who walked, sat or stood excitedly around the fighting arena, expressing their interest for the cock-fighting by way of loud laughter punctuated with tremendous shouting.'[27] As can be seen from the schematic plan of a south Balinese village (chapter 4, p. 90), in the centre the market place and the cock-fighting arena (*wantilan*) lay directly opposite the palace of the ruler. This made it easier for the lord, as the 'owner', to control and to tax the market (*pasar*) and the cock-fights (*tajen*).

As far as Bali is concerned, it was rather a peripheral part of the wide world of the European seafarers until the first half of the nineteenth century. Raffles substantiated Bali's remoteness with respect to sea-trade as being a result of the poor access for ships: 'having an iron-bound coast, without harbours or good anchorage, it has been in a great measure shut out from external commerce, particularly with traders in large vessels'.[28] In writing about its inhospitable coasts for harbours, Raffles was especially referring to the coral reefs which fringe Bali's coastlines and upon which many ships were wrecked.[29]

Yet it is obvious that from early times Bali has been involved in the Asiatic sea-trade: the biggest collection of early Indian trade pottery from the whole of Indonesia has been found at Sembiran, a Balinese village at the north coast. Foreign ships presumably anchored there in the first and second centuries AD (see chapter 2, pp. 20f).[30] Balinese royal edicts, issued in the tenth and eleventh centuries, show that the villages of Julah and Bhanwa Bahru had been fortified settlements, functioning as harbours and market places for interinsular and long-distance trade. At that time the north coast – facing the Java Sea – gave access to the sea-trade in the Archipelago and to the shipping routes between China and India.[31] From the German cosmographer Sebastian Münster (1498–1552) we learn that in the sixteenth century Bali was already peripherally involved in the flourishing trade in spices. He refers to the fact that many 'gentlemen' lived in the harbour town of Tuban (in the present province of east Java), conducting wholesale trade in

*Plate 10   Balinese with his fighting cock at a ceremony to appease
demonic forces*

textiles such as silk and cotton cloth. They owned ships which they called '*jonken*' (that is junks). In Tuban they were loaded with pepper and sailed 'to Balie' (Singaraja, Julah or Tulamben?), where the pepper was exchanged for poor-quality cotton cloth. The acquired textiles were shipped to the Moluccas (for example, to Ternate) where the Balinese cloth was exchanged for nutmeg, cloves and other products which were, in turn, brought back to Tuban.[32] Seafaring Bugis, Malays, Chinese, Arabs and so on purchased rice, cattle, skins, cotton cloth and coconut-oil in Bali in exchange for thread, Chinese silk, Indian brocade, glass trinkets, ironware and Chinese coins. Later, weapons (including gunpowder and lead) and, above all, opium were sold. However, not only goods but also people were traded. A great demand for slaves arose from the Dutch East India Company, which suffered a shortage of workers in agriculture and the crafts as well as servants for the households at their headquarters in Batavia, in the outposts of the Archipelago, and also at the trading posts along the shipping route to Europe (above all in Cape Town). Within the network of the Indonesian slave trade, Bali played a prominent role as a supplier. Whilst at the start resident 'burghers' in Batavia procured slaves for the main market there, it was the Chinese who controlled the Asian slave trade from the end of the eighteenth century. The Balinese contractors were the lords who profited by the sale of prisoners of war, criminals who had been reprieved (to slavery) after receiving the death sentence, negligent debtors, and those widows and daughters who had been 'confiscated' by means of the *hak camput*. The Indonesian slave trade was halted for the first time during the short British interregnum (1811–15) by the Lieutenant-Governor of Java and its dependencies, Thomas Stamford Raffles. The reason for this was the anti-slave trade law passed by the British Parliament in 1807. However, this did not prevent French and British slave-traders in the following phase from increasing their stock of people, whom they sold on the French sugar island of La Réunion (Ile de Bourbon). A further demand – this time from the Netherlands Indies Army – arose in the context of the Java War (1825–30), a war in which followers of the Javanese prince Diponegoro opposed the colonial power. To reinforce the latter, soldiers were 'enlisted', not always of their own free will but often by the coercive incorporation of bought slaves.[33]

Even after the issuing of strict anti-slave trade prohibitions by France and the termination of the Java War (both in 1830), the slave trade continued to exist to a moderate extent. We can glean this from Zollinger, for example, who in 1845 describes the following incident in Kuta. When the Netherlands emissaries (amongst others, the Swiss Zollinger) met the Prince of Badung in the house of the Danish trade master Lange, Chinese coins were loaded on to a ship at anchor, whereupon one of the sacks opened and

four little packets to the value of four silver guilders fell onto the floor. A young kuli snatched up the coins and put them in his pocket. He was caught red-handed and brought before the Dewa [the prince]. The deed was quickly proven and the sentence even more rapidly pronounced. The verdict was that the man had to be 'krised' (stabbed with a *keris*) . . . Mr L. [Lange] stepped between the two [i.e. between the prince and the thief] and declared to the Dewa that the punishment was too severe . . . The matter was settled in that Mr L. could bring the condemned on to one of the ships and if the man liable to punishment did not want this, the death penalty had to be put into effect. The thief was in fact brought on to one of the ships in our presence . . . Under such cruel methods of jurisdiction, slavery appears to be a very humane form of punishment.[34]

Zollinger's report also makes us aware of an unfolding process, that is, of the dissociation of the Balinese from their originally stronger domestic orientation and the introduction of external influences, which marked the start of the islanders' irreversible road to the market economy. Whilst at first Singaraja (kingdom of Buleleng) on the north coast was the only trade enclave with a bazaar-like character being sailed to by freight ships, the kingdom of Badung in south Bali was drawn increasingly into foreign trade in the nineteenth century. Even though other kingdoms with suitable coastlines had small harbours and anchorages, Kuta, which lay on the isthmus joining the Bukit Pecatu Peninsula with the island mainland, proved to have many natural advantages. It had two harbours: in the western part of the isthmus that of Kuta (*pantai barat*), which lies in the lee of the south-east trades; and Tuban on the east side of the isthmus (*pantai timur*), whose roads are protected from the Javanese west monsoon. However, the off-shore coral reefs were a disadvantage in both cases.

The organization of the pre-colonial foreign trade must now be considered. As the harbours were seen as the 'possession' of the lords and foreign trade their domain, it lay within their power to lease out trade to contract-bound Chinese trade lords (*subandar*). Being managers of foreign trade, the latter had a monopoly in their realm of trade. Responsibility for the actual buying and selling of goods was transferred by the *subandar* to their subordinate compatriots. If trade masters did not possess their own boats, shipping was ceded to Buginese and Madurese contractors. As a quid pro quo for the payment of high trade-leasing fees, the *subandar* enjoyed their employers' protection.[35]

After the abrupt decline in the remunerative slave trade (1830), the interest of the lords and their trade masters turned towards the export of agricultural goods. In addition to rice and other export products, coffee, tobacco and sugar gained in importance. However, the most profitable field was the import and marketing of opium from Singapore and Calcutta – not only for the lords granting concessions, but also for the importers and their sales agents. The retail network was so closely meshed that even inhabitants of remote villages became addicted. As Geertz remarks, the island-wide demand for this narcotic was an important stimulus of the turn to a market economy: in order to buy opium, the addicts were forced to sell their products and labour in order to get cash.[36]

A new dimension of the incorporation of Bali into the international trade network opened up after the arrival in Kuta (1839) of the Danish merchant-adventurer Mads Johann Lange. Within a few years Kuta was rivalling the north coast harbour of Singaraja in importance. When Zollinger sailed in with a Dutch battleship, six years after Lange had set up in Kuta, he was surprised not only by the 'European luxury' of the trading post, but also by the four foreign cargo sailing-vessels lying at anchor, three of them from Europe. Over a hundred people permanently occupied the living and business quarters. Balinese princes, Dutch commissioners, European researchers and captains met there and enjoyed Lange's well-known hospitality. For a good ten years, Lange was the most successful and influential *subandar* in Bali, acknowledged and patronized not only by the lords of Badung but also later by the Netherlands Indies government in Batavia (after the efforts of the Netherlands Trade Company failed to establish its own trading post in Kuta). As a confidant and mediator between local princes and Dutch colonial civil servants, Lange enjoyed the patronage and goodwill of both. The Dane, who was later awarded Dutch citizenship by the colonial government, traded in everything which promised profit, buying Balinese products at fixed prices set by himself through his well-functioning market network – regardless of fluctuating world market prices. He paid Balinese suppliers with imported Chinese perforated coins (*pis bolong*) at an exchange rate fixed by himself, shipped the export products in his own modern fleet or sold the goods to captains whose cargo ships lay at anchor, and sold provisions to whaling boats for internationally recognized currencies. European assistants supervised trade and did the bookkeeping. In Lange's most brilliant period the yearly turnover of goods amounted to several million silver florins.

Only ten years after the opening of his trading post, Lange's trade activities suffered their first serious setback. The reasons for this were, among others, the sea blockade against Bali, which was imposed by the colonial government during the Dutch – Balinese wars of 1846, 1848 and 1849. But internal Balinese disputes between rival lords were also detrimental to foreign trade.[37] Despite great efforts on the part of Chinese merchants, the trade emporium of Kuta diminished further in importance after Lange's death (1859). After a short period of incorporation into interinsular and international trade, the village of Kuta reverted to a peasant and fishing village, only to re-emerge in the last quarter of the twentieth century to claim world attention, this time as an international tourist resort (see chapter 8).

The change from favourable to unfavourable phases of trade does not alter the fact that many inhabitants of south Bali were, even before Dutch subjugation at the beginning of the twentieth century, familiar with the market economy. It is true that indigenous exchange systems continued to exist on a reduced scale and that everyday goods were bought and sold in village market places. However, in the cities Chinese, Arab and Javanese shop owners had established themselves and wealthy Balinese could stock up with new commodities.

4

Social Organization

Regardless of the tradition scholars represent, they all agree that Balinese social forms display an enormous spectrum of variations. Thus, the Dutch legal scholar and colonial civil servant V. E. Korn dedicated his principal work to a detailed description of the extremely varied rules of social life in Balinese villages.[1] Finding a common denominator for the variety of outward manifestations leaves even renowned academics with a sense of despair, for 'Neither simplicity nor uniformity are Balinese virtues';[2] 'The complexity of the Balinese society is notorious';[3] and 'The social organization is, in fact, heterogeneous and confusing in respect to its essential aspects, and at times completely differing. We are dealing here with what I would call an "ordered anarchy".'[4] The Balinese themselves are also aware of this confusing complexity. With regard to the sphere of the village they express this as 'other village, other *adat*' (*len desa, len adat*). The differences, however, do not stop short at comparisons between villages. Further *adat* realms, for example, govern the actions of individuals within their families or kinship groups, in irrigation associations, voluntary organizations and – at a higher level – in the vassal areas of earlier kingdoms. One of the scholars who tries to go beyond the pure description of phenomena relative to this complex social organization and interprets it as the result of a process of development on a continuum is L.E.A. Howe.[5] Thus, sections of the present chapter follow his argumentation.

To begin with, the central concept of *adat* will be explained and changes over space and time set forth. Attention will be directed first to the so-called Bali Aga. They live mainly, but not exclusively, in the mountainous parts of central and east Bali; some also live in villages on the northern and eastern coast and on the island of Penida. Bali Aga display some socio-cultural attributes that are different to those in the lowlands. Subsequently, foreign influences from the Hindu-Javanese kingdom of Majapahit will be referred to, which were grafted especially on to the Balinese substrate of communities in the low-lying plains from the middle of the fourteenth century (see chapter 2, pp. 34–6). Because the ideology of hierarchical descent groups is expressed through the Balinese caste system, its principles of organization as well as the rules and practices of interaction between members of different castes and different positions will be explained. Subsequently, the aspirations of Balinese groups to raise their position in society (after the externally induced step backwards into the fourth caste) by referring to supposed links to the Javanese nobility will be touched on. The ostensibly clear hierarchical structure of society stands in opposition to the fact that the Balinese also belong to overlapping lineage and caste groups. They were formerly the subjects of rival rulers and they are simultaneously members of temple congregations, ward organizations and village communities, and can belong to irrigation associations based on egalitarian principles. Thus, the tensions encompassing Balinese society are evident; but so also is one particular characteristic of the island population, namely the marked endeavour to harmonize apparently irreconcilable opposites.

Adat

The knowledge communicated and imparted by the ancestors is referred to as *adat*. The word is of Arabic origin and includes the ideas of 'habit', 'custom' and 'practice'. Within the Islamic judicial system, it is customary law which is used in those cases that cannot be solved unambiguously by employing authorized sources. In Indonesian linguistic usage, the meaning of *adat* is more comprehensive and is described by Sutan Takdir Alisjahbana:

Like other early traditional cultures in history, the Indonesian people, prior to the arrival of Indian culture, had evolved a style of thinking at once complex, all-inclusive, and highly intuitive. This style of thought was closely bound up with the enormously important position of religion in the cultural life of Indonesian society . . . Most of his [i.e. man's] knowledge and his arts were subsumed in the intellectual legacy he had received from his forefathers, and which he called *adat*. This *adat* was very different from what we call custom or convention today. Its meaning was not simply wider, but more particularly went far deeper. It included everything we call law nowadays; and it went much further than law in determining the needs and the actions of individuals and the community. It ordained the ceremonies of marriage, birth and death, the times and the methods for sowing rice, building a house, praying for rain, and many other things. . . . Indeed from one point of view, *adat* was simply a social expression of the community religion, in as much as it was not a human creation, and in its exercise men were still constantly watched over by the spirits and supernatural powers ruling the community.

Because the *adat* which regulated the entire life of the community was dominated by spirits and supernatural powers, that communal life was inevitably static and deeply conservative. Its roots lay in the obscurity of the past, when the ancestors laid down the *adat* once and for all, or as the Minangkabau say: 'It doesn't crack with the heat or rot in the rain.' In such an environment the world 'old' had a special significance, denoting something venerable, sacred, powerful and full of wisdom.[6]

Even though the *adat* includes action and behavioural maxims established for all time in an ideal typology and is irrevocably connected to religion, it is in reality not static but subject to change over space and time. Reasons for this can be either innovations induced from within society or externally imposed constraints which stimulate or force change. It was not in all regions of the island that the rulers of Bali – being of East Javanese noble descent – could assert their influence and establish to the same degree the Hindu-Javanese type of caste and class structure from the middle of the fourteenth century onwards (see pp. 75–82). Village economic units were neither equal in size nor equally included in higher-order economic systems. Administrative changes during Dutch colonial rule in Bali (from the middle of the nineteenth century in north Bali and from the beginning of the twentieth century in south Bali) limited the authoritative powers of indigenous communities to a greater or lesser degree (see chapter 8, pp. 203–10). Recent measures towards unification within the framework of the general striving in Indonesia for modernization plus increasing urbanization are jeopardizing certain elements of the *adat*, and are gradually replacing them with uniform standards. Tension between members of a community can arise when the *adat* (not least because of its integrated religious components) changes more slowly than external conditions; 'traditionalists' maintain the indispensability of the *adat* and 'modernists' endeavour to take advantage of new freedoms (see chapter 8).

Original (Mountain) Balinese

Travelling from the south coast inland, the visitor to Bali encounters striking differences in the landscape (see chapter 1). On the easily accessible, densely populated plain, coconut groves fringe the coastline. Landwards, these are replaced by excellently irrigated wet-rice complexes where villages multiply and the courtly establishments are found. The population here is divided into castes and possesses a clear hierarchical structure. This zone is often referred to as 'the cradle of Hindu-Balinese culture'. Above an elevation of about 600 m (as on the steep slopes near the coast) dry-field cultivation replaces wet-land fields. Maize and tubers are the main agricultural products in this transition zone between the plain and the mountains. Access to villages situated on ridges between the deep gorges was and sometimes continues to be impeded, especially in the rainy season. Thus population density decreases. Even though these villages are connected with the economy and markets of the plain, the village folk, who are mainly commoners, are socially and culturally orientated towards the mountains. On the adjoining mountainous land, coffee plantations hidden under shade-giving trees already existed in the first half of the nineteenth century, and were later joined by fruit and vegetable gardens and in recent times by groves of cloves and citrus fruit. Balinese cattle and occasionally goats are bred in areas of low-intensity cultivation.

The flanks of the volcanoes are still partially covered with tropical rain forest. The mountainous country is the main settlement area of the so-called Bali Aga ('Mountain Balinese'), or Bali Mula ('Original Balinese'). This notion is misleading because, even though this group may have some primary characteristics in common with east Indonesian peoples, they were, in the pre-Majapahit period, subject first to Buddhist and later to Hindu influences which, to a certain degree, affected their practices even without the formation of castes (see chapter 2, pp. 22–7).[7] The Hindu-Javanese impact during and after the Majapahit period affected the Bali Aga village communities to a lesser extent. An indication of this is, for example, that the dead are not cremated. The corpses are either buried, thrown into a gorge (as they were until recently in Sembiran) or exposed on rocks (as in Trunyan). The rank system on the basis of age seniority may be considered as another characteristic feature of Bali Aga villages. Compared with the strictly hierarchically ordered descent groups in the southern heartland, status differences are less pronounced.

Without falling prey to geodeterministic thought, we must consider that the extreme natural and cultural variety of Bali is conducive to the formation of diverse forms of economic and social organization. The technical aspects of work and organizational forms of peasant societies must take natural surroundings into account alongside human variables. If we turn to the sparsely populated mountain areas, their peripheral position since the fourteenth to fifteenth centuries with regard to political power and economic centres of the plain is conspicuous.[8] Communication and the exchange of goods and services between the periphery and the ruler's palace (as the centre) were not impossible but were difficult, thus impeding closer integration of the mountain villages into the socio-economic and socio-political network of lower-lying areas. That the economic system was different and its base rather weak was influential in limiting the interest of the throne in fully subordinating and controlling the mountain areas. The new rulers concentrated much more on securing potentially profitable tracts of land on the plain and on the piedmont. As the rival lords' wish to rule the desirable and favourable zones almost entirely absorbed the military forces (recruited from

among their subjects), there were insufficient troops for costly
campaigns in the less-attractive mountainous areas. Recent
research reveals that despite this the Bali Aga did not live in
closed villages completely out of touch with the lower-lying
areas. Evidence can be furnished that village communities on
the southern flank of the Batur volcano were occasionally
obliged to carry out compulsory labour at the palace of the
principality of Bangli and had to provide frontier-defence for
the ruler. In a modest way, the mountainous areas maintained
certain supra-regional economic ties from the nineteenth century onwards.[9] It is known that royally sanctioned trademas-
ters (Indonesian: *syahbandar*; Balinese: *subandar*) marketed
cattle from the highlands in addition to lowland products and
slaves. Thus the rulers living in the south could derive some
benefit from the mountains without full territorial domination
and without direct taxation. It is often overlooked that in
earlier times the power of a ruler was manifested by the
number of subjects he controlled rather than by the area of his
sphere of influence. The inclusion of mountain inhabitants in
ritual obligations to the court and military service was less
intensive than on the plain because no regal governor (*punggawa*) lived in the area to control the Bali Aga. The Brahman
priests (*padanda*) carried just as little weight in the religious
rituals of the markedly inward-looking village communities.
Thus, the reason for the contrast between the Bali Aga villages
and those on the plain should not be attributed solely to the
physical-geographical framework: it is also a result of the
limited influence of the feudal system of the plain to foster
change. As the caste hierarchy in Aga villages is missing,
nobility-related title groups are inapplicable, as is the status
symbol of the Balinese high language (*alus*).[10]

As with other Indonesian villages of early times, a distin-
guishing characteristic of the land-tenure system of many, but
by no means all the mountain villages was communal land
ownership, which was transferred, according to the *adat*, to
heads of families as plots for usufruct, sometimes rotating on
an annual basis.[11] The ceded areas were measured to ensure
that the subsistence needs of a family were covered and that
these would be modest surpluses for redistribution during
community rituals and for sale in the market place. Pasture

lands of the village jural community were used collectively. With the exception of the Aga village of Tenganan (regency of Karangasem), which is in some respects a special case, the surplus produced was small and, in accordance with the rather egalitarian ideology typical of the village population (which the nobility referred to as *sudra*), individual gainful endeavour was less desirable. Respect was on the basis of ritual status rather than the accumulation of goods.

Horizontal and in some cases vertical delimitations arise when persons belonging to different agnatic kinship groups live in the same village. Thus, members of the same descent group (*soroh*) feel united because they are of 'the same kind', that is, their origin can be traced back to a common – real or fictional – forefather (*kawitan*). The perception of difference is founded on the singularity of the diverse origins of ancestors.[12] In contrast to the widespread real or quasi caste system of the south, by which the various descent groups are strictly ordered hierarchically on the basis of the divergent social rankings of the various deified ancestors (as the 'origin'), the *soroh* of the *sudra* – for example, in *Aga* villages – exhibit a lesser degree of social difference as well as fewer title groups. In any case, it is important that a common point of origin unites members of one and the same *soroh* both by descent from a common founding father and also spatially, through the same place of origin. The internal collective articulation of a descent group is thus expressed mainly through the preparation and performance of festivals in the temple of its common ancestor.[13] Analogous to the Boda communities of the Sasak on Lombok,[14] the village structure of the Bali Aga is gerontocratic. Within its territory, the council of elders is responsible for law and order whilst village priests (*pamangku*), who work closely with them, watch over religious observances and function as mediators between the real world and supernatural forces. The 'village assembly', which is made up of married villagers (often the eldest son of a family), is presided over by a council of elders; thus, it is not headed by a single official as in other Balinese villages. When a member of the council of elders retires or dies, either his eldest married son or the next youngest married villager moves up and takes his place on the ladder according to the principle of age seniority. This is expressed visually by the seating arrangements in the meeting hall where not only the council of elders assembles but also where village gods are thought to be present, and where closely knit worldly and religious village affairs are debated.

A further characteristic of Aga villages is their dual structure, which takes into account the Balinese world view of the equilibrium of opposites and tries to harmonize the polarity of uranic and chthonic forces. Such pairs of opposites are, for example, masculine vs. feminine; landwards (*kaja*) vs. seawards (*kelod*); the direction of the sunrise (*kangin*) vs. the direction of the sunset (*kauh*); above (*ke luhur*) vs. below (*ke teben*), and so on.[15] In the eyes of the Lowland Balinese, especially of the gentry, Bali Aga are considered to be stupid, backward,[16] bumpkins – not being 'men of Majapahit' (*wong* Majapahit).

The general disdain for Mountain Balinese values arises out of, for example, the '*wong* Majapahit' version of the legend about the early Balinese local king of Pejeng (a village in the transition zone between the plain and the mountains). It furnishes evidence for the idea held by many Balinese that the pre-Majapahit era is to be looked upon as the demonic 'Dark Ages' and that salvation – and 'modern times' – first began with the arrival of the legendary Majapahit minister and commander-in-chief Gajah Mada. The last king of Pejeng, namely Dalem Bedaulu,[17] is thus depicted as a half-demonic ruler with the head of a wild boar and the body of a man. The magical powers of the *dalem* (king) were so impressive that, deep in meditation, his head could rise into the sky. One day, one of his ministers became so worried about the 'headlessness' of the king that he cut off the head of the first animal trotting past – a wild boar – and placed it on the torso of the ruler. The king, who was appalled at his unfortunate appearance, withdrew from this point onwards and forbade all his subjects to look at his face. Gajah Mada, who had heard about the boar-headed King of Pejeng, wanted to find out for himself about this extraordinary ruler. The Javanese nobleman managed to win the favour of the Balinese king. On the occasion of his meeting with the *dalem*, Gajah Mada was allowed to choose the food and the beverage for their meal together. The clever Javanese decided on boiled rice, *kangkung* (*Ipomoea reptans*), and water from a jug with a long spout, things which could only be eaten or drunk with the head tilted backwards. It was therefore impossible for the boar-headed king to hide himself from his noble Javanese guest during the meal. Full of shame and anger over the artfulness of his guest, Dalem Bedaulu burst into flames. Even today, the demonic local king with the head of a wild boar is known to every Balinese, as he appears in mask plays (*topeng*) and is also pictured – in colour – as the dark ruler, as opposed to the shiny, white and wise Gajah Mada.

Was Bali's early history, from the late ninth century until 1343, as gloomy as many Balinese – and western scholars – assume? Recent studies provide evidence that this was not the case.[18] The Bali Aga were neither remnants of Polynesian tribes that had fled into remote mountain areas after the invasion of Majapahit troops nor were Bali Aga villages isolated. Royal edicts (*prasasti*)[19] written on bronze plates point out that by the late ninth century a Balinese king personified the head of the social hierarchy (see chapter 2, pp. 24–7). He represented not only the political but also the economic order. *Prasasti* of the eleventh century indicate an extension of the royal sphere of influence. Wälty (1995) also emphasizes that there existed different types of settlements and communities in the tenth century. Three of them will be mentioned briefly.

Kintamani   In the very first edict, issued in 882, an unnamed king orders the building of a Buddhist monastery, with an adjoining hospice (as a shelter for travelling traders and other persons) on the royal hunting grounds of Kintamani. Levies from carpenters, weavers and holders of livestock should contribute to the maintenance of the monastery, the shelter for the travellers and the temple of the Firegod.

Serai   In an edict issued about 940, the inhabitants of a royal hunting ground plead for a reduction of taxes (which was granted). The petitioners are called 'the king's servants in the hunting ground'. They are ruled by a lesser lord or official.

Julah   In a *prasasti* issued in 922 the community is referred to as inhabitants of the fortified harbour settlement of Julah. They are headed by a market officer who was also the harbourmaster. The petition is addressed to the King Ugrasana and details complaints about attacks and pillages of the town.

Ugrasana grants a tax reduction and gives permission to the inhabitants of Julah to loot ships stranded on its coast (thus being an early version of the Balinese *hak tawan karang* (see p. 231, note 29). He further requests the community to increase its population dramatically by taking in new settlers.

Thus the edicts issued between 882 and about 940 illustrate how different types of settlements were integrated into an emerging early Balinese kingdom. Map 5 shows the Batur region and the north coast around the year 1000. It contains both the location of the *prasasti* and the villages mentioned in the royal edicts.

Seen from a wider Balinese perspective, the late ninth century is marked by the transformation of tribal societies into a class-divided society, the latter being characterized by the differentiation of social and system integration.[20]

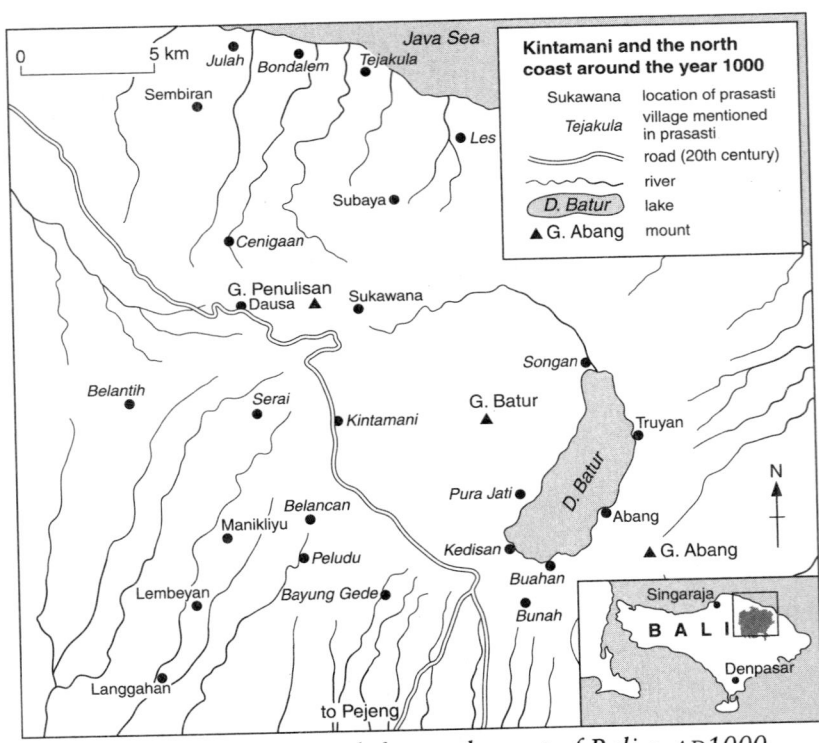

Map 5 Kintamani and the north coast of Bali c. AD1000

In class-divided societies traditional practices and kinship relations, even tribal identifications, remain very prominent . . . Class-divided society is marked, however, by some disentangling of the four institutional spheres [i.e. symbolic orders/modes of discourse, political, economic and legal institutions]. The polity is separated in some part from the procedures of economic activity; formal codes of law and punishment exist; and modes of symbolic co-ordination, based in written texts, make their appearance.[21]

Among the nobility (that is, the officials) a distinction was made between officials who dealt with the more secular aspects of the administration, on the one hand, and Buddhist monks and Siwaitic priests who were concerned with religious/legal matters, on the other hand.[22] A precondition for the process of homogenization of the administration was the use of written charters which enabled rules to be laid down that were valid across time and space. ,

Even though representatives of Bali Aga villages agreed to abide by the rules imposed by the king, they were allowed to keep their autonomy in *internal* village affairs. This applied particularly in relation to their temple systems and temple associations. In other words, villages at that time were dependent in external affairs on royalty whilst internal affairs were largely determined by the villagers themselves. This laid the foundation for the diversity that is evident in the social organization and institutions within the so-called Bali Aga villages until today. Yet all these villages have at least in common a council of elders (see pp. 71ff) who deal with the internal affairs.

Lowland Balinese

Balinese lowland culture was based for at least 1,000 years on a wet-rice economy, the main working principle of which was that the land belonged either to individuals or to corporate groups and that water represented collective property. In this favourable zone the gentry established its palaces, which are drawn into a hierarchical network. Inland, the proportion of the nobility in comparison with the rest of the population declines, as does its economic, cultural and political significance. Balinese kings and other nobles trace their origins and their civilization back to the Majapahit dynasty.[23] In the middle of the fourteenth century, at the time of the Majapahit King Sri Hayam Wuruk, the legendary prime minister and commander-in-chief Gajah Mada is said to have conquered Bali and made it a province of the greater Indonesian empire. However effective the Majapahit political control over the kingdom of the Indonesian Archipelago may have been, the socio-cultural influence of this period is uncontested. Thus Bali in particular became familiar with the ideas of Hindu-Javanese social organization and state structure. As a result, many cultural innovations were absorbed. The general focus of the Balinese nobility was less on Samprangan, where the first palace (Javanese: *kraton*; Balinese: *puri*) was built, than on Gelgel, because descendants of the Javanese Susuhan Kapakisan had moved their *puri* there before the end of the fourteenth century (see chapter 2, p.37).[24] It appears to be a proven fact that the only time the whole of south Bali was politically united under a single central ruler was during the so-called Gelgel period. In the first decade of the seventeenth century, Klungkung became the seat of the Dewa Agung, a title which designates the highest-ranking *satria* court on Bali.[25]

The Hindu-Javanese influence created new forms of status rivalry, above all in the lowlands of south Bali. Here, with agricultural productivity decisively higher than in the mountains, social systems of reference extended even beyond the village. Ideologies from hierarchically ordered descent groups, which share certain attributes with the Indian caste system, spread from the courts, particularly from Gelgel. The four main categories of the Balinese caste system are collectively referred to as *caturwangsa*, whereby the first three castes (those of the gentry) are called *triwangsa*:

		Castes	Titles
caturwangsa (all Balinese)	*triwangsa* (nobility)	*brahmana*	Ida
		satria	Dewa Agung, Dewa Gede, I Dewa, Anak Agung, Cokorda, I Gusti, etc.
		wesia	Gusti

		Within the *sudra*, the title groups of Pande, Pasek, Pulasari, Bandesa, Sengguhu, etc., are attributed higher status than 'ordinary'commoners
sudra	{	

The title I Gusti is granted to people belonging to the Satria Jawa or Arya caste. Balinese *lontar* scholars furnish evidence that after the conquest of Bali (1343) certain high Javanese officers of Gajah Mada's army became very influential officials at the courts of Samprangan and Gelgel. In this early phase, the ministers (*patih*) were given the Satria Jawa or Arya title Rakrian Apatih (or Krian Apatih) and later I Gusti. Even the highest-ranking *satria* in Lombok (who is still alive in 1995), Ratu Agung I Gusti Agung Gede Jelantik Teges, the grandson of the last Balinese king of Lombok, uses the designation I Gusti Agung. The title refers to his descent from the ruling dynasty of Kediri in east Java (Satria Jawa, Arya). This is evidence for the high status of certain I Gusti, who are often mistakenly considered to be *wesia*. Even the Gusti – who belong to the *wesia* caste – often trace their origin back to meritorious companions of Gajah Mada. It is said that the Gajah Mada followers Tan Mundur, Tan Kaur and Tan Kobur received their title Gusti (without I!) in this way.

It is true that some of the I Gusti are of Brahman descent, for example, I Gusti Ngurah Sidemen and I Gusti Dauh. After their ancestors had been awarded the duties of a ruler, the former Brahman families were considered *satria* and given a title according to their actual function. Within the ruling caste, descendants of the first Majapahit vassal king (*adipati*, 1352–80) at Samprangan/Bali, Dalem Ketut Kresna Kapakisan, enjoy highest esteem and are called Satria Dalem. The founder of the Kresna Kapakisan dynasty is the youngest son of the venerated east Javanese Brahman high priest Danghyang Kapakisan, who, after the conquest of Bali, was summoned by Gajah Mada to become his personal advisor (see chapter 2, p. 36). After the displacement of the royal palace from Gelgel to Klungkung, the ruler and his successors to the throne were granted the honourable title I Dewa Agung, and others without royal functions the title I Dewa.

Plate 11 *Siwa priest on the occasion of a Puja Wali ceremony at the Bebengan Lingsar temple, Tanjung*

As can be seen from these examples, there are important nuances in status within a single caste. This is also true for *brahmana*. Members of the *brahmana paksa buda*, for example, the Brahmans of Budakeling, Wanasari and Batuan, trace their origins to the Javanese priest Danghyang Astapaka. For their part, the *brahmana paksa siwa* regard the younger brother of Danghyang Astapaka, namely Danghyang Nirartha (synonymous with Danghyang Dwijendra or Ida Batara Sakti Wau Rauh[26]), as their progenitor. He is supposed to have established many temples and to have decisively revitalized Hinduism during his legendary missionary travels (*dharma yatra*) through Bali, Lombok and Sumbawa in the fifteenth and sixteenth centuries.

Balinese explain the strata within the Brahman caste as deriving from the various positions on the social scale of the missionary Hindu priest's five wives, which in turn had an influence on their offspring. His first wife was said to be the daughter of a priest from the Javanese kingdom of Daha (Kediri), who bore him a daughter Dalem Melanting and a son Danghyang Wiraga Sandhi (*syn.*: Batara Padanda Sakti Kemenuh). The latter became the founder of the Brahamana Kemenuh line, which commands the highest respect in Bali. As his second wife, Danghyang Nirartha chose the daughter of a priest from the east Javanese kingdom of Pasuruhan and produced four children: Padanda Sakti Kulon, Wetan, Lor and Ler. Descendants of this union call themselves Brahmana Manuaba. The third marriage, with a Brahman's daughter from the small east Javanese kingdom of Blambangan, produced the three children Ida Padanda Keniten, Ida Sakti Telaga and Ida Padanda Isteri Rai. The Brahmana Keniten trace their origins to this marriage. After a sojourn in the village of Mas (Gianyar, Bali), Danghyang Nirartha subsequently married the respected (in the eyes of *wong* Majapahit) but not royal daughter of the Balinese Bandesa Mas. The son of this marriage and later Padanda Gede Mas is said to be the founder of the line of the Brahmana Mas. The fifth and final wife, with the lowest status, was Ni Brit, a servant of Bandesa Mas. Her two sons, Ida Patapan and Ida Bindu, are looked upon as the founders of the lowest-ranking Brahman line, the so-called Antapan Mas.[27]

With respect to the term *brahmana catur* ('four Brahman lines of descent') only four of the five above-mentioned lines of descent are indicated. This is perhaps because the mothers originally came from four different regions. A further possible interpretation, that the fifth wife (Ni Brit) was not classified on account of her low social status, would be worth investigation.

The title group *sengguhu* may be employed to demonstrate how Balinese who are socially classified as lower than the gentry try to raise their position by reference to legendary Javanese Brahman priests. According to the Babad Pasek,[28] the Javanese priest Mpu Dwijaksara was supposed to have been summoned by Gajah Mada to go to Bali in the middle of the fourteenth century to supervise the *pujawali* ceremonies and see that they were carried out correctly, thereby ensuring happiness and prosperity for the island. Sang Kulpetak, accompanied by his devout servant I Guto, was supposed to have gone to Bali at the same time. On account of the close contact to Sang Kulpetak, his companion gradually mastered the holy *weda*, the *mantra* and *mudra* just as well as his master, and I Guto's behaviour and manner could not be distinguished from that of a priest. On his walking tours through the villages I Guto came into contact with 'uninformed' peasants who only knew the Javanese Mpu Dwijaksara by name. They therefore mistook the servant for the Brahman priest.[29] In mistaking his identity, a villager had asked the presumed Mpu Dwijaksara – who was none other than I Guto – to come into his simple home and assist with a ritual for the dead. The flattered servant celebrated the ritual faultlessly but, on account of his caste membership, without authority. Mpu Dwijaksara caught him unawares and took him to task. After the villages realised the mistake, the real priest granted the remorseful I Guto permission (as the mistaken one = *sengguh*) to carry out certain ceremonies for the dead (*pitra yadnya*) on request, because of his religious knowledge and good intentions. This special right is vested in the descendants of I Guto (*sengguhu*) up to the present day.[30] As Balinese nobles classify the *sengguhu* only as elevated fourth-caste members, this title group has to defend itself against its allocation to the *sudra* caste.

Major differences from the caste system in India arise from the fact that in Bali the class of the 'Untouchables' is missing and that – apart from a few exceptions – gainful employment is not bound to caste differences. There are also fewer caste-specific taboos. A notable exception is the position of Brahman priest (*padanda*), which is open exclusively to men and women of the priestly caste. For pious Balinese, religious devotion is based less on reflection and prayer than on intuitive experience in the community. The main duty of the priest is to mobilize his acquired knowledge in order to enter into contact with God. For the great mass of believers, the experience of God ensues from the *padanda*. His income is confined to the (net) proceeds of the sale of water which he has consecrated (*tirta*). In addition, priests may also accept gifts from families and temple congregations for rendering religious services to them. As the 'purest' among the living, manual occupations – regarded as impure – are forbidden to them. Likewise, they are the only group which is subject to dietary restrictions, for example, chicken meat is forbidden, but duck is not.[31] The food offered by host families or congregations must be presented on new plates. If the host cannot fulfil these requirements, the food must be offered to the *padanda* in fresh banana-leaf cones. In the past, judicial roles also fell to the *padanda*, and they functioned as royal advisers as well. Their preferential position is manifested in the fact that in earlier times, Brahman priests could not be sentenced to death, neither did they have to pay taxes to any ruler. In return, their service to the *raja* consisted in praying for the welfare of the kingdom and strengthening the ruler spiritually.

The occupation of blacksmith (Pande Besi) is vested exclusively in members of the *pande* title group. The smiths declare themselves to be members of the ruling class and try, as the latter do, to prove their noble origins with the aid of family trees, although other Balinese rank them only as higher-class *sudra*. Thus, conflict is inevitable – not only with the *satria* but also with the *brahmana*, as *pande* (contrary to Hindu doctrine) choose priests from their own ranks and consecrate water to *tirta* themselves. The towers (*bade*) upon which the smiths carry corpses to cremation places – for example, in the village of Marga – display seven roofs, the same number as are accorded only to *satria* elsewhere. In Marga, deceased *pande* are cremated in a coffin in the shape of a black bull, a coffin-type which is usually reserved for men of the ruling class. Butchers, potters and textile-dyers belong to the few occupations which are considered to be impure. They command correspondingly low respect. It is only the low *sudra* who maintain their livelihood by carrying out these income-generating activities.

The Balinese caste system is rather less rigid than it may seem at first glance. As already mentioned, the highest-ranking Balinese royal family (that is, the one from Klungkung) is said to have originally belonged to the Brahman caste and to have changed over to the *satria* caste only after it had assumed the ruling function. The identification of the Balinese elite with the Hindu-Javanese nobility and its followers appears to have first developed around 250 years after the 'conquest' by Gajah Mada.[32] With fictitious genealogies (*silsilah*) the Balinese gentry tried to trace their direct descent back to high-ranking Javanese personalities. As a case in point, the royal family of Karangsem tried to raise the value of their position by creating a 'son of god' (Batara Alit Sakti). Up to the present day such genealogies provide conflict-ridden material for discussion among rival ruling factions. In extreme cases, certain unpopular members of the *satria* caste are even discriminated against for being power-hungry social climbers from the caste of commoners (cf. the controversies surrounding the origin of the Pamecutan dynasty in Badung). A certain vertical mobility within Balinese society can be substantiated in that, for example, deserving subjects could be raised to the lower nobility by the ruler, and this authorized them to bear the title Gusti. Shifts in status also occur through the legal marriage of a Balinese nobleman with women from the *sudra* caste. The children of such a marriage automatically receive the status of their father, whilst their mother remains in the fourth caste, but in a higher position than commoners living outside of the palace.

Rules of Social Interaction

The presence of the *bangsa* becomes conspicuous in the multiplicity of hierarchical groups, whose interactions are subject to certain rules and practices. Members of the *triwangsa* (about 7 per cent of all Balinese) as well as certain higher-ranking *sudra* groups attach great importance to the adherence to good manners that is associated with certain positions. Contrary to the system in India, caste rules are restricted principally to fixed social conventions. A lack of good manners is a serious reproach to a Balinese. Concern over the observance of proper manners at forthcoming meetings can render both partners psychologically insecure and inhibit their behaviour if, for example, the two persons concerned are not clear about their respective differences in status. This characteristic Indonesian insecurity phenomenon is expressed by the Malayan word *malu* (Bal.: *kimud, kemad, lek*), whose meaning is often incompletely translated as 'ashamed', 'shy', 'timorous' or 'full of reverence'.

In social interaction with those of higher-ranking position, a person ranking lower in the hierarchy must be careful to play his assigned role and demonstrate his position. When a *sudra* greets a nobleman, he must bow his head as a sign of respect. Pavilions in palaces exhibit tiered platforms which allow people to walk or sit at a height appropriate to their status. In conservative circles of the highest nobility it is usual even today for servants, who are often offspring of earlier bondmen, to approach their masters on their hands and knees, pressing their heads to the floor. It is an honour to catch sight of the dust on the king's feet, not to mention the whole person! The substance of this view is expressed in what used to be the courteous form of addressing a king: Bukpadan Cokor I Dewa.[33] According to the *adat* from Karangasem, illegitimate children of a nobleman and a *sudra* mother must behave subserviently towards their father. As long as they live in the palace, they are obliged – as so-called *astra* – to take the role of humble servants. On the other hand, illegitimate children both of whose parents come from the gentry are integrated fully into the father's family and assume the caste position of the father. At communal meals, the highest-ranking starts to eat, and no one is allowed to leave before he declares the meal to be over. In the early phase of mass tourism, this rule of etiquette created unexpected problems. In 1967, I remember how tourists kindly invited Balinese local guides to dine. The problem was who should be served first and who should summon the guests to eat: the noble Balinese employee or the paying guest (who, being an outsider, is in the eyes of the Balinese a *jaba*)? Until as recently as around 1970, the incompatibility of this 'east/west' question of etiquette was elegantly circumnavigated by the Balinese guides accepting the invitation but eating in a separate room; members of the *triwangsa* were actually served there before the tourists. Further insecurity arose out of the situation in locally owned travel companies and hotels, that employees belonging to different castes had to take on higher- or lower-ranking functions irrespective of their social position.

The introduction of appropriate levels of verbal communication whose rules were to be followed when members of different castes and caste levels conversed went hand-in-hand with the acceptance of the caste system (cf. chapter 1, p. 5). When two Balinese meet for the first time, they start to speak in *madia*, 'the middle language', which can be considered a language of compromise between *kasar* ('low language') and *alus* (the 'high language' of the nobility). In conservative east Bali the conversation in such cases begins in *alus*. As soon as the interlocuter's caste membership is evident, the *sudra* remembers the basic rule that as a fourth-caste member he must continue to speak in *alus* out of respect, whilst the nobleman addresses him in *kasar*. In contrast to the Balinese *kasar* language, *alus* is nuanced and contains sophisticated poetic paraphrases. Courtesy requires that a person referring to himself does not use the high language. However, well-educated Balinese address their parents and the elderly in *alus* as a sign of respect.[34] Within the nobility itself, depending on the region, *kasar* or *madia* is used. The person spoken to in *alus* answers in the low-caste language (*kasar*). Whilst in urbanized Denpasar and in north Bali *kasar* and *madia* are spoken almost exclusively, inhabitants of the conservative regency of Karangasem mainly use *madia* and *alus*. The language of instruction in the rapidly growing provincial capital of Denpasar is *kasar*, but in east Bali *madia*. Priests, readers of *lontar* texts, puppeteers (*dalang*) and other classically trained Balinese also know Old Javanese (*kawi*), Old Balinese and occasionally Sanskrit. The Indonesian national language, Bahasa

Indonesia, is taught in the schools at all levels. As a further idiom, the school-children learn English as their first foreign language and sometimes Japanese, French or German as well. Only the older Balinese, who were taught by teachers from the Netherlands, speak Dutch.

Villagers and *Banjar* Members as Corporate Groups

Even though Balinese society is clearly stratified by caste and ranking within castes, it should not be forgotten that the Balinese are also members of numerous other overlapping caste groups in addition to their affiliation with kinship groups of various ranks according to their origins. Whilst the inclusiveness of a descent group is manifest mainly in community rituals in the temple of its common ancestor, the other groupings play a more important role in everyday life. In pre-colonial Bali, the commoners' living space was restricted mainly to their village (*desa*) and its subdivisions (*banjar*), whilst the network of noblemen (priests, rulers) was organized at a supra-village level over large regions. Royal civil servants were responsible for the amalgamation of village communities within a kingdom. They were either residents of the capital city or were sedentary nobles in villages and responsible for the implementation of royal edicts. As the extent of power assigned to a ruler's house also correlated with the number of commoners in their domain, the rulers made a point of extending their sphere of influence at the cost of that of their rivals. The commoners were quite aware of this game of intrigue between rival potentates. They also knew how to use the situation to their advantage by promising to serve obediently and pay tribute to those rulers who were prepared to guarantee them the better conditions.[35] Such a change from one ruler to another is expressed in the Balinese term *matilas*.

As the social structure of the Balinese is inseparable from religious concepts and ceremonies, the activities of diverse corporate groups are concentrated on specific temples. At the same time the various temple congregations are made up of diverse members. This can be substantiated, for example, by the categorization mentioned by H. and C. Geertz[36] (and found particularly in the southern lowland) into village area, *banjar*, irrigation association, title group, kinship group, voluntary associations, and groups concentrated around Brahman priests. Consequently, we shall turn our attention to the significance of the village and the *banjar* as corporate groups. After the family and kinship groups, the *banjar* is the most important reference group in the life of a commoner. On the one hand, *banjar* are clearly defined territories within a village (*desa adat*). In this sense, *banjar* are residential units – to a certain extent the 'address' of village inhabitants. On the other hand, *banjar* as neighbourhoods form socio-political groups in village life upon which certain duties, rights and authority devolve. In certain cases membership of a *banjar* in the sense of it being a socio-political entity is not identical with the *banjar* 'address'.[37] In order to avoid the ambiguity of the concept, *banjar* will be understood here in its meaning of a socio-political group.

The members of a *banjar* comprise adult men who can prove the completeness of their identity through a female partner – usually a wife, but sometimes a sister, mother or daughter. This regulation has validity because certain duties falling on the *banjar* are gender-specific. These duties include, for example, the presentation of offerings for temple ceremonies and for *banjar* meetings and so on, duties that are exclusively reserved for women. Widows, single men and sometimes newcomers as well need not adhere to all the conditions of the *banjar*, but are merely 'half-obliged' (*setengah ayahan*). The old and frail can withdraw completely and be represented by their married sons.

Among the most important duties of the *banjar* are the maintenance and restitution of the ritual purity of the *desa adat*. Each *banjar* has specific tasks and ritual duties to fulfil for the benefit of the village temples. From this it can be concluded that the village as a religious-magical authority is ranked above the secular autonomy of the *banjar*. As long as the purity of a *desa* as a whole is guaranteed, the autonomy of a *banjar* is not affected and the independence of the grouping is stressed. *Banjar* activities can be very mundane, for example, improving roads through community work or restoring the meeting-house (*bale banjar*). The *banjar* is generally responsible for public institutions and even more for public welfare, which requires not only material support but also assistance in ritual matters. In the preparation and practice of *rites de passage*, such as the tooth-filing ceremony, *banjar* members are called upon to participate alongside family members and relatives. In time-consuming work, women prepare offerings for the gods (*banten*) or to appease the demons (*caru*). The elderly can accompany the ceremonies with songs, others can take part in a ritual day-puppet show (*wayang lemah*). Even more obvious and time-consuming is the obligation of all *banjar* members to participate in the burial or cremation of the deceased.[38] The men must construct the wooden coffin as well as a richly decorated corpse-supporting tower (*bade*) of bamboo, made according to requirements relating to the caste or rank of the deceased. According to the *adat* of the Marga blacksmiths, it is the duty of its young members to carry the empty coffin to the place of incineration, whilst the married men of the *banjar* bring the *bade* with the corpse to the cremation ground. The rest of the *banjar* members accompany the funeral procession. On arrival at the cremation ground, the corpse is transferred from the *bade* to the coffin, which is then placed on a pile of wood collected by *banjar* members and set alight by a flare or a glass lens. Only the family members remain at the cremation site for the actual burning of the corpse, along with a few men whose duty (prescribed by the *banjar*) it is to see that the corpse, which slides through the trap-door in the bottom of the coffin, is fully incinerated.

A further task of the *banjar* is in social control and surveillance of the actions and behaviour of its members in relation to the *adat*. For example, men armed with sacred spears (*tumbak*) move through the residential areas of the *banjar* of the large municipality of Sanur on the day of transition between the old and the new *saka*-year (on Hari Raya Nyepi) and monitor the obligatory regulations about rest and the ban on lighting fires.[39] The *banjar* is legally permitted to interfere, using sanctions against members who do not follow the rules of behaviour according to the *adat*, and fines may be incurred. Especially serious offences against the *banjar* rules are punished by the exclusion of the wrongdoer. This means that he loses his share of *banjar* ownership and the plot of land on which his family compound is built is withdrawn. He also loses the right, in accordance with the *adat* to a funeral in the village cemetery and subsequent cremation. He becomes an outsider without the security of the *banjar* community and must look for a new life far away from his native village.

Once during the 35-day Balinese month, the *banjar* members congregate for a meeting in the *bale banjar* or, where there is none, in the temple of origin (*pura puseh*). A *klian banjar*, elected for a specific period of time, functions as chairman of the *banjar* and is helped in his work by various assistants. Each member has legally recognized equal rights without regard to his caste membership. Even the chairman of the *banjar* has no particular authority, as he is merely there to organize and to guarantee the implementation of decisions. For example, he supervises community work and is responsible for the collection of *banjar* contributions.[40] Resolutions of the *banjar* council are framed by common consent according to the fundamental ancient Indonesian principle of *musyawarah untuk mufakat*, that is, discussion with the aim of reaching a consensus. Usually, after extensive lobbying, the decision has already been taken before the assembly gathers, so that the procedures of the meeting take place in a quiet and dignified way.

Many *banjar* have considerable wealth at their disposal. This includes real estate, for example the *bale banjar* and a hall where cock-fighting takes place (*wantilan*). In addition to their function as assembly halls, *bale banjar* take on the role of informal meeting places where men can call in to chat, have a drink and eat a snack after work. In the wealthier *banjar*, a television set stands in the meeting-house if only few inhabitants have access to a set. During the day, children may play table-tennis on the terrace or practise on *gamelan* instruments belonging to the *banjar*. Until the Indonesian federal government issued a law in the late 1970s concerning the prohibition of gambling and as a result rigorously limiting cock-fighting (*tajen*), a substantial amount of money flowed into the coffers of the *banjar* from binding betting fees. The money in the *banjar* till is invested in internal *banjar* economic activities. The *barong* and *rangda* masks are stored very safely. In certain communities, the *banjar* community reactivates their magic, radiating powers once during the 210-day year. Some *banjar* possess their own rice granary (*lumbung*) in which 'taxes in rice' from *banjar* members or sheaves of rice from *banjar*-owned fields are kept to be redistributed on ceremonial occasions.

In contrast to the *klian banjar adat*, who is responsible for *adat* matters within his sphere of influence, the *klian banjar dinas* (today officially called *klian dusun*) is entrusted with the implementation of edicts issued by the regional or national governments, a responsibility going back to the time of the colonial regime.

The word *desa* (village) in its territorial sense has several connotations. In Europe, the word 'village' can mean, in its strictest sense, the built-up and inhabited central part of the village territory, or in a wider sense it can encompass the built-up *and* open areas within the village boundaries. Similarly in Bali and other Indonesian islands: on the one hand, *desa* can mean the part of the village which originally lay within an area bounded by a wall or fence and upon which the family compounds (*pakarangan*) and the village temples stood; on the other hand, it can mean the whole territory over which the village community as a corporate group exercises legal rights. In the following, the concept '*desa adat*' will be understood in its broad sense, that is, as a village territory with its family compounds, temples, agricultural areas of various kinds and even uncultivated reserves of land. The rules of village behaviour laid down in the holy village regulations (*awig-awig*) refer to these boundaries.[41]

Because the village territory is (according to the ideas of the villagers) in the last instance the property of the gods which is temporarily managed by people and run by families, the primary goal of each village community as an *adat* jural community is to guard the ritual purity of its territory and to restore it to this state when there has been a disturbance. Actions and events which render village territory and its inhabitants impure transgress the *adat* and are detrimental to cosmic harmony. The main function of a *banjar* (subordinate to a *desa*) lies within the sphere of the secular and the visible (*sekala*), as in the regulation of human interaction and the accomplishment of certain tasks for the village temples. The institution of *desa adat* is, as we saw above, responsible for the magic-religious domain and for the relationship between the villagers and the invisible (*niskala*). Whilst the *desa adat* possesses primarily symbolic functions and defines social relations, it is the *banjar* that is responsible for its realization.[42]

The group of heirs to family compounds and the heads of immigrated families who have been awarded land for a *pakarangan* from the *desa adat* make up the authorized members of a village community (*krama desa*).[43] If a villager dies without offspring his own or adopted), his right of usufruct over agricultural plots as well as the ground upon which his compound stands is returned to the village estate. This expresses

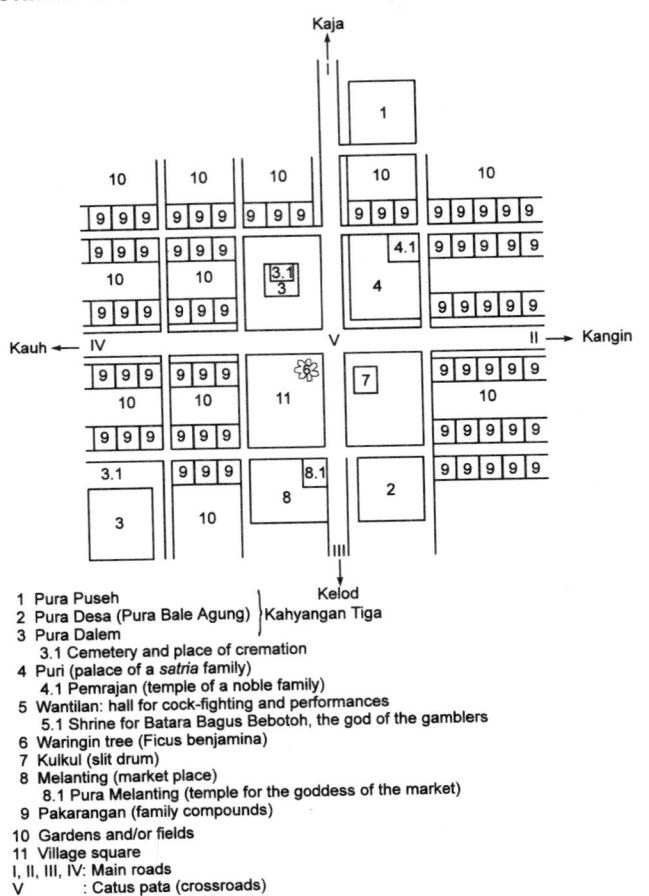

1 Pura Puseh
2 Pura Desa (Pura Bale Agung) } Kahyangan Tiga
3 Pura Dalem
   3.1 Cemetery and place of cremation
4 Puri (palace of a *satria* family)
   4.1 Pemrajan (temple of a noble family)
5 Wantilan: hall for cock-fighting and performances
   5.1 Shrine for Batara Bagus Bebotoh, the god of the gamblers
6 Waringin tree (Ficus benjamina)
7 Kulkul (slit drum)
8 Melanting (market place)
   8.1 Pura Melanting (temple for the goddess of the market)
9 Pakarangan (family compounds)
10 Gardens and/or fields
11 Village square
I, II, III, IV: Main roads
V   : Catus pata (crossroads)

Figure 4.1 Schematic plan of a south Balinese village

clearly the fact that it is the *desa* community as a corporate group, and not the *banjar*, that has the exclusive right of disposal over its own village land.[44] Also belonging to the *desa adat* are the village temples in which all members of groups belonging to the village worship and are supplied with holy water (*tirta*). The members of the village community as a religious congregation must keep up their duties in these temples, maintaining them and organizing sacred observances.

Ideally, the village incorporates three *pura*, which are designated collectively as *kahyangan tiga* ('the three holy temples'). They are the *pura puseh*, the *pura desa* (syn.: *pura bale agung*) and the *pura dalem*.[45] The *pura puseh* ('navel temple') is the temple of origin in which the village community worships its purified and deified ancestors. Due to its uranic value, it lies in the 'godly direction', that is, towards the mountains and/or east of the village core (see chapter 5, pp. 98ff). In the centre of the village – and thus in the intermediate area between earthly and godly activity – lies the *pura desa*. The *pura dalem*, in addition to being the temple of death, is the temple of chthonic powers where, amongst other things, the deceased who are not yet fully purified are remembered. This temple is attached to the village cemetery (*sema*) and to the cremation ground (*setra*). In accordance with the value of cardinal directions, the *pura dalem* lies in the direction of the sea and/or the western part of the village. Sometimes it is isolated from the actual living area (cf. figure 4.1). It is conspicuous that the *pura dalem*, the cemetery and the place of incineration belong to the village, but funerals and the subsequent purification ceremonies are conducted by the *banjar*. Consequently, these rituals comprise one of the connecting links between the *desa* and *banjar* institutions.[46]

The traditional head of a *desa adat* is the *bandesa adat*. The observance of the holy village regulations lies within his authority, and he is responsible for the temples in which village-specific celebrations take place. When confusion over the interpretation of rules relating to behavioural matters arises, the villagers seek his advice. The position of a *bandesa* cannot be compared to that of the chairman of a community because a *bandesa* has no power whatever to authorize the implementation of legal or political decisions. As we mentioned earlier, this power lies in the hands of the *banjar* community.

Plate 12   Temple priest (pamangku) *leading prayer for the temple congregation*

Village assemblies (*sangkepan desa*) usually take place once in a Balinese month, which has 35 days, and if possible in the *pura bale agung* or *pura desa*. In addition to duties related to the management and maintenance of sacred and profane village property and routine administration, one of the main tasks is the delegation of responsibilities and the organization of the 'birthday celebration' of the temples (*piodalan*), which takes place once a year (210 days) and is aimed at purifying the village territory and the entire temple congregation. In this case, too, the village sees to the religious-ritual aspects and delegates the necessary preparatory tasks to its *banjar* communities. In villages where the number of *krama desa* has become so large that a full assembly is hardly possible, representatives are delegated to attend the meeting, for example the chairman of the *banjar* (*klian banjar*), the assistants of the *bandesa* and the temple priests (*pamangku*).

Villages, which were created as political-administrative entities during the colonial regime (Indonesian: *desa dinas*; Balinese: *perbekelan*), are composed not only of various *banjar* but often of several *desa adat* together. The borders of the political communities, however, do not always correspond with those of the *adat* villages. It is the duty of the *kepala desa* (Indonesian) or *perbekel* (Balinese) to implement and control the decrees and edicts of the national and regional governments within his area of authority.[47]

Subak Associations

One of the most important institutions of an agrarian, economic and religious character in wet-rice areas are the *subak* associations (*sekaha subak*), which were established over a thousand years ago. Their members comprise not only landowners but also mortgagees, tenant farmers and share-croppers of plots which lie in the same *subak*. A *subak* can be defined as a gravity irrigation complex whose water supply comes from a higher (in the direction of the mountains) common source, for example, from a river which has been dammed. The water is then directed into the many terraced plots by way of an ingenious distribution system (cf. figure

4.2). The area of the approximately 1,300 Balinese *subak* varies greatly according to topographic and hydrographic conditions. On steep river embankments they can be less than one hectare whereas in the favourable areas of the great alluvial plains they can cover several square kilometres. As *subak*

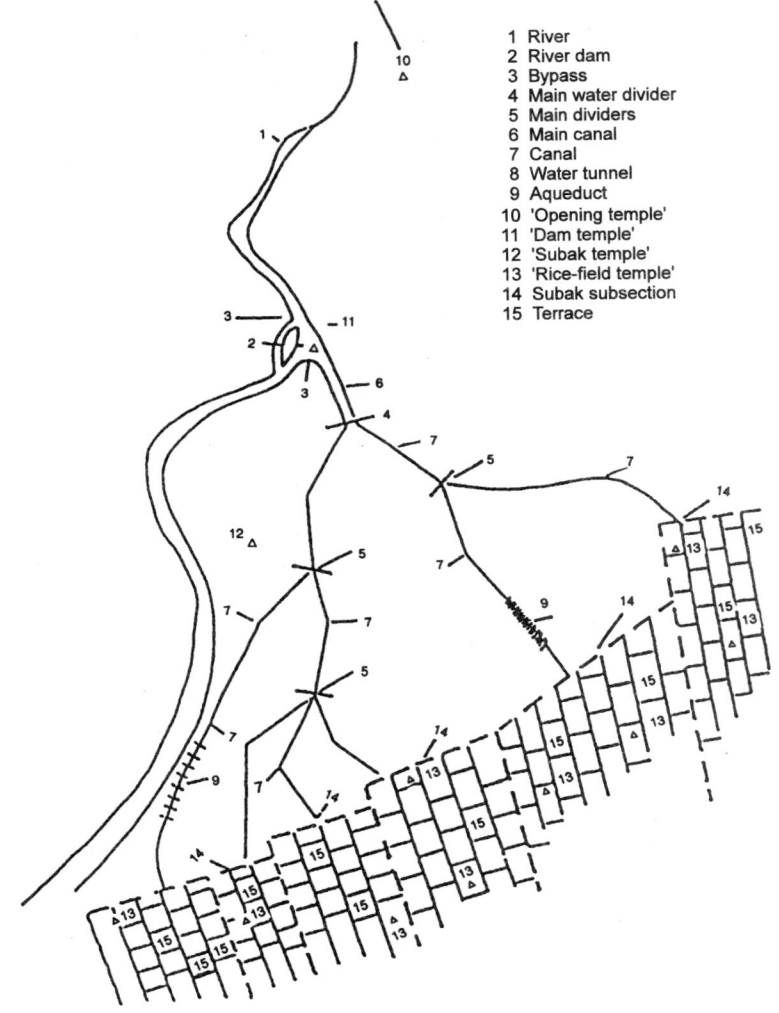

1 River
2 River dam
3 Bypass
4 Main water divider
5 Main dividers
6 Main canal
7 Canal
8 Water tunnel
9 Aqueduct
10 'Opening temple'
11 'Dam temple'
12 'Subak temple'
13 'Rice-field temple'
14 Subak subsection
15 Terrace

Figure 4.2 Schematic diagram of preliminary waterworks for a 'typical' Tabanan subak

fed from the same river are often connected with one another, regulations about water rights have to be worked out and implemented not only within a single irrigation complex but also among separate ones. Conflicts between *subak* associations may occur in low-rainfall years, when irrigation systems positioned higher up-stream draw off so much water that the supply to the lower-lying areas is seriously impaired. In pre-colonial times, the king and his governors were called in to mediate in cases of disagreement because they were not directly involved in *subak* matters and their opinions were thus considered to be impartial.[48] Rulers were not only arbiters in questions of conflict over irrigation matters, they also initiated the construction of royal dams on the upper and middle courses of rivers and promoted the consequent necessary rituals. Because wet-rice was the main source of nutrition as well as one of the sources of royal revenues, the control of water supplies was decisive in the well-being of the people and the wealth of the ruler. Rivalry for power between rulers, for example between Mengwi and Badung, was often expressed in struggles for water rights.

As *subak* often cover areas overlapping village territories, they are composed of members from different village communities. With the exception of cases in which village rituals are affected by the *subak*, village and *subak* are separate *adat* jural institutions. If a peasant possesses or works plots in two or more *subak*, he is obliged to be a member of each of the respective associations. When decisions are made at compulsory meetings, all members have equal rights regardless of caste membership and other rank positions, but also independent of the size and water requirements of their property and whether it belongs to them or whether they cultivate it as share-croppers. Both the amount of water tax imposed and the services to be furnished are, on the other hand, decided according to the quantity of water drawn. Terms of membership and the rights and duties of members of a *subak* are laid down in regulations which are often, for prestige reasons, drawn up in the name of the king or confirmed by him.[49] They contain not only clauses with respect to organization and technical matters, but also rules with regard to *subak*-related sacred matters. The former account for specifications concerning water distribution, taxes and other fees, expected achievements, sanctions against theft of water or against damage or neglect of the irrigation installations, and instructions for arbitration in the case of arguments between members.[50] The sacred aspect of a *subak* association is not exclusively expressed through regular offerings of sacrifices and the communal performance of religious festivals in the irrigation temple, but also in the fact that – similar to the case of the *desa adat* – the infringement of the specifications is regarded as a violation of the divine order, resulting in a destabilization of cosmic harmony. For example, offences by individuals are feared for their negative consequences, such as poor harvests.

The decisive body of the *subak* community is the gathering, which must be attended by all members. If they are unable to attend, members are required to name a representative. Meetings occur regularly once in the 35-day month or, for urgent matters, are fixed according to need. The place of assembly is the *subak* temple. The chairman (*klian subak*), who is either elected by the members or appointed in rota, has assistants to help him. The summoning and conduct of the gathering are

Plate 13   A typical subak *in east Bali*

among the duties of a *klian subak*. He records the list of members and registers the area and position of the plots as well as their owners or cultivators. Other duties concern the control of work done in the *subak* and the organization of patrols to monitor adherence to granted water limits. As agricultural modernization programmes initiated by the government affect particularly wet-rice cultivation, the *klian subak* is also responsible for the implementation of government ordinances through the *subak* association. He and/or the assembly sets the punishment when offences against the *subak* regulations occur. Usually, the offender is fined and in extreme cases his water rights are withdrawn.[51] The assembly meeting is concerned with the planing and realization of work on irrigation installations, the improvement of terraces, and the timing of the wet-rice cultivation; it also organizes the preparation of religious community rituals. Further, it debates adjustments to the *subak* regulations arising from changes in the external frames of reference.

The *subak* association (*sekaha subak*) draws its income from the entrance fees charged to new members, annual fees dependent on area and share of water, and also from exceptional taxes. Further revenue flows from fines and from the contributions of members who would rather render their share of obligations to the community in a monetary way instead of partaking in work themselves. The work at hand in the immediate area of irrigation is done by special water associations (*sekaha yeh*) which are headed by a *pekaseh*. *Subak* members who do not belong to this water association compensate for the work that arises for the *sekaha yeh* with a water tax (*sawinih*).[52] The money received by the *subak* associations flows to the *subak* fund. Its wealth and assets include the material infrastructure of the irrigation complexes (if not state-owned) as well as the technical equipment. Where a *subak* temple is granted fields (*laba pura*), the profits are redistributed during specific temple festivals. The handing over of a certain portion of the harvest to the *subak* association serves the same purpose. In agricultural matters, too, it is clear that the Balinese is a member of a collective whose aim it is, through behaviour in conformity with the *adat*, to reconcile and therefore to harmonize the sacred and the profane within defined boundaries.

5

Religion and Beliefs in Practice

Orientation in Space and Time

Small though the island of Bali is, the culture of the Balinese is by no means homogeneous. Geographical factors and historical events have often had divisive effects and have occasionally produced divergent mixtures of Old Balinese, Indian, Indo-Javanese and sometimes even Chinese culture within a very small area. Diversity deriving from place, time and cultural patterns (*desa*, *kala*, *patra*) is an integral part of Balinese culture and the Balinese self-image. Consequently, what follows here can be no more than an attempt to adduce the overarching characteristics of Balinese religion and to explore these fundamental religious concepts and principles. Special emphasis will be placed on lived faith as it accompanies and determines the lives of the Balinese from birth to rebirth.

In contrast to many members of western societies, who have lost their innate sense of space and time, the Balinese are always spatially and temporally orientated, whatever the situation. They feel at home and at one with themselves as they adjust to the calendrical system and cardinal points. Mountains, rivers, roads, crossings, walls, gates and buildings of all kinds are unmistakable points of orientation in a cosmically interpreted world, a world in which human beings view themselves as images of the cosmos in miniature, reflecting total agreement between what is inside and what is outside. Another fundamental religious and philosophical concept – dualism and the balancing of opposites – shapes the physical environment: the layout of villages, temples, compounds and houses. Both dualism and the view of the human being as the cosmos in miniature imply a harmonious equilibrium between man and nature and are consequently of special interest to the industrial or post-industrial world in its struggle to rediscover ecological systems.

Balancing Opposites

The Balinese world lies between two antagonistic poles from which divine and netherworldly forces or energies can emanate. They are mutually dependent and make sense only in synergy. The world view of an agrarian society is shaped and inspirited by the practical experiences of working and cultivating the land. Through his daily work man discovers that nature's inexhaustible creativity is ultimately a result of germination, maturation, wilting and death. On the one side of this process stand the powers of fertility and life, operating from above: the sun, which is considered male, the mountains and the upper courses of rivers, whose waters fertilize the fields. The forces working from below include the receptive female soil, where growth and decay meet, and the sea, which brings illness and death to the coasts, while also serving as a source of useful, vital energy.

In accordance with these everyday experiences and following the equally clear example of cosmic antagonisms such as day and night or sun and moon, Bali's autochthonous society ultimately divided all phenomena – natural, cultural and social – into two conceptual categories, attributing them to the uranian (heavenly or belonging to the upper world) or chthonian (earth-bound or netherworldly) sphere. Both of these inherently ambivalent spheres can be controlled and even directed by proper ritual behaviour. Out of formless chaos this elementary dualism (*Rwa Bhineda*) thus created an orderly world with clear-cut points of reference for individual and social behaviour.

Throughout Bali the volcanoes, from which life-giving water flows to human beings and plants, are considered the centres of the uranian powers. The highest of them, Gunung Agung, is both the focal point of the Balinese world and a central point of reference to the direction from which all good things are expected. It is the seat of the Almighty Siwa, who resides there in his manifestation as Mahadewa together with his divine ancestors. This explains the classification of the concepts of sun, mountains, Gunung Agung, ancestors and fertility as belonging to the uranian sphere. The influences brought to bear from this direction, known as *kaja* or *kaler*, are in general positive, fertile and divine. Their effect is downstream, from top to bottom, from mountain to sea. To benefit from them, one turns away from the sea towards the mountain, for everything that lies below, whether earthly or netherworldly, exerts its ambivalent or threatening influence from the direction of the sea, operating upstream, from bottom to top. Consequently, the way to appease the chthonian powers or to exorcise them, together with illness and death, is to turn away from the mountain towards the sea.

A second axis, defined by sunrise (*kangin* = east) and sunset (*kauh* = west), runs from east to west, at right angles to the mountain–sea axis. As the sun rises, it brings light, day and life – all uranian forces associated with mountain, height and *kaja* – from the east. Once the sun has passed its zenith and moves westwards towards the sea, it enters the chthonian sphere and is associated with *kelod*, earthly and sea. There it temporarily sinks into the underworld, where death and the provisional end of all earthly, visible things take place.

The lines of these two axes yield a system of co-ordinates with varying force fields crucial to orientation in everyday and ritual behaviour, as well as to the geographical, architectonic and social arrangement of living space in general. Thus the topmost, mountainward, easternmost point in every compound, temple or village is particularly well suited for contact with the uranian powers. Conversely, the burial and cremation grounds and the chthonian temples of a village will always be located downwards, towards the sea (see chapter 4, p. 90).

The Human Being as the Cosmos in Miniature

The step from the twofold to the threefold quality of all things was undertaken in the attempt to balance out the antagonisms and oppositions innate in agrarian dualism and thereby to establish harmony. As human beings become part of this system, their living space becomes a middle world between the upper and the nether world. Now everything has three zones or components. *Nista* signifies things that are located down or low; *madia* means middle and neutral, designating the torso of things; and *utama* means high and lofty, designating the head of things. Everything in the world has an allotted place. The highest, holiest spot is reserved for the gods and ancestors. It belongs to the sphere of the upper world and heaven. The lowest places are home to demons and evil spirits and belong to the sphere of the netherworld. The middle world is inhabited by human beings. As a microcosm, or world in miniature (*buana alit*), they are a mirror of the great world (*buana agung*), the macrocosm, and thereby participate in all three worlds.

The way the tripartite division is translated into physical form clearly demonstrates that this principle, in conjunction with the dualistic axis of mountain–sea, sunrise–sunset and zenith–nadir, is as decisive to the ground plans of villages, compounds and houses (foundations, walls and roof constructions) as it is to the tripartite layout of temples or the vertical arrangement of shrines and altars.

Understanding the Balinese world also presupposes knowledge of a further system of classification, according to which five elements – earth, fire, water, wind and atmosphere – determine the tangible world and the essence of all material things. The Hindu teaching of the five elements (*Panca Mahabuta*) would undoubtedly be compatible with the Old Balinese concept of the nature of the world, particularly with the pivotal Balinese sanctification of animated nature and its elements.

The doctrine of Panca Mahabuta posits that, as the world in miniature (*buana alit*), the human being is a faithful copy of the world at large (*buana agung*). The five elements are also found in the body, the microcosm of the macrocosm. In other words, in material terms the human organism is analogous in structure to the outside world and receives positive or negative impulses from it. But these divine or demonic influences can be kept in check through a life of ever-increasing purity and appropriate – meaning ritually correct, – behaviour in the right place at the right time. At death the five elements constituting the body return to their origin; now the soul is liberated and pure, ready for reincarnation or continued existence as a deified ancestor.

From Birth to Rebirth

The five sacrificial rituals (*panca yadnya*) of Hindu-Balinese religion are named after the focus or principal addressee of a ritual cycle. Thus *dewa yadnya* (rituals for gods and deities) is the common term for all ritual activities, offerings and prayers centred on the worship of the gods and the ancestral deities in their temples. *Buta yadnya* (rituals for spirits and demons) relate to the pacification or exorcism of forces and powers capable of interfering with the positive course of things. *Resi yadnya* is the general term for rituals in which various categories of priests and priestesses are consecrated. As the aim of this book is to explore the Balinese way of life, this chapter concentrates on *manusa yadnya* and *pitra yadnya*, rituals connected with human beings and their souls.

The first of these two series of *rites de passage* begins with the wedding ceremony and the subsequent act of legitimately begetting a child, continues during pregnancy, strengthening the embryo in the womb and bringing about a felicitous birth for mother and child, and then marks the various stages of growing up until, as an adult, the young person starts his or her own family. These rites of transition, known as *manusa yadnya*, are arranged by parents for their children. They comprise a succession of ritual complexes designed to promote spiritual and physical welfare and gradually free the young person from impurities deriving, on the one hand, from what may have been a flawed former life and, on the other, from the natural circumstances of physical birth.

The second group of transitional rituals – *pitra yadnya* – embraces the cult of the dead and the subsequent purification of the soul. These ceremonies essential for deliverance from the torments of hell, for heavenly existence, rebirth or trans-

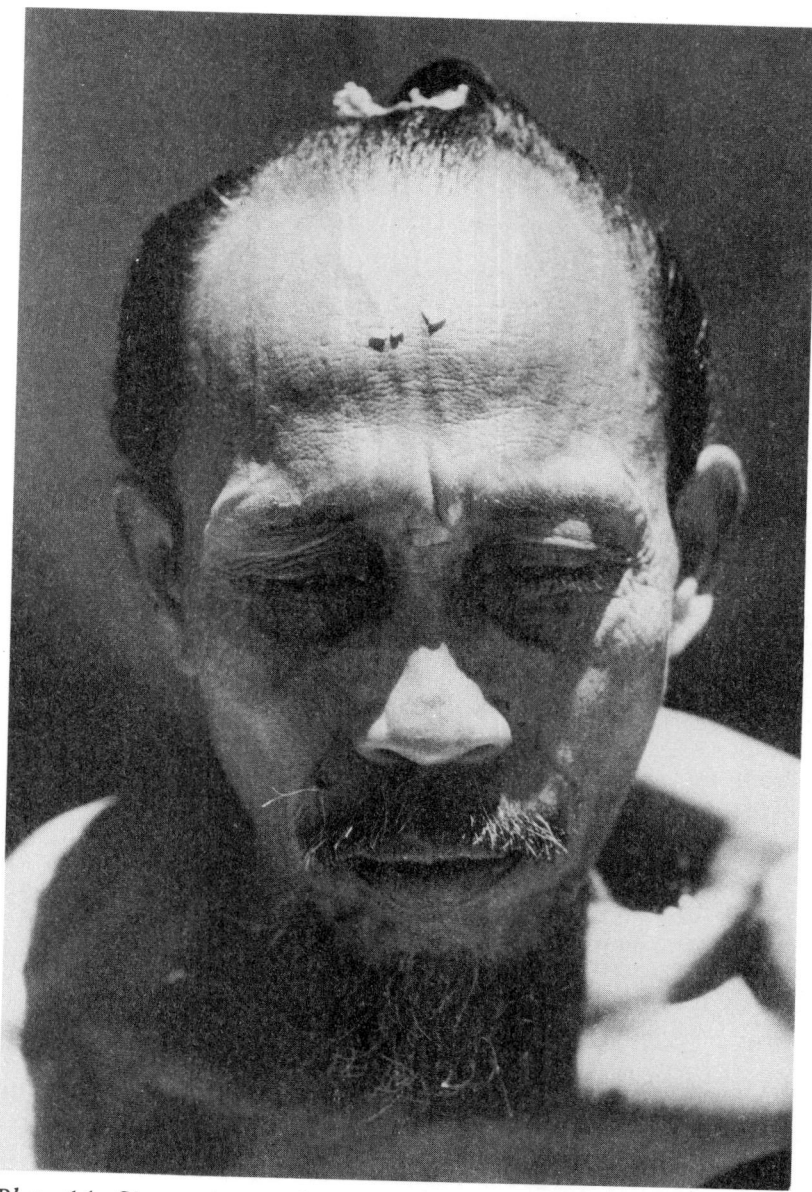

Plate 14 Siwa priest with soaked rice grains (wija) placed on his forehead

Plate 15   Daughter of a king's family of Karangasem praying in the family temple of Puri Madura, Amlapura

formation into a deity, must be performed for parents and grandparents by their children and grandchildren. Several kinds of holy water (*toya tirta*) produced by various categories of specialized priests and priestesses are used for purification, that is, ritual washing, and serve to purify ritual objects, religious sites and individuals involved in religious rites. It is this holy water that has led Agama Hindu Bali, the Hindu-Balinese religion, to become known as Agama Tirta, 'Holy Water Religion'.

Weddings and Marriage in the Balinese System of Belief

Weddings and marriage are a part of divine revelation. If they are to endure before god and human society, marriages must, therefore, be consecrated in a wedding ritual (Balinese: *masakapan*, Sanskrit: *wiwaha*), in accordance with the divinely ordained order of life (*darma*). All Balinese regard marriage as an express goal in life, granting them the right to establish a household and have children of their own. It also gives the husband, as representative of the household, a seat and vote in the political organizations of the village.

In accordance with fundamental Hindu legal treatises and locally interpreted traditional laws (*adat*), all members of the Hindu-Balinese religion must marry, the self-evident goal being to beget children and thereby guarantee the continuity of the patriliny. During the wedding ritual the bodies of the marital partners, as 'seedbeds' for conception and birth, are symbolically cleansed. This renders the couple mature for sexual relations, which will culminate in the birth of pure children with strong characters – as vessels for the reincarnation of good and pure souls.

There is a further reason for begetting children of one's own: only they can perform the rituals for the dead and for the purification of souls – rituals indispensable to the liberation and rebirth of the soul, which redeem any existing debts before god, shorten the period of torment in hell and prepare for a successful reincarnation or transformation into a deity. Thus the Balinese consider it their sacred duty to marry and have a family in order to maintain the patrilinear line of descent and preserve the benevolence of the ancestors to attain a good rebirth. That eternal bachelorhood should render a man negligible in society, and childlessness and impotence be considered grounds for divorce, is not surprising under the circumstances.

Arranged Marriages and Free Choice of Partners

Arranged, ritually planned marriages (*mapadik*) between families related by blood or friendship are, for a variety of reasons, considered safer and more satisfactory than marriages between comparative strangers. Status- and title-related rivalries between castes, subcastes, clan and temple organizations are a source of latent or even manifest conflict in Bali. Such conflicts can become particularly threatening and virulent if a marriage between unequals impairs status or is not agreeable to the ancestors. The basic principle is that a woman of caste cannot marry a man of lower caste unless she is ready to risk her status, title, inheritance and the inheritance of her children and to bring shame and perhaps even loss of status upon her whole family.

Arranged marriages within a family or clan are intended not so much to promote emotional bonds between the families of groups linked by blood or friendship as to preserve the established social, individual and cosmic hierarchy, thereby preventing tension and conflicts arising in the earthly and spiritual realm.[1] The castes, subcastes and clan associations trace their origins back to a mythical point of reference, which thus becomes a source of religious obligations, rights and group identification. All this becomes particularly manifest in the family or clan temple, where one's own deified ancestors are worshipped. A woman who marries a man from outside her own ritual group is released from her family and temple of origin and joins her husband's family and ancestors. But if she marries within her own family or clan group, her family's working and ritual authority is retained.

Among the *brahmana*, *satria* and *wesia*, arranged marriages within the family group are often aimed at maintaining religious purity. Partnerships of this kind, which preserve the ancestral quality of the patrilinear and matrilinear line equally, are considered particularly strong and sacred. This explains the preference for patrilateral parallel or cross-cousin marriages (first cousin = *misan*). Where ties of this kind cannot be established, alliances between second cousins (*mindon*) are striven for. The *jaba* clans, the so-called *dadia*,[2] frequently favour marriages consecrated in, and ensuring the survival of, their own ancestral temple (*tunggal paibon*).

But apart from respecting clan and ancestral interests, Hindu law and Balinese tradition also consider private interests and wishes compatible with *darma* and give lovers whose relationship runs counter to family-political considerations a chance to marry legitimately and legally. An adventurous or desperate woman has the right to flee her parents' home or to be abducted by her lover or his friends in order to escape the consequences of parental arrangements and free herself from parental domination. Thus, providing a young woman fulfils the social criteria of marriageability, she can defy her parents wishes respecting the formation of alliances by making use of her right to elope or be abducted. Today the institution of marriage by elopement or abduction (*ngrorod*) – not to be confused with wife capture (*malegandang*), which is prohibited and was, even in feudal times, an aristocratic prerogative only during military campaigns – is particularly widespread in urban agglomerations.

The Status and Role of the Wife

According to Hindu law (Manawa Dharma Sastra), women are subject to the will first of their parents, then of their husbands and finally of their sons, and are consequently not free to act independently. A woman leaves her parents' home and follows her husband, often moving into her in-laws' compound for the first few years, until her father-in-law or the village or area council grants her husband property for personal use. The head of the new household is once again the husband, who may own the house, garden, rice-fields and cattle, and passes them on in the patrilinear line. The husband also represents the family before the law, before god and before the deified ancestors, who are often his own.

And yet, thanks to the strongly gender-specific division of labour that marks the Balinese way of life, the wife's lot is by no means an intolerable one – particularly as women control the traditional markets and certain trade relations, giving them leverage of their own. They also tend to hold the purse-strings at home, for their dowries and their own incomes are at their disposal: by law, everything that a woman earns or has received as a gift (including the marriage portion) belongs to her. Women also own their clothing and jewellery and the family's small livestock, a not insignificant economic commodity. In case of conflict or divorce, they are entitled to a share of the jointly acquired assets, the amount being determined by a judge and by public opinion.

According to Hindu law, a wife must be faithful to her husband. She must keep house with skill and maintain the house altar and the sacred places of the compound (Manawa Dharma Sastra V: 148; VIII: 299; and XI: 177). The husband must protect his wife and children from enemies and from associating with people who might bring harm upon the household. Should he abuse his wife, be impotent, neglect to support his family appropriately or marry a co-wife (*madu*) without the approval of his first wife, the injured spouse may return to her family. If she succeeds in convincing the court of her husband's guilt, she receives custody of her children. In practice, however, alliances, property ownership and children tend to complicate divorces.

Should the wife neglect her duties, be proven adulterous, have concealed an incurable physical or mental ailment or remain childless, she can be 'thrown away', that is, sent away, by her husband – if she has come into the family from outside through *ngrorod*. The situation can become more difficult if a marriage has been preceded by scrupulous preparations and an engagement, and if divorce would endanger a carefully wrought set of politically significant alliances. In such cases the husband may go to live with a lover while continuing to support his wife. If a marriage is in obvious conflict with the principles of Agama Hindu Darma, application for annulment may, under Indonesian law, be submitted to the appropriate district court (*Pengadilan Negeri*) within six months by the families of the husband and wife, by the spouses themselves or by an authorized civil servant.[3]

The Basic Elements of the Wedding Ritual

The Balinese wedding ritual is primarily a ritual of purification and legitimation, legitimating sexual relations between husband and wife and declaring their marital bond compatible with Darma and thus legally binding before god.

How lavish the ceremony is depends on the financial circumstances. But whether performed on a small (*nista*), medium (*madia*) or large (*utama*) scale, the basic elements of the ritual and its significance before god remain the same. The couple are led in a festive procession to the bridegroom's compound, where they are received at the gate. There offerings (*caru, segehan*) are distributed in the street and by the gate to banish demons and keep them from entering the compound. The first rite upon entering the compound is also directed at these potential mischief-makers: an exorcistic purification ceremony and offerings induce them to move away from the site of the sacred activities and the participants of the ritual.

Now the most important part of the ritual can take place: the couple are freed from blemish and sin, and the 'seedbed' for impregnation, conception and birth is symbolically purified (*madengen-dengen*) by a priest or a priestess, preparing it for the reception of a pure soul, in other words, a good, healthy child. After a ritual consecration of offerings and a prayer, the couple take in the essence of these offerings. Thus fortified and purified, they walk three times round the altars in which the gods and ancestors have settled. The bridegroom carries a hoe, a piece of sugar cane and a magic *dadap* twig (*Erythrina subumbrans*), at the end of which dangles a pot and a woven basket containing coins. The bride carries a marketing basket containing raw rice, spices and various useful plants, which she 'sells' to her husband. The bridegroom pierces a woven mat, symbol of the bride's purity and virginity, with the phallic *keris* dagger; the 'purchased' plants are

planted behind the ancestral altar (*sanggah kemulan*) to promote fertility. Finally, the bride and bridegroom cut or tear a
cotton thread which has been stretched between two *dadap*
twigs: a new stage in life has begun and the newly-weds now
pray together for the first time at the altar of the Hindu trinity
and the deified ancestors.

On the following day or at some later date, the young couple
visit the compound and family temple of the bride's parents to
ask for their blessings and to allow the daughter to bid farewell to her original temple association. If the bridegroom's
family are not related and thus not members of the same
temple association, she now transfers to her husband's family
and ancestral group, acquiring a status and title for herself and
her future children appropriate to her origin.

Conception, Pregnancy and Birth

During the sexual union of husband and wife in the pure
seedbed of the female body, sperm (*kama petak*) and egg
(*kama bang*) meet. The fusion of 'white' and 'red' elements in
the fallopian tube produces a foetus (Sang Hyang), which
establishes itself in the womb, takes on human form within
one month and develops into a fully developed human child in
five Balinese months. According to the palm-leaf manuscript
Widhisastra Siwa Sumedang (Gria Carik, Sidemen), the foetus
(*manik*) created by the energies of the god Brahma is bestowed
feelings after one month and granted the ability to remember
and forget after two.

The embryo can grow properly in the womb only if, from
the fourth month on, it receives tangible support from the *yeh
nyom* (amniotic fluid), *lamad* (*vernix caseosa*, that is, the fatty
layer), *ari-ari* (placenta) and *getih* (blood). As Kanda Mpat or
Catur Sanak, elder siblings, these elements plus 108 helpers
(*babu* and *nyama bajang*) accompany, protect and nourish the
nascent life.[4]

The four siblings – brothers or sisters, in accordance with
the sex of the embryo – become inseparable companions from
before birth until beyond death. As long as the Kanda Mpat
are treated well and provided with offerings, they fulfil their

roles as tutelary spirits; otherwise they are transformed into demons, bringing disaster and death.

In their magical relationship to human beings, the four siblings possess both divine and demonic powers, and change their names and seats in the body according to a person's age. The five material elements – Panca Mahabuta – which determine in the fifth month that the developing being will be human, also have both a divine and a demonic nature. Skin, arteries, flesh and bones, on the one hand, the face and the senses of touch, hearing, taste and smell, on the other, can thus be identified and associated with the basic cosmic elements, the demonic guardians of the cardinal points, the five deities Iswara, Brahma, Mahadewa, Wisnu and Siwa, and their colours, white, red, yellow, black and mixed hues.[5]

Now the time has come for the pregnancy ritual, *Magedong-gedongan*. Performed for the welfare of mother and child, its purpose is to anchor the embryo firmly in the womb, thereby creating the conditions for a good birth. The ritual focuses on the joint prayers of the spouses before the altar of origin (*sanggah kemulan*) in the family temple. Sanghyang Guru, Siwa in his manifestation as divine teacher and educator, and the deified ancestors are entreated to confer good fortune, health, protection and blessings for a long life on the mother-to-be and her child.

Before the pregnant woman and her husband may enter the sacred district of the compound, they must undergo a cleansing ritual to purify them physically and spiritually. This act of pre-prayer cleansing, known as *mabiakala* or, in High Balinese, *mabiakaon*, is a basic element of all Balinese rituals (*yadnya*), which might otherwise be impeded by demonic powers and evil spirits. In other words, before the Balinese address the divine powers they must first banish the negative forces from themselves and the site of the ritual. This is done with the help of special sacrificial offerings to appease the *buta kala*, magical holy water (*toya panglukatan*) to cleanse body and soul, and, finally, by hand gestures (*natab, ngayab*), the individual who is performing the ritual turning his back to the gate and motioning the mischief-makers to move behind him and away from the house.[6]

Occasionally the prayer is followed by a highly symbolic ritual in which the embryo's four siblings participate, their physical presence represented by aromatic ingredients in a small, four-chambered medicine box (*ceraken*). In front of the entrance to the family temple, two three-forked branches of the magic evergreen *dadap* tree are stuck into the ground and connected with black yarn. From one twig hangs a receptacle made from a particularly large *kumbang* leaf; it is filled with water containing living creatures from the river or rice-field – small fish and crabs.

The pregnant woman now stoops to walk back and forth three times beneath the yarn and finally tears the yarn with her torso, symbolizing the removal of all possible obstacles to the further course of her pregnancy. The husband, shouldering a pointed bamboo pole, now steps up to the *kumbang*-leaf receptacle and jabs it forcefully enough to send the fish, crabs and water sloshing out and on to the ground. So easily shall the amniotic fluid and the child leave the womb during the birth. To influence the child to come out head first, care is taken to ensure that the water animals return to their element head first.

From now on mother and father must adhere strictly to certain behavioural maxims dedicated to the physical well-being and character formation of the child. Thoughts and actions must be guided by a pure heart, behavioural models being drawn from, among other things, the Hindu-Javanese epics, whose teachings the parents should become acquainted with. The husband is expected to be calm and considerate at home, to harbour no improper thoughts and use no indecent language. He should also avoid certain inappropriate jobs and may under no circumstances participate in the washing of corpses. Even nowadays many Balinese men leave their hair uncut throughout their wife's pregnancy.

The early stages of pregnancy in particular are a time for the mother-to-be to eat foods that pregnant women tend to crave, for instance sour fruit in spicy sauce (*rujak*). She may under no circumstances accept food from people who are temporarily impure (*sebel, cuntaka*), and dishes containing fresh blood, roasted pig or octopus are taboo.

Thus prepared, the woman awaits the birth of her child,

which is so happy in the womb that it will leave there only at the urging of its four siblings. The Kanda Mpat promise the new earthling help in finding a way out into the world and protection during life in the middle world – providing they are given as much love and attention as the physical parents receive.

Now the amniotic fluid opens the gate to this life; blood and *vernix caseosa* protect the infant at the left and right, and the placenta pushes from behind. The miracle of birth has become reality thanks to Brahma, the creator and procreator (impregnation), Wisnu, the protector and sustainer (pregnancy), and Siwa, the divine teacher and educator. The command to be born and enter the visible world (*sekala*), which means dying in the invisible world (*niskala*) of the beyond (Widhisastra Siwa Sumedang), comes from Batara Guru. The child, its siblings and the 108 helpers (*bajang*) leave the womb and are welcomed into this world with offerings of reception (*banten pemapag rare*). As the birth, or, to be more exact, the exit from the uterus, renders mother and child impure for 42 days, the pregnant woman has had to leave the couple's house several days before the birth and move into the pavilion in the chthonian western part of the compound, where the infant will now spend its first 42 days (a 35-day Balinese month plus a 7-day week). The period of seclusion tends to be shorter today, as most Balinese women give birth in obstetric clinics or hospitals.

Hospital and clinic births have not displaced the central birth-related ritual, the solemn burial of the placenta (*ari-ari*). The father collects the most important of the Kanda Mpat elements from the clinic or hospital and takes it home. There the afterbirth is washed with pure, flower-scented water and then placed into a halved coconut along with flowers and ritual money. The shell-halves have previously been inscribed on the inside with the magic syllables *Ong*, *Ang* and *Ah*. The two halves of the coconut are now put together again, wrapped in a white cloth and tied up with white yarn or sugar-palm fibre.

The father of the child sits down quietly before the grave and holds the coconut containing the placenta in both hands. Girls' placentas are buried on the left side of the stairs to the couple's home, boys' on the right. With a *mantra* to the Earth

Mother Pretiwi, the afterbirth is given back to the five elements as if it were a human corpse, washed, bathed in scented water and wrapped in white cloth. Though *ari-ari* has died in the middle world, it lives on in the beyond.

After the funeral the grave is covered with a black stone (*batu bulitan*) and decked with sweet-smelling flowers plus a bunch of spiky pandanus leaves to protect *ari-ari* from domestic animals and evil spirits. Finally, a symbolic cremation fire (*tabunan*) is lit on the grave, with embers of charcoal, rice spelt and fibrous coconut shells. A simple bamboo altar (*sanggar cucuk*) is anchored in the ground next to the grave for the offerings to Panca Mahabuta and the Kanda Mpat.

The First 210 Days of Life

The Javano-Balinese *uku* year comprises thirty seven-day weeks, making a total of 210 days. It is also divided into six 35-day periods. Other calendrical systems affecting the temporal order in Balinese ritual life will not be dealt with here as they have no relevance to the major rites of transition. Dates for these rites are fixed calendrically according to the Javano-Balinese *uku* year and to the astrological calendar, with specialized priests calculating the days on which constellations will be propitious (*dewasa*).

The first ritual event in the life of the newborn child is independent of the calendar. It takes place when the navel cord is shed, *lepas aon* (also: *kepus odel*), for with it the child also throws off the impurity originating from its physical connection with the placenta. The navel cord and various hot spices are packed in a woven palm-leaf receptacle and stored away at the foot of the cradle. Above the head of the cradle, in the mountainward, uranian direction, hangs a carved offering-platform (*palangkiran*) for Ida Hyang Kumara, the god of infants. The eternally childlike son of Siwa will protect the infant until it loses its first baby tooth. Every day offerings are placed here to exert a favourable influence on the growth and health of the child; and every time the child receives mother's milk or fine pulp of young coconut, the four siblings in their bamboo seat are fed as well.

Twelve days after the birth, the soul has become so firmly anchored in the child that the parents can now give it an individual name and inform the rest of the family of the birth. The period of twelve days also plays an important role for the *pitra yadnya*, for it is twelve days after the cremation that the *ngroras* ritual, with its concomitant soul purification (*mukur*, see pp. 125–6), frequently takes place. Once again the parallel course of events in this world and the beyond, in the realm of the visible (*sekala*) and the invisible (*niskala*), manifests itself.

In certain regions of Bali, a clairvoyant priest (*balian tenung*) with the ability to communicate with the ancestors and thus to establish whose soul has been reincarnated in the newborn child is summoned to the ritual of the twelfth day (*ngroras rahina*). The central event of the ritual is the purification of mother and child with exorcistic holy water (*tirta panglukatan*), which is requested at the hearth (Brahma), the watering place (Wisnu) and the house temple (Guru). The god of infants receives gifts, and the four siblings of the infant, who must be indulged with gifts in accordance with the unborn child's earlier promise, receive new names.

Forty-two days, in other words one month (thirty-five days) and one week after the birth, the mother's period of impurity, resulting from the birth of the child and the death of the placenta, comes to an end. The period of careful abstention is over (*tutug kambuhan*), and after a purification ritual for mother and child, the woman can return to her husband and her daily and religious activities.

The offerings on this day are prepared in the colours of the deities endowed with the purifying, cleansing powers so vital to the mother: red for Batara Brahma, who has his seat in the kitchen and is master over the fire; black for Batara Wisnu, who presents holy water to the mother at the bathing place and is ruler over water; white and yellow for Batara Guru, the divine teacher and educator in the family temple. Naturally the Kanda Mpat and Sanghyang Kumara, the child's guardian angel, also receive small offerings.

The purification ritual of the forty-second day is known either as *tutug kambuhan* (end of abstention) or *macolongan*, referring to the exorcism of the four siblings' helpers or servants. Useful though they were during pregnancy, they have now become mischief-makers and must be sent back to their place of origin. The exorcism of the *bajang colong*,[7] whose survival potentially imperils the existence of the child, is part of a colourful ritual often held during the three-month festival (*nelubulanin* or, in High Balinese, *nigang sasihin*), after 105 days or then after 210 days, on the child's first birthday by the Javano-Balinese calendar.

The child and its four siblings now move into a new stage of existence and come into contact with the forces of nature for the first time. A dangerous transition is ahead, which, depending on geographical location and status, must be confirmed by a multi-part ritual after 105 or 210 days. Form and content of the ritual are similar throughout Bali, though there are differences in detail depending on the village, time or social pattern (*desa, kala, patra*). The following basic features pertain to Karangasem in eastern Bali, where the *bajang colong* are often exorcised after 210 days, in conjunction with the first time the child comes into physical contact with the ground (*ngenteg* Pretiwi).

After 210 days the child ceases to be a divine creature and becomes an earthly being in need of protection. Up to now it has been carried around by its parents, elder brothers and sisters or other relatives; now, at the beginning of the *moton*, before the sun rises, the child makes contact for the first time with Earth Mother Pretiwi in front of the family's altar of origin: for the first time the infant's feet are allowed to touch the ground. While the morning ceremony in the household temple is a quiet family affair, the subsequent afternoon rituals of purification and offering are colourful festivities to which a Brahman or Buda priest (*padanda*) or priestess is normally invited.

The first phase of the ritual is aimed at removing the troublesome *bajang* powers from the child's vicinity, while transferring some of the impurity still clinging to the infant to them in the process. During this ritual, which is performed by women, a squash (*beligo*), a banana blossom (*pusuh*) and sometimes a cucumber (*ketimun*) temporarily take on the role of the child, becoming changelings. Further *bajang*, in the guise of a duck egg, a black stone and the sheathing base of a coconut palm bearing anthropomorphic chalk drawings, also participate in the ceremony. The squash is decked out with the child's jewellery – fontanelle plate, wrist and ankle bracelets and finger-rings – perfumed and then dressed in one or more sacred cloths (*wangsul* or *gedogan bajang*).[8]

The ceremony, which is analogous for changeling and child, often begins with a ritual bath in purifying holy water. Following a long blade of bamboo grass and a broad *kumbang*-leaf canopy, the procession now pulls the *bajang* round the offerings and the clay bathing receptacle (*paso, pané*) several times. The woman carrying the *beligo* squash symbolically pounds rice during every circuit, just as the mother holding her child will do later on. Rice pounding is a symbolic act emphasizing that growth and fertility are vital to life.

After these circuits, the changeling is brought before the priest, who treats it as if it were a child, cleansing it and sprinkling it with holy water. Next, the women fan the essence of the offerings towards it and rock it lovingly to the strains of a lullaby. Then, however, the squash is prosaically undressed, carried outside and thrown away at the next street corner. At this point the genuine child celebrating its birthday becomes the focal point of the priestly purification ritual. It is decked out and dressed in a sacred *bebali* cloth for its first appearance before the priest and Batara Siwa.

Before the infant is ready for the priestly ceremony, it must be freed from further impure elements. To this end the child is first carried round the offerings several times and subsequently taken to the ritual bath to be cleansed with *tirta panglukatan*. Then it is held over a flat, water-filled clay basin. The water, which is compared to a 'pond of life', contains things that will be important in later life: an inscribed lontar leaf stands for intelligence and wisdom; Chinese coins are associated with wealth, but also with gambling fever; grains of rice and kernels of corn represent industriousness and diligence; gold and silver rings, the need for jewellery or vice. Various river animals – small fish, crabs or eels – bring life to the symbolic pond. What the infant grabs with its right hand will be bestowed upon it in abundance in later life. During this divination ceremony, known as *magogo-gogoan*, a loosely woven basket of cocks (*guungan*) is held over the child's head as a protective roof. Finally, a chicken picks the remaining impurities from the infant's fontanelle. Only now can the priest perform the ritual haircut.

Balinese *rites de passage* (*manusa yadnya*) all have a single purpose: to free growing individuals from the impurities of birth and the blemishes and sins of previous lives, thus preparing them spiritually and physically to marry and start a family of their own. The ritual haircut after 210 days denotes the symbolic removal of one more element considered impure or unclean.

The priest or priestess uses a large pair of scissors to cut five locks of hair from the infant's head, taking them from the sunrise and sunset sides, from mountainward, seaward and the centre, in accordance with the cardinal points ruled by the most important deities and demons. The hair is put into a rolled-up, cylindrical coconut leaf (*blayag*), which is placed on to a sacred, striped cotton cloth (*wangsul, gedogan*) and carefully laid into a silver bowl. Depending on the priest's views, the hair is buried either by the altar of origin, and thus returned to the Earth Mother, or thrown into a nearby river or

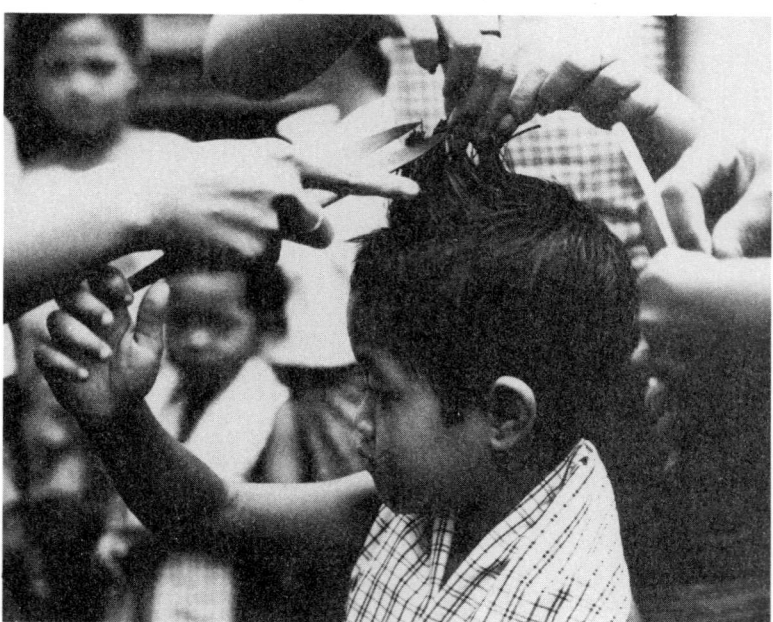

Plate 16   Hair-cutting ritual in Tenganan Pageringsingan

the sea. The Widhisastra Siwa Sumedang lontar book uses the term *maligia rare* for the infant's ritual transition from divine creature to ordinary mortal. This establishes a further parallel with the invisible world, where the *maligia* soul-ritual leads to total purity of the soul and its entry into the highest of all heavens.

Maturity Holidays and Tooth-filing

The cycle of *rites de passage* resumes with the first recognizable signs of growing up and the attendant end of childhood. For girls, the onset of menstruation marks the time for a rite of transition (*menek kelih, ngrajasvala*); for boys, it is generally when their voices break. From now on the young people are under the influence of Semara and Ratih, the gods of love, who bring uncertainty and temptation into their lives but also take over important protective and guiding functions in this difficult pre-marital period.

This explains why Semara, Ratih and their heavenly male and female nymphs, Widiadara and Widiadari, play so central a role in the *rites de passage* undergone during this period. They are depicted on cloths and mats in a close embrace, in the style of Balinese *wayang* figures, and even receive their own offering place.

The actual initiation rites are preceded by a three-day period of seclusion (*ngekeb*) dedicated in part to the symbolic encounter with the male and female principle in the form of Semara and Ratih. During this time, the initiates' mothers give the young people food, spices and drinks in the six basic tastes – sweet, sour, salty, tart, bitter and burning hot (*sadrasa*) – as a symbolic lesson in finding the proper measure of all things. Finally, the initiates grasp the fringe of an undyed cotton cloth decorated with a drawing of the gods of love (*wangsul, gedogan*) between their thumb and forefinger and let Semara and Ratih pass gently over their cheeks.[9]

The tooth-filing ceremony (*matatah*), in which the six upper (uranian) canine teeth and incisors are evenly filed off, is designed to reduce the following six human passions to a reasonable level:

1 *kama*, lust, sensual desire;
2 *kroda*, anger, ire;
3 *loba*, greed;
4 *mada*, arrogance;
5 *moha*, intoxication through passion or drink;
6 *matsaria*, jealousy, envy.

The lower, chthonian teeth remain as they are, for desire and passion should never be killed off completely. The important thing is for men and women to learn to establish a balanced, harmonious relationship between the two hearts beating in their breasts. The candidates lie on a mattress covered with a woven mat, placing their heads on a soft pillow wrapped in a sacred cloth to elevate it above the profane realm. Their bodies too are covered to the neck with ritual cloths to safeguard them from danger. A spittoon, mirror and silver container for hammer, chisel, file and towel are the basic requisites for this painful but courageously borne priestly procedure.

As tooth-filing is very expensive, it is sometimes postponed

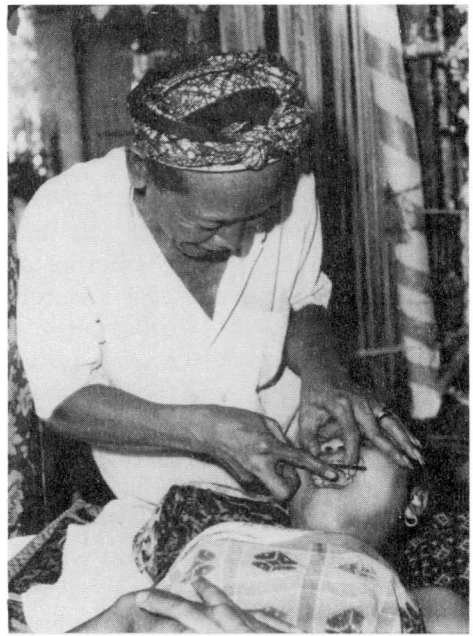

Plate 17   Tooth-filing ceremony at Sukawati

until a person's marriage is sanctified, meaning that it takes place at the close of the circle of *manusa yadnya*. Women generally have their teeth filed between the onset of menstruation and marriage, men between the age of sixteen and death, in extreme cases only after they have died.[10]

Death and the Purification of Souls

The Balinese death cult and soul purification ritual can be understood only with reference to two concepts central to the Hindu-Balinese faith: belief in the correspondence of macrocosm (*buana agung*) and microcosm (*buana alit*) is based on the idea that the cosmos and human beings consist of the same five material elements (Panca Mahabuta):

1 *pretiwi*: earth/all parts of the body of firm consistency;
2 *apah*: liquid/water and blood;
3 *teja*: fire, light, warmth/body temperature;
4 *bayu*: air, wind/breath;
5 *akasa*: atmosphere, sky/very fine bodily substances like hair or nails.

These five materials are in the womb during pregnancy and together form the unrefined human body (*stula sarira*), which consists of three layers (*trisarira*), body, spirit and soul. In the vertical, hierarchical order of things, the unrefined body belongs to the lowest of the three worlds. At death it disintegrates into its constituent parts again, decomposing and returning to the macrocosmic dimension of the Panca Mahabuta; ashes to ashes, dust to dust.

The process is different for the two higher levels of being: the refined body (*suksma sarira*), consisting of feelings, desires, thoughts and wishes; and the soul (*antakarana sarira*), the most refined, divine substance. Both are released from the corpse (*sawa*) once the death ritual has broken their bonds to the body. Liberated, they set out on their journey to the world of the ancestral souls.

The order of *manusa yadnya* dictates that parents are responsible for the purification and ritual protection of their children prior to marriage; once married, the younger generation takes on the sacred obligation to care for their parents and grandparents in old age, during the transition between the worlds and in the next world. The death cult and rites for the purification of souls (*pitra yadnya*; *pitra* = ancestral soul, *yadnya* = ritual) afford descendants the opportunity to express their gratitude and repay their debts to their progenitors, both out of love and in the interest of their own physical and spiritual welfare. Their task consists largely in ritual responsibility for the processes that enable the soul to break away from the dead body, allow soul and body to move into their respective worlds and afford the soul a smooth, undisturbed reception in the next world.

Temporary Burial

The elements of the death cult most commonly encountered in Bali are the washing of corpses, ritual purification, separation of body and soul with the aid of special holy water, cremation, and consignment of the ashes to the sea. Exposing the corpse to the natural elements (as practised in the mountain village of Trunyan) and burial (as performed in the Bali Aga village of Tenganan Pageringsingan, in several villages in the vicinity of the sacred mountain peaks – where gods and ancestors might be disturbed by the smoke from cremations – or among certain Old Balinese clans) are the exception and will not be considered here.[11]

In view of the religious principle that simple (*nista*), medium-(*madia*) and large-scale (*utama*) rituals are equally pleasing in the sight of god, the poorer strata of society could theoretically afford to limit themselves to simple cremations without having to endure the unpredictable perils of a temporary burial. But status-consciousness, the social obligations of the living towards the dead or the simple need to break up the daily routine with a festive occasion often lead to a temporary burial until the family has accumulated the funds necessary for a large cremation or until there is an opportunity to participate in a collective cremation organized by an aristocratic family, the priesthood or *banjar*.[12]

Burial temporarily places the soul (*atma*) under the protection and power of Durga, goddess of death, who reigns over cemeteries. One's mortal remains are, however, returned to Earth Mother Pretiwi, as representative of the Panca Mahabuta. In principle, and in line with the lontar texts (Tattwa Loka Kreti, Upacara Patiurip), cremations should not be put off longer than a year; otherwise the soul will be claimed by Batara Yama, god of the underworld, and become a wretched, unpredictable spirit burning in the fires of hell. The curse these spirits place on their negligent progeny remains a constant threat until the cremation has taken place. Three days before the burning, the soul is called back (*ngulapin*) to allow the mortal remains (*tawulan*), either in the shape or the company of effigies, to be washed, purified and burnt.

Cremation

A medium- or large-scale cremation may easily take on the character and dimensions of an Old Indonesian merit festival of the type still celebrated on Nias a century ago or still common today among the Sadan-Toraja in Sulawesi, the Batak in Sumatra or the Ngaju-Dayak in Central Kalimantan. Large cremations are often so expensive, time-consuming and labour-intensive that they outstrip the powers and possibilities of a single family. When that happens the family

Plate 18   *Taking care of the dead: women with anthropomorphic effigies*

*Plate 19   Coffin in the shape of a black bull being carried to the
cremation ground by members of the blacksmiths' youth association
from Marga*

becomes dependent on help from relatives and friends, and
above all on the assistance of the *banjar* and the know-how of
specialists. Paying tourists are increasingly beginning to feature as sources of finance as well.

Demands on the time of the many Balinese with jobs in the
tourist, service and government sectors have increased so dramatically over the past years that weeks of voluntary communal work (*gotong royong*), as supplied in the past, have become
virtually unthinkable today. In the spirit of growing individ-
ualim and ever-greater time pressure, the family and *banjar*
now perform only some of the necessary tasks (*karya*). These
include construction of the cremation pavilion (*bale gumi*) and
simple altars, the preparation and serving of food to guests,
and the transportation of the towers (*wadah*, *bade*) and ani-
mal-shaped coffins (*patulangan*) to the cremation ground.

Yet the religious sense and knowledge of the Balinese, rather
than waning, continues to grow (Parisada Hindu Dharma,
Eka Dasa Rudra 1979), and that has led to a significant

increase in the number of cremations performed and an inevitable shift towards the professionalization of certain tasks. Thus various offerings, cult objects and, in particular, textiles can now be bought at Balinese markets. The construction of massive towers for transporting corpses and of coffins artistically fashioned in the shape of winged lions, bulls, white cows or fish with elephant tusks – formerly the traditional domain of the *banjar* – often falls to specialized professionals today. This means that the centuries-old job market for professionals in the production of offerings (*tukang banten*) has now been joined by a new job market, one that is developing into an ever-more important socio-economic component of Balinese life, which would lose its meaning without offering rituals, cremations and the purification of souls.

The Purification of Souls

After cremation, a soul that has been spared a sojourn in hell moves directly to the lowest ancestral heaven. It is accompanied there by its four siblings (*Kanda Mpat*), who have been waiting for it. Though it is now liberated from the unrefined body and cleansed of material impurities, its links to the refined body have not yet been broken. Its thoughts, feelings and wishes are still sullied by worldly flaws, which must be removed as thoroughly as possible through the ritual of soul purification (*mukur*). Only then, in its even purer or totally pure condition, can it become an ancestral soul (*dewapitra*) and enter the heaven of the gods, from where it can direct and protect its family's destiny on earth.

The *mukur* ritual grants the soul the purity it requires for reincarnation. But as the Balinese faith holds that rebirth takes place in accordance with *karma*, the divine balance sheet of good and bad acts, the soul remains connected with its *karma* even after the purification ritual. The *mukur* ritual thus tacitly assumes that the soul has passed its test in the realm of Yama and been found free enough of defects by Jogor Manik, guardian of hell, to move directly into heaven.

Like cremation, soul purification is a lustration ritual, with holy water and fire once again figuring as the principal means of purification. But here the deceased are represented by symbolic images, effigies, which are animated and inspirited by an initiated high priest (*padanda*) and then ultimately separated from the purified soul in a symbolic cremation. The ashes of the symbolic seat of the soul (*sekah*, *puspalingga*), which is made out of *Ficus* leaves and flowers, are treated like the ashes of a body after cremation: they are placed in a young, yellow coconut and taken to the sea or a river flowing into it to be scattered. The transportation towers (*bukur*) used for this purpose are slimmer than cremation towers; they are made of light wood and totally covered with white cloth and gold tinsel. Once again the number of vertically arranged, pagoda-like roofs indicates the rank and cast of the organizers of the ritual.

Unlike cremation, *mukur* is a pure, uranian-orientated ceremony (*karya ayu*) and may therefore never be performed in impure or magical places. The courtyard of a compound or family temple, an uncultivated garden or a complex of linked, fallow rice-fields would, for example, be appropriate sites. Whether the ritual is performed on a low, medium or large scale, in other words, *nista*, *madia* or *utama*, is a factor in determining when the ritual takes place. Simple *mukur* ceremonies are often held immediately after cremation, either on the same evening or the following day, but in any case within twenty-four hours. Three other possible dates connected with cremation are *tutug katelun*, three days later, *tutug roras*, twelve days later, and *tutug bulan pitung dina*, forty-two days later.

When wealthy upper-caste families organize elaborate, expensive soul purifications on the highest level (*maligia*), less-affluent Balinese can let the souls of their deceased relations follow (*ngiring ka puri*, *ngiring ka gria*). In such cases the date of the ritual depends, not on the cremation, but on a specialized priest, who calculates a propitious date (*dewasa*) on the basis of calendrical and astrological constellations.

Now the soul has become a virtually divine ancestral soul and can enter the heaven of the gods. But it will become a genuine ancestral deity (batara, dewa) only after a further ritual, *ngalinggihang*, in the course of which it will take its place in the family or clan temple, thenceforth to be worshipped as Batara Kawitan, a divine ancestor.

Sacred Places and Districts

The word 'temple' generally brings to mind generously pro-portioned edifices containing architecturally self-contained structures. A Balinese temple, *pura*, on the other hand, is not a building or covered area containing a statue of a god as the focus of religious worship. Balinese *pura* go back to megalithic ritual places. The invisible gods of Bali do not reside permanently in the temple. As they occasionally allow themselves to be invited down from their world above the volcanoes, they need a place open at the top, through which they can come down and settle on their seats.

In line with this concept, buildings to receive the gods and divine ancestors are constructed within the open temple area bounded by hedges or walls. The enclosed district also contains numerous shrines and altars for the deities themselves, constructions known either as *palinggih* (seat) or *pasimpangan* (visiting-place), depending on whether they are meant for the gods of one's own temple or for divine guests from neighbouring temples. To reiterate the point, Balinese temples are not monumental edifices. The walls and gates enclosing the sacred grounds tend to be architecturally more impressive than the pavilions, shrines and altars standing inside the open inner area.

One of the common clichés used to sell Bali to the world is the image of the 'island of a thousand temples' – a vast understatement. Balinese *pura* are omnipresent, ranging from the simple, domestic sacred area to the extravagant state temple, from the modest shrine where the rice goddess is worshipped in the rice-field to the lavish baroque of the temple of an aristocratic family. Each Balinese *adat* village has three public *pura*, known as *kahyangan tiga*, which may be visited by members of all strata and castes: the uranian temple of creation or origin (*pura puseh*), located mountainward, in the purest part of the village; the village temple (*pura desa*), with its large assembly hall for the traditional village council (*bale agung*); and the chthonian temple of death (*pura dalem*), which is attached to the cemetery and is located seaward, low and hence in the most impure area of the village (see figure 4.1, p. 90).

Plate 20   Taman Ayun, temple of the royal family of Mengwi

But the *pura* supported by the village population at large are vastly outnumbered by temples belonging to genealogical groups or associations. This latter category includes both the household temples of individual families (*sanggah, pemrajan*) and the temples of origin of whole clan associations, which are known as *pura dadia, paibon, pura kawitan* or *pura panti*, depending, among other factors, upon the size of the group.[13]

But it is not only as members of territorial or genealogical groups that the Balinese participate in rituals. They also maintain special temples as members of specific occupational groups or voluntary associations, going there periodically to establish contact with the gods and to pray for blessings and prosperity in their work and on the land. Thus *ulun carik* is a temple for the irrigation society of a specific canalization system; *ulun danu* belongs to the irrigation society that obtains its water from the mountain lakes; *ulun pasar* is for traders and market-stall holders; and *ulun segara* is for fishermen.

The more or less supra-regional district temples, originally the state temples of the old autonomous princely dynasties, also deserve mention. They include such temples as the Pura Kehen in Bangli or Pura Taman Ayun in Mengwi. Six temples (*sad kahyangan*) already renowned as places of nature worship long ago and beyond the boundaries of the old empires continue even today to retain their importance throughout Bali. The most famous of them are the Pura Uluwatu complex, which sits atop a rock jutting into the sea on the Bukit Peninsula; Goa Lawah, the bat-cave temple near Kusamba; and the mountain temples of Lempuyang in Karangasem and Batukau in Tabanan. Naturally, no list would be complete without the Pura Besakih, mother temple of Bali. Spiritual and religious centre of the universe for all Hindu Indonesians, it is a place to worship not only Trimurti, Brahma, Wisnu and Siwa, but many kings and princes of bygone days, who are now divine ancestors.[14]

Offerings

The art of the offering (plate 21) is perhaps the most varied creative expression in Bali, conveying charm, refinement and

*Plate 21   Huge offerings ready to be carried to the temple and
presented to the gods*

at times humour. Yet it is by intention an ephemeral art. The diverse biscuits of rice dough, once offered to the gods, who merely enjoy their essence, *sari*, are taken home to be eaten. The intricately fashioned palm-leaf decorations and freshly picked flowers wither in a day or so. It is of interest that the indigenous term for offering, *banten*, reflects the transitory nature of the art. In the folk etymology *banten* is derived from *enten*, implying being conscious or waking up momentarily, then falling back to sleep again. This interpretation is in many ways apt, for offerings are unique vehicles for expressing the idea that the aesthetic repose which they initiate is a fleeting encounter. The scholar Maquet[15] has drawn attention to the parallelism that exists between the aesthetic vision, which is non-discursive, disinterested and outside or beyond secular time, unfolding instead in sacred time, and intuition, which is immediate and total and belongs to the meditative mode of consciousness. All aspects of the art – the occasions for which offerings are made, the process of creating them, the ingredients used, their external appearance – highlight how suitable offerings are as objects to generate aesthetic perception and contemplation in their makers and beholders alike.

Offerings are an integral part of the five ritual cycles, *panca yadnya*, mentioned earlier. While there is some variation in the offerings presented throughout Bali, their size and ornateness is determined by the ceremony at hand and the level at which it is performed – whether large, medium or small. Offerings, as well as their multifold composite parts, all have names. While the *plutuk* palm-leaf manuscripts attribute meaning to certain individual offerings, in general terms worshippers point out that offerings are suitable vehicles to express homage and thanks to the supreme god, Sang Hyang Widi, and his emanations. Demons, *buta*, who are disruptive to ordered community life also need to be appeased.

Offerings are primarily made by women, with the exception of certain offerings of animal flesh, which must be prepared by men. Many offerings are produced in the household compound, although on the occasion of a temple anniversary they are sometimes prepared in the kitchen of the temple complex. The creation of offerings for large cermonies is supervised by a female specialist in the art, who is often from a brahmana household.

The women gossip and chat together in groups while making offerings, especially if this for a larger ceremony. Thereby a contented, light-hearted atmosphere is generated, which lays the basis for atuning the thoughts imperceptibly to the art of fashioning offerings. Through their co-ordinated and united effort the women become increasingly absorbed in the work. This state of absorption is intensified by the detailed prescriptions that have to be followed in producing offerings and the emphasis that is placed on 'purifying the thoughts' (*nyuciyang pikayun*) during the work. This mode of consciousness is contemplative in intent, the discursive activities being gradually silenced as the creator of the offering becomes engrossed in the art.

Aesthetic perception is further encouraged by the ephemeral nature of the ingredients used for offerings. They come in all sizes and shapes. The smallest are *banten jotan*, which consist of a few grains of cooked rice on small squares of banana leaf and are placed daily in relevant spots in the compound. The main substances of offerings are rice and rice cakes, fruit, betelnut, fruit and flowers. Woven or plaited palm-leaf containers are produced as well. All these natural substances are short-lived in their freshness and beauty, and hence they help to stimulate the aesthetic attitude of disinterestedness or, in Buddhist terms, detachment – a state in which greed and clinging are held at bay. Before offerings are actually presented, incense is lit and they are purified with clear or holy water, *tirta*. Only then is their essence wafted to gods, ancestors or demons.

Demons require special offerings. These are placed on the ground and include chicken, pork, fish, ginger, arrak, palm wine and white wine. Balinese explain that these are given in order to appease demons so that they go home in peace. Demons are also propitiated with loud metallic music from gong ensembles.

Once made and placed in a ritual setting, offerings display an exellence and integrity of design which further stimulates in the worshipper a disinterested vision. This is exemplified by the elaborate offering called *bebangkit*[16] fashioned for all large ceremonies. In its entirety it reveals an underlying structure which parallels the patterning of the universe as conceived by the people. It is adorned with biscuits, *jaja*, that represent the four cardinal points. The cosmic dualities, mountain–sea, day–night, sun–moon, male–female, are also reflected by the biscuits, which are essentially forms of miniature art. For example, the biscuits called *segara gunung*, 'ocean and mountain', shows on one side a mountain and on the other the ocean where a man sits in a tiny boat, surrounded by fish. A humorous note may, moreover, be added to the biscuits of the *bebangkit*, motivating an imaginative outlook which rises above everything limited and mundane. A tiny dog may be depicted on a biscuit, eagerly waiting to snatch the offerings placed on the ground for demons. So the dynamic variables of this splendid offering are balanced in a unified configuration which enables the beholder to gain an awareness of the Totality, Sang Hyang Widi. All offerings, even less-elaborate ones than the *bebangkit*, express aspects of the cosmic order.

Palm-leaf hangings, *lamak*, are also associated with offerings. *Lamak* often have as their central motif an elegant, stylized feminine figure with a fan headdress, who symbolizes earth and fertility. They often adorn altars, where they are placed next to tall decorated poles that bend gracefully during festive occasions. Together they represent the unity of the female and male principles, and hence too form a symbol of totality.[17]

Specific genres of dance and drama performances deserve attention here, for they are presented to the gods as offerings in sacred time-space. They too sustain an aesthetic vision. They fall into the sacred category *wali* – implying offering or rite – and are always given as an integral part of rituals, in particular on the occasion of a temple anniversary. While they all seem to be of indigenous origin, subsequent Hindu elements may have been added.[18] The dances are all communal, the participants being drawn from the village or temple community. They require little or no training for the most part. While there is some variation in the genres included in the *wali* category, among the most famous are the girls' dance *rejang*; the *baris*, performed by a group of men; and the day-time puppet performance, *wayang lemah*. In line with their sacred

Plate 22   Girl of the village of Asak (east Bali), ready for the
rejang *dance on the occasion of* Usaba Kasa

orientation, these genres are performed in the inner courtyard of a temple (*jeroan*).

There are diverse forms of *rejang*, involving somewhat different costumes and choreographic formations. It is, however, always a processional group dance. Undulating as they advance accompanied by the gamelan music, the women or girls pay homage to the shrines that act as 'seats' (*palinggihan*) of the gods who have temporarily descended into small anthropomorphic wooden figures, *pratima*, which are dressed and adorned with flowers for the ceremony. Later these effigies are taken in procession in special portable shrines to be bathed in the river.

Like *rejang, baris* is a ceremonial dance given during a temple anniversary, but by men and boys. *Baris* implies a line of soldiers[19] and although there are several kinds of *baris*, the dance is both religious and martial, the dancers essentially acting as protectors of the temple effigies. The dance is distinguished by the sacred weapons that the men carry – spears, lances, shields or *keris*. During the dance, the men form rows and march rhythmically in unison to the gamelan music.

The day-puppet show is performed without a screen, on the ground, in daylight or dusk while a brahman priest recites ritual incantations. The few puppets required are set up against a string stretched out between two branches of a luminous plant, *dadap*. Two musicians who play percussion instruments, *gender*, accompany the story narrated by the *dalang*, poet-priest. A standard *wayang lemah* show is said to be given for the celestial beings, not for humans.[20] Indeed, it is hardly audible to the few bystanders.

A day-puppet show, like other *wali* performances, is of short duration. But then, much of Balinese art is characterized by its transitory nature. Sculpture and architecture made from soft volcanic rock have to be renewed frequently. Music and dance-drama performances are ephemeral. Cremation towers and biers go up in flames in a few minutes. This transitory element highlights the important principle of transformation, *metamahan*, in the culture, that is, that flux is inherent to all things. Social change too entails transition from one position to another. Even the cosmos is ordered: cosmic events follow one another with regularity (day–night, rain–drought, and so forth). This principle of transformation is particularly marked with offerings. Through their fleeting beauty they temporarily instil an aesthetic vision which is explicitly reverential and contemplative in intent. So by association with what is orderly, pure and divine, the worshipper participates in the cosmic pattern and learns to reflect these qualities in daily life.

6

Myth and the Artistic Tradition

A great many myths have been perpetuated and disseminated in Bali. These have also profoundly affected the arts. We need only to watch a dance drama performance to experience the unfolding of facets of divine–human relationships on the stage, or enter a palace or temple to encounter statues and reliefs of mythical beings or cosmic symbols of earth, heaven, trees, water and life.

The myths are also deeply rooted in the daily life of the villagers, the content of the stories forming part of a conceptual map which acts as a guide to the moral code of the society. This is evident in the recurrent analogies and references made to mythical characters. For example, it is immediately clear to others that a person said to be like the coarse, ignoble Prince Dursasana from the great epic, the Mahabharata, is rough, haughty and contemptuous of others. These are vices abhorred by the villagers, who value solidarity, a quality threatened by anyone who presents himself as better than others. In contrast, a handsome youth may be compared to the comely Prince Arjuna. Like Arjuna he too may have a 'roving eye' (*mata keranjang*). Such figures of speech enable the villagers to structure and order their experiences by incorporating them into a framework shared and comprehended by all.

Most Balinese myths are derived from the Hindu-Javanese classical literature which flourished at the courts of East Java between the eleventh and the fifteenth centuries. A few are also of indigenous origin. Myths are generally drawn from the following literary sources:

1 The Mahabharata: nine of the eighteen volumes (*parwa*) of the epic are known in Indonesia.[1] The earliest versions of the *parwa* are in Old Javanese prose, but they show similarity to the Sanskrit.[2] The central theme of the epic concerns the tragic conflict between the five Pandawa brothers and their first cousins, the hundred Korawa brothers. This culminates in the Great War, the Bharatayuddha, in which the Korawa, who are ogres incarnate, are defeated, and the eldest Pandawa brother, Yudistira, is crowned king of Nastina. *Parwa* myths are among the most popular in Bali as they deal with so many complex and varied issues. The heroes of most of the stories are the Pandawa brothers, begotten by gods – gentle Yudistira, powerful Bima, comely Arjuna and their younger twins, Nakula and Sahadewa. Their mentor is the brilliant and wily prince Kresna, an incarnation of the preserver god, Wisnu.

2 Myths associated with the *parwa* through recounting adventures pertaining to characters known from the Mahabharata. The most familiar are perhaps Sutasoma (a story of Buddhist origin), Arjuna Wiwaha, the Bharatayuddha and Bima Swarga.

3 The Ramayana: the epic resembles the Mahabharata in language, but is a long poem, *kakawin*, which closely follows the rules of Indian prosody. Myths recount the abduction of the beautiful Sita by the demon-king Rawana. With the help of the monkey-god Hanuman, Prince Rama rescues her from his clutches.

4 Mention should be made of the court chronicles, the *babad*, and the Panji romances, known in Bali as Malat. Although they are not overtly sacred, the stories do not clearly distinguish between legend, myth and fact, and they also exemplify fundamental truths.[3]

Of the literary sources, the Balinese revere most the Mahabharata. It is a 'history' in the sense that it validates and explains the present, justifying the authority of the aristocrats, formerly the 'god-kings'.[4] Although the power of the senior *satria* has waned considerably, remnants of their divine status are still evident today in what Geertz[5] has called the status title system or system of prestige. So villagers still address *satria* by such titles as Dewa Agung Gede (supreme great god) or Cokor I Ratu (at the foot of the lord) (see chapter 4, pp. 76–8).

The mythology also indicates propositions about the universe – the macrocosm – as well as implying an ethical system involving the study of the person – the microcosm – as both a social agent and the bearer of moral and metaphysical values. Two extracts from the epic – a monumental work, which includes complex political, spiritual and social issues – are incuded in order to give an idea of its significance.

The first story derives from the first book, the *Adiparwa*. The Lord of the Dead, Yama, is concerned that earth is similar to heaven. There is no conflict on earth and people do not become ill and die. Brahma comforts Yama, telling him that this state of affairs will soon change. Indeed, soon afterwards Indra meets the rice goddess, Sri, who is weeping. Her tears fall like lotuses into the river. When asked the reason for her sorrow, Sri explains that she has seen Siwa and his wife, Uma, making love on a mountain and she is jealous of their happiness. Indra is moved by her misery and strikes the couple with his mighty thunderbolt. As a punishment Siwa sentences him and Sri to be incarnated as humans on earth. There, like ordinary mortals, they experience grief and joy.[6]

The story provides a powerful metaphor of the cosmos. With the banishment of Indra and Sri to earth, the world emerges as it is and radical separation occurs between what the Balinese refer to as the imperceptible world of supernatural beings, *niskala*, and the perceptible world of men, *sekala*. The indigenous people stress that these two cosmological spheres must be kept separate in order to avoid chaos and to maintain harmony and peace. Mediation may, however, be sought between these spheres – primarily, as we shall see, through the arts.

The second extract is from the Bismaparwa, which includes the well-known Bharadwadgita. The Great War has broken out and Prince Arjuna enters the fray with his charioteer Kresna. But Arjuna is confused and reluctant to fight against enemies who include family and former teachers. Kresna forcefully admonishes him with the words: 'It is unworthy, Arjuna, as a *satria*, not to fight in war. One who has "pure knowledge" realizes that the body is transient. A *satria*'s sacred duty, *darma*, is combat. In an attitude of detachment, he ought to focus solely on his *darma*, and not be swayed by feelings of sadness or joy. If killed he would ascend to heaven. If victorious he would gain supremacy on earth.' Kresna then reveals that he is Wisnu incarnate.[7]

Plate 23   Writing on a lontar *palm-leaf*

Darma here implies individual and caste duty and virtue, as well as 'ultimate reality'.[8] Such ethical statements are scattered throughout the epic. They also occur in Old Javanese poems. These literary works are still understood today as presenting a metaphorical world-view and insight into life in general.

Another reason why the classics have maintained their significance in Bali is that they were written down on palm-leaf manuscripts in Old Javanese (Kawi). This language has sacred overtones and, once written, it is thought to fix the religious dogma and uphold eternal truths. Hence manuscripts are kept in shrines, often in Brahman households.

Manuscripts and Language Patterns

Palm-leaf manuscripts are carefully copied and preserved. The characters are incised with either a sharp knife or a stylus and then rubbed with a mixture of lamp soot and oil to darken them. Traditionally manuscripts were largely produced by high castes at courts. Gelgel was particularly known for its literary activity in the fifteenth century. Here there were apparently also court singers (*angidung*) who composed texts and music.[9]

Still today the old texts are chanted and translated in male study groups called *seka pepaosan*. These are made up of about ten men and are often linked to the courts. They included mainly high castes, but also villagers with a scholarly inclination. A profound knowledge of the classics can be gained in these groups, which tend to meet on ritual occasions. *Pepaosan* is basically a process: one man chants a section from the text while another paraphrases in the vernacular. As Zurbuchen writes, this implies that 'voices' of both the present and past are heard simultaneously.[10]

Such literary fluidity has been a characteristic feature of Balinese society from at least the tenth century, when Old Balinese kings commissioned charters in Old Balinese and Sanskrit. The content of the charters may also have been explained to the general public in colloquial Balinese. A unique example of the use of two languages, and even two scripts, is the Belanjong pillar of Sanur, dated AD 914 which tells of the victories of King Sri Kesari Warmadewa. The incription on one side of the pillar is in Old Balinese, in Pre-Nagari script, while the inscription on the other side is in Sanskrit, in the Pallawa-derived Old Javanese script.[11]

These literary events illustrate, moreover, the ease with which the classical tradition, stemming from the royal courts, was entwined with the 'little', or folk, tradition. It is also evident in other spheres. Aristocrats were traditionally patrons of the arts and undoubtedly stimulated their development.[12] They owned some of the finest *gamelan* orchestras and elegant court dancing was a model for village dances. As patrons they were further instrumental in linking the arts to village life. They gave spectacular public dance-drama performances or shadow plays for high castes and peasants alike. In these the *sudra* servants, the *panasar*, must already have had crucial roles. They do not appear in the great epics, but belong instead to the folk sphere. They were the main mediators in the plays, as they still are today, interpreting and exploring the myths dramatized on the stage, which are derived for the most part from classical literature. As such the servants mediate between the *satria* and the predominantly *sudra* audience, between the world of mythology and that of humans.

In fact, the ability to achieve ever-new blends of ancient tradition and external influences – from Hindu, Chinese, Islamic and later, of course, western sources – has given Balinese culture both resilience and flexibility over the years.

Dance-drama and Music

Dance-drama, music and myth are intimately related on the islands, their common element being imitation by means of rhythm, which is expressed in words, sounds, light and movement. While the themes of the stories are often wide-ranging, especially in the shadow play, the main plots are always drawn from the mythology. These are then danced out in steps, attitudes and gestures accompanied by lyrics or dramatic orchestral music.

All the genres considered here – the shadow theatre, *wayang kulit*, the human dance-drama, *wayang wong* and *gambuh*, the masked dance, *topeng* and operetta, *arja* – are communally based and hence can be regarded as expressions of the collective experience. The most frequent occasion for a performance is the anniversary of a temple, *odalan*; it is customary to have some form of entertainment on each of the three final days of the festival. The temple congregation pays for the performance, which is presented in one of the courts of the temple or the village community hall.

The shadow theatre and the human and masked dance-dramas are generally assigned to the *bebali* group, which implies that they include a sacred element, although they also stimulate and entertain spectators. *Arja*, on the other hand, is essentially a secular dance-drama and as such belongs to the *balih-balihan* group.[13] It is important to remember that each show is a creative work, and as such is a unique event given to the audience in accordance with what is called *desa, kala, patra*, a particular place, time and custom. Performances these days are also serialized on television or radio, which have been available for the last fifteen years in even the most isolated villages, and are given in a modified form to tourists.

Mention has already been made of the servants who have a special place in most performances. The comic, often spicy, interludes add an element of freedom to the plays, whereby new angles and possibilities are suggested to the spectators.

It is of interest that the plastic arts also continually draw villagers' attention back to dance-drama and the mythology. Reliefs and statues on palaces and temples crystallize mythical themes, while the iconographic features of the images reflect those of the characters in the theatre. Because these images are hewn out of soft volcanic stone they are frequently renewed, ensuring the continuation of a tradition that is invigorated by the creative spark of the individual craftsman.

Plate 24 *Ramayana epic: Rawana carrying off Sita*

The Shadow Play: *Wayang Kulit*

The shadow play is deeply rooted in myth and poetry and is the most revered and conservative form of theatre for reasons that will emerge as we examine its various components: the *dalang*, the poet-priest, who brings a play to life; the stories; the puppets which are the actors; the music; the stage; and the actual performance itself. So we shall give particular attention to this genre.

The earliest reference in Indonesia to what may be the shadow play is to a performance, *wayang* (meaning puppet play or dramatic performance in general), from a stone inscription in central Java, dated AD 906.[14] In Bali the royal inscription Prasasti Anak Wungsu, of the eleventh century, mentions a *wayang* performance, as well as *topeng*, the masked dance. In any case, it seems that the shadow theatre came from Java to Bali between the eleventh and the four-

*Plate 25 The stage of the shadow theatre (*wayang kulit*)*

teenth centuries. It is of interest that the first outsider to describe the Balinese shadow play was Chinkah, the Siamese master of a junk that landed on the island in 1846.[15] In line with the traditional role of aristocrats as art patrons, the king of Klungkung gave a performance for him.

During a shadow theatre performance given at night, *wayang peteng*, the shadows of the puppets are projected on to the screen of a temporary booth, where they dance in the flickering light of a coconut-oil lamp. The predominantly male spectators watch these silhouettes while the *dalang*, who sits cross-legged in the booth, manipulates the puppets and narrates a story from classical literature. Myths pertaining to the Mahabharata and Old Javanese poems (*kakawin*) are the most frequently dramatized, for they deal with issues ranging from political intrigue and spiritual and moral striving to themes of love. Yet the *dalang* often ad libs skilfully, especially in the subplots, while adhering to the mythological framework of the stories.

The shadow theatre is frequently chosen for a temple anniversary because the plays are thought to be appropriate because of their religious and moral content. It is also cheaper to perform than the other genres which require a troupe of actors or musicians. A shadow play may also be performed in conjunction with the celebration of a domestic event, such as a birth or a marriage, and may then be given in the household.

The *dalang* is the creator and sole narrator of every play. In theory *dalang* should be *brahmana*, but in practice most are peasants, *jaba*. It is estimated that there are about 110 *dalang* on the island, the majority of whom are male[16] (although, in line with modern developments, there are now a few female *dalang*). *Dalang* tend to be highly mobile, sometimes travelling some distance to give performances. Rarely do *dalang* make a living from their art, though, for a show is not a commercial enterprise. The primary occupation of most *dalang* is rice cultivation.

Dalang have an essentially three-fold role in society: as teacher, albeit an informal one, entertainer and priest. Hence, like all people who have a religious role in the community, a *dalang* must be consecrated. In folk etymology *dalang* is derived from *galang* (bright or clear), implying a man who clarifies the poetic higher truths and metaphorical language of the literature for the benefit of the audience. In this light it is unsurprising that most of the spectators are male, for traditionally they were deemed to be the active perpetuators of the culture, and special stress was laid on their literary, religious and philosophical knowledge.

However, a play which lasts for about three to five hours does not just attract adults; children – mainly boys – make up the front rows of any performance; they squat on the ground or stand at the side of the crowd. As stories are sprinkled with humorous and often bawdy episodes, they too can enjoy them. Moreover, a performance is a relaxed, informal occasion. So it is relatively easy to walk away early or go and sit at a stall to sip tea, lime juice or coffee, while eating a variety of food, such as cakes or nuts, or to chat quietly with others, who for the most part come from the same area. In the background a few groups of villagers may also sit huddled in a dim light, playing gambling games. The attention of the audience need only be sporadic, for the basic outline of the stories tends to be known and they often have a disjointed quality.

The *dalang*'s role as priest comes to the fore in a special type of the night or day performance, *Wayang Sudamala*, which is exorcistic in intent. *Sudamala* connotes the destruction of bodily blemishes or deformities[17] and the main occasion for Wayang Sudamala is for a child born in the week of Tumpek Wayang who is thought to be prone to illness or to injury by the demon-king Kala. During the elaborate *sudamala* rite, which follows the performance, the *dalang*, with the help of eminent puppets, creates special purificatory water. This is given to the child to drink in order to purify him spiritually and to restore a sense of well-being in his family.

The art of the *dalang* is passed down through the male line. The main teachers of an aspiring *dalang* are usually his older relatives, but he also learns from observing different *dalang* perform. Numerous demands are made on an accomplished *dalang*. These include literary and dramatic skills and spiritual knowledge. The *dalang* must know the mythology and the archaic language of Kawi, as well as being fluent in the different Balinese speech levels. Only then can he be eloquent in spoken recitation on the stage. He must know how to play the music and make the puppets dance gracefully. It is also essential that he be acquainted with the mystic treatise the Dharma Pawayangan,[18] which contains the philosophical background of the shadow theatre, including religious incantations, *mantra* and rules of conduct for a *dalang*.

The puppets are the actors on the stage. A standard collection includes about a hundred puppets, which can be classified into different groups:[19]

1 the celestial beings, whose higher morality cannot be understood;
2 the high castes, the *brahmana*, *satria* and *wesia*. The *satria* are by far the largest group in any collection. In plays based on the Mahabharata or Old Javanese poems, the Pandawa and Korawa, and their respective followers are the warriors and administrators. They are also the main protagonists of plays. Members of the Pandawa camp are relatively virtuous and refined while the Korawa are coarse and rough. Yet no polar-

Plate 26 Shadow puppet: Siwa, the Lord Teacher (Batara Guru) of the Balinese

ization between the groups is possible because there are shades
of difference between characters;

3 the *sudra* servants, the *parekan* or *panasar* (the base ones,
those who are at the basis of society). In contrast to most other
characters, they do not appear in the epics but stem from the
folk tradition. They are uncouth and idiosyncratic-looking, in
line with their marked individuality in a play. The four most
important servants are Tualen (plate 27) (the equivalent of
Semar in Java), who in local myths descends from the supreme
god, Sang Hyang Tunggal; his quick-witted son Merdah;
Delem, who is pompous and overbearing; and his shrewd,
ironical younger brother, Sangut. Tualen and Merdah serve the
Pandawa – or more virtuous – camp, while Delem's and Sangut's masters are their antagonists;

Plate 27   Shadow puppet: silhouette of Tualen

4 the ogres, *raksasa*, who represent the 'wild', and are greedy, coarse and impure: they support the ignoble group;
5 scenic figures: by far the most important is the Kakayonan, the Tree of Life or Cosmic Tree;
6 others, including animals and chariots.

As new puppets are always made by copying old ones, their form, design and body colours remain relatively the same, and collections are fairly standardized across the island. Indeed, puppets have a lingering affinity with figures on reliefs on east Javanese temples dating from the twelfth to the fourteenth centuries.[20]

Puppets are made of cowhide and each has a buffalo or wooden handle with thin rods which are attached to the hands to manipulate their arms. Each puppet is painted and delicately chiselled, so that spectators can recognize individuals by their silhouettes, which often appear only fleetingly on the screen. However, the puppets do not only represent mythical characters, for a unitary system underlies their iconography. Conventions determine the particular combination of features of the puppets, the most important concerning the facial features, the costume – especially the headdress, and body colours. These characteristics are part of the shared experience of the people. As such the visual dimension in a performance acts as a richly symbolic system, communicating directly with the spectator. This can be shown by a few examples (see figure 6.1).[21]

Headdresses are the main indicator of social status. Two imposing and elegant examples are the *candi utama* (supreme royal headdress) and *candi kurung* (royal headdress). They are associated with spiritual power and the office of king, and hence are worn by such senior figures as Kresna or the god Siwa.

Eyes are an immediate clue to character type. Most Pandawa have almond-shaped eyes (*panyurianan sumpe*) indicative of their refinement and self-control. On the other hand, Korawa and ogres, who are coarse, hot-headed and often disruptive, have round, bulbous eyes (*panyurianan dedelingan*).

The hand gestures of puppets are an intriguing feature that few scholars have examined. Scholarly *dalang* and Brahman

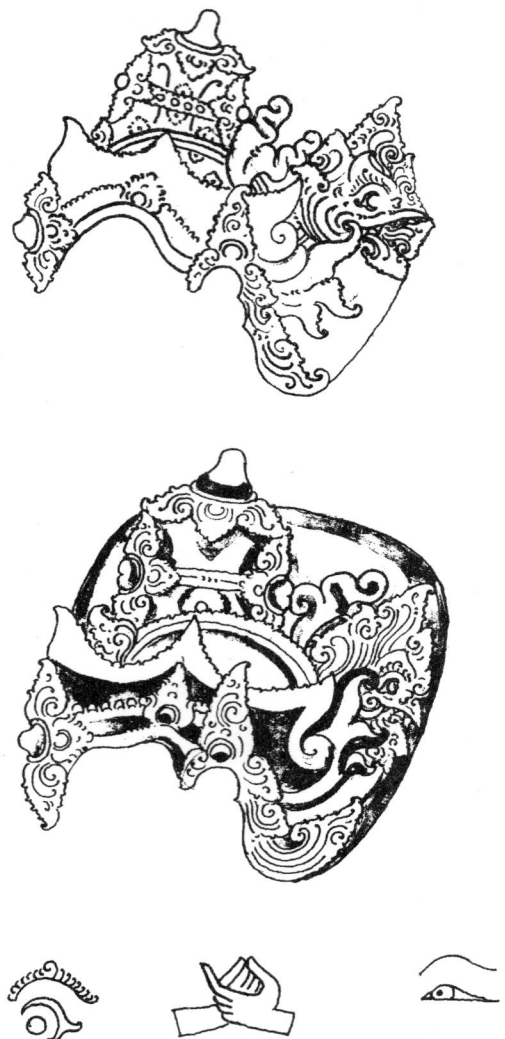

Figure 6.1 Drawings by a Balinese craftsman of headdresses and
important features

priests who were interviewed point out that they are all based on ritual hand gestures, *mudra*. This is exemplified by the hand of the god Sang Hyang Tunggal, which forms a distinct *mudra* called *redaya-mudra* (heart-*mudra*). Balinese explain that through their ritual hand gestures, the characters all worship the gods and beg forgiveness, if need be, for their base actions.

The body colours of puppets are rich in symbolism that we can only touch on here. They subtly express an individual's personal and mystical qualities. In brief: yellowish-white, light blue or green, described as 'cool' colours, connote purity and nobility, while 'hot' reddish or brown tones signify coarseness and boldness and are generally used for ignoble ends. Each of the features clearly intensifies the message of the others. So refined, noble characters have light body colours and slit eyes, and ogres tend to be reddish with round eyes. It is noteworthy that all theatrical genres follow these iconographic principles.

All the puppets are said to 'dance' on the stage, thus revealing the cosmic rhythm of the drama. In moving the puppets, the *dalang* adheres to certain conventions, for dance is essentially an extension of appearance. Hence refined characters dance gracefully and swing their arms gently, while their coarse counterparts dance proudly and jarringly and move their arms flamboyantly.

The vast number of battle movements, too, clearly reflect the world of the shadow play. *Satria* in particular are involved in battle, love and courtly exploits. Of these the first predominates, for conflict is intrinsic to every play. Combat is usually a personal contest in which *satria* may beat with clubs, shoot with bows and arrows, stab with the *keris*, slice with knives, hurl stones, strangle, wrestle, fling the opponent to the ground, submerge him in water, or tear him apart.

Special attention should be given to the percussion music that accompanies a performance, which the ethnomusicologist McPhee described as 'the most sensitive form of musical expression existing in Bali'.[22] The repertory of compositions, which sparkle with intricate figurations, are played by an ensemble of four metallophones, known as *gender*.[23] Each *gender* has ten keys suspended above bamboo resonators. The musicians strike the keys with light wooden mallets, and the shock produces a soft, yet metallic sound that accords with the precise, yet delicate and transparent lacework of the puppets.

The ensemble is divided into two pairs of *gender*. The larger one, *pengumbang*, is predominant; the smaller, *pengisep*, has a higher pitch. They enrich the tonal quality of the lower pair by doubling their parts an octave higher. Great technical skill and rhythmic co-ordination is required of the musicians to produce the varied compositions that are played during scenes of strife, tenderness, playfulness, sorrow or dismay. In order to co-ordinate their parts, the instruments are placed close together, the musicians of each pair sitting opposite each other, so that each can carefully watch the movements of the other (figure 6.2).

The scale, known as *slendro*, belongs to the regular pentatonic scheme. Yet the Balinese regard it as being composed of

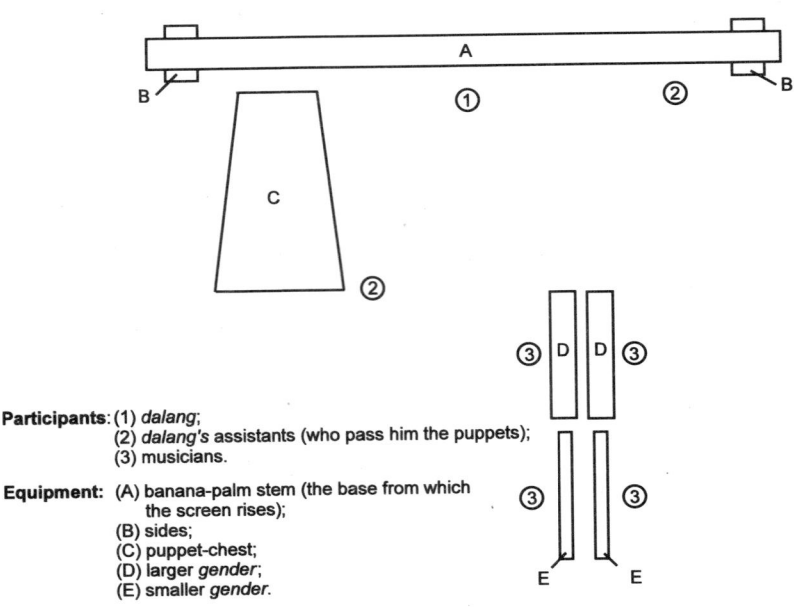

Participants: (1) *dalang*;
            (2) *dalang's* assistants (who pass him the puppets);
            (3) musicians.

Equipment: (A) banana-palm stem (the base from which
            the screen rises);
            (B) sides;
            (C) puppet-chest;
            (D) larger *gender*;
            (E) smaller *gender*.

Figure 6.2   The stage of the shadow theatre

unequal intervals, which is evident in practice. There is, however, no notation, although the repertory played during a performance is standard. It is therefore not surprising that each district and ensemble has its own style of playing.

There are basically two types of composition. The first is non-rhythmic, archaic and static. It is played softly and accompanies certain songs sung by the *dalang* or quiet scenes of love, grief or death. The second type is dynamic and vigorous and accompanies departures to wars, pursuits and flights.

The most elaborately constructed composition is the opening Pamungkah, when two-voiced passages alternate with animated sections in 3- and 4-part polyphony, the mood constantly oscillating between calm and agitation. It is followed by an *andante* composition, Alas Harum (perfumed forest), while the *dalang* chants the opening stanzas of the story.

From that point the music is largely incidental. It announces entrances, and specific compositions accompany different situations. The melody Rebong perhaps deserves special mention as its liturgical cadences have a peculiarly graceful quality. It is the music for love scenes; during these the *dalang* may sing in a sweet, languorous voice such poetic lines as:

The crimson lily (*gloriosa superba*) is sought by the white *madori* flower.
The bud has opened out; the lovely centre is displayed.[24]

After its initial soft and slow tempo, Rebong changes and becomes loud and animated when the scene closes with the burlesque advances made by one of the servants to the lady-in-waiting. A *dalang* also punctuates the dialogues by rapping the side of the puppet chest with a gavel held between the toes of his right foot. During battle scenes this tapping is energetic and loud. The *gender* music is intrinsic to every performance and adds a unique sonorous beauty to the drama.

It is of interest that both the *gender* music and the stage, together with the equipment shown in figure 6.2 have symbolic value to the people: they are said to symbolize the macrocosm. The music represents the harmony of the cosmos and the interrelationship of everything in it. The screen is the sky or face of the world. The puppets represent all that exists in it. The lamp is the sun. The banana stem into which the puppets are placed is the earth. The *dalang* is god, who is invisible to the audience.[25]

The *dalang* carries out a complex set of rites before beginning a standard evening performance. Numerous *mantra* are recited invoking the gods to descend into him, for it is they who ensure that the spectators will enjoy the show. This is clearly demonstrated by the *mantra pasikepan*:[26]

> Yes, supreme god, Sang Hyang Tunggal,
> Grant me magical power,
> [So that] demons and witches are happy,
> [So that] the people are happy,
> [So that] the gods are happy,
> All that exists in the world be happy and worship,
> and so depart in happiness.
> AM AH [Sky Earth]

So the *dalang* is thought to be a mouthpiece of the gods when narrating a story on the stage that is a replica of the universe. This increases his authority in the community. However, his role as 'worldmaker'[27] who continually creates and recreates mythical worlds out of those already at hand comes to the fore only when we watch an actual performance. It is then that the varied stimuli of light, dance, gesture and sound are orchestrated. The orientation of the shadow theatre and the *dalang*'s role as worldmaker are best shown by extracts from dialogues in an actual dramatized story. The following examples are taken from a performance that took place in the 1980s in the village of Tegal in Gianyar. It was given by the now deceased *dalang* I Ewer, of low caste, who was highly esteemed for his profound literary knowledge. The story was drawn from the Old Javanese poem Sutasoma, which is Mahayana Buddhist in orientation. In the story Prince Sutasoma is called Batara Buda, Lord Buddha. It recounts how one night Sutasoma, like the historical Buddha himself, leaves the palace to go and meditate on Mount Meru. In the woods he encounters three wild creatures, an elephant-headed giant, a serpent and a tigress, whom he tames and who become his faithful pupils.

As in all performances, only the skeleton of the plot is derived from the classics and I Ewer improvised considerably, interspersing the main plot with evocative episodes which reflect the life of the people. This is vividly illustrated by these dialogues. Here the servants have a crucial role. In all stories dramatized it is they in particular who interpret the classical literature. The other characters all speak Old Javanese (Kawi), which is inaccessible to the predominantly Balinese-speaking peasant audience. The servants translate and often elaborate extensively on what the others say.

The first dialogue takes place when Prince Sutasoma encounters a tigress which is about to devour her cubs. Sutasoma admonishes the tigress to desist from this wicked deed, and the following discussion ensues between the price, his servants, Tualen and Merdah, and the tigress. Sutasoma and the tigress speak Old Javanese and the servants translate and comment in Balinese.[28]

Merdah We are deep in the woods close to the mountain [i.e. Mount Meru, Siwa's abode]. The branches of trees overarch the path where it is cold and dark for no sunlight penetrates the thick foliage. Father, look at the waterfall tumbling down the cliff.

Tualen Dah, Dah [Merdah, his son], its spray is carried to us by the wind. A tigress is now emerging from a cave. She is snarling as she approaches her cubs whom she wishes to devour. They are too weak to flee and are crying in fright.

Sutasoma Stop, stop, tigress! What are you doing?

Merdah Mother tigress, desist from this wicked act. Remember you brought them into the world. You are committing two wrong deeds in one, for you are neglecting your two roles: to be their parent and spiritual teacher. Consider the consequences. You will have to suffer [*sangsara*] one thousand years in hell.

Merdah [expanding on Sutasoma's words] You are setting your cubs a poor example. It is moreover from you that they should learn how to perform the correct ceremonies [*yadnya*]. If they are not taught properly they too will become bad parents, cruel and greedy. They will also not treat you well when elderly.

Tualen   Yes, mother tigress, listen to Sang Sutasoma who has compassion [*kapiolasan*] for all that lives. It is important that you understand the meaning of *darma*, duty and virtue.

Tigress   I wish to devour my children because I am hungry. All the animals have fled and hence there is nothing to eat.

Tualen   In her hunger, mother tigress has forgotten that these are her children. She no longer knows her limitation.

Sutasoma, in compassion, offers his body to the tigress as food (see plate 34). But as she licks his blood it acts as the elixir of immortality (*amerta*), and she becomes aware of her wickedness. She worships the prince and asks to become his pupil.

The second dialogue takes place later in the story, when Sutasoma goes to meditate. The gods are fearful that demons will now destroy the world and they send celestial nymphs to disrupt his meditation. Tualen and Merdah describe the scene:

Merdah   Celestial nymphs are floating in the sky, light emanating from them. They can be likened to yellow hibiscus, fragrant jasmine and other blossoms.

Tualen   The god Indra himself now descends, disguised as a nymph more beautiful than the goddess of the moon, Ratih. She is upright as a *keris* and moves with grace. In wonder at her loveliness, the sun god Surya hides behind the mountain peaks so that it becomes night. Seductively she invites Sang Sutasoma to make love to her [*ngaryianin kesemaran*].

Yet he is not disturbed for his thoughts are pure [*pikayune nirmala*], being deep in meditation [*tapa*].

By failing to be disturbed, Sutasoma demonstrates the steadfastness of his meditation.

This performance highlights a number of features which are characteristic of any shadow play performance. All stories have instructive value. In the Sutasoma story this comes to the fore in the prince's teaching to the tigress, which is reprimanded for her wickedness in wishing to devour her cubs. Thereby she is neglecting her two roles, as parent and as spiritual teacher. She is also setting them a poor example, for it is from her that they learn how to behave properly and to conduct the requisite rites. Moreover, the cubs will grow up cruel and greedy, mistreat their mother and not perform the rites for her once she is deceased, for they know no better. The issue of correct behaviour between the older and younger generation is one that often crops up in theatre and in real life. The ethical values and philosophical principles embedded in the texts are, however, contextualized by the servants in terms familiar to the villagers. In Steiner's evocative words, it is evident that the servants use language on the stage not as a passive mirror, but as 'an intensely energized beam of light, shaping, placing, and organizing human experience'.[29]

The servants, however, have multiple roles in plays. They are mediators, translators, commentators, clowns and jokers, as well as village sages who have sanctioned disrespect to question and critize the speeches, behaviour and intentions of their masters. It is also largely through them that the aesthetic quality of the narrations is enhanced. As is evident in the second dialogue above, stories are often replete with poetic imagery or figurative modes of speech, analogies and metaphors (*pratiwimba*) that give ambiguity and phonetic echo to words, triggering various emotions in the spectators, and suggesting new relations and meanings into ideas and qualities derived from the texts.

Energy and tension is furthermore imparted to the conflict of ideals by the inevitable complementary opposition played out on the stage between two camps, which generally leads to loud and often violent warfare. This accords with an important ontological principle in Bali, that creation and order derive from chaos and disorder; both sides are necessary to offset and complement one another. The Old Javanese treatise Korawa-crama points this out in relation to the Pandawa and Korawa, but it is applicable to all opposing camps: while both groups, the Pandawa and Korawa, are bitterly opposed, they 'are each other's counterpart and indispensable completion . . . The equilibrium between the groups should ever be maintained.'

Indeed, a *dalang* may recite a short incantation after a performance in order symbolically to bring back to life any hero who has been killed, regardless of his allegiance.

This mythical world of motion and drama that unfolds on the stage still has deep religious significance for the people. This is exemplified by the shadows cast on the screen. Balinese sometimes refer to them as *maya*, illusion, because they allude to the illusory and transitory nature of all appearances within human experience. This was indicated in the fourteenth-century Old Javanese poem Arjuna Wiwaha, which is still popular today and hence frequently serves as the basis for performances and paintings. In the poem Indra explains to Prince Arjuna that all appearances merely ensnare the senses and are an illusion. This the god illustrates by referring to the entraptured spectators of a puppet-show, who forget that the moving and talking images are carved leather – a display of sorcery with no reality.[30]

So the shadow theatre emerges as a vehicle that stimulates a contemplative and aesthetic vision in the beholders, and instructs and entertains old and young alike. It is therefore perhaps not surprising that the shadow theatre has left a profound influence on the other traditional arts.

Dance-drama: *Wayang Wong*

The dance-drama *wayang wong* will be dealt with only briefly here as it is by no means as ubiquitous as the shadow theatre. Essentially it evolved into its present form in the capital cities of Gelgel and Klungkung in the seventeenth and eighteenth centuries, from where it was disseminated to smaller satellite courts.[31] Nowadays, it is still performed in such villages as Wates in Karangasem, Mas, Pujung Kaler and Batuan in Gianyar, or Tejakula in Buleleng, in association with the religious festival Galungan, or the subsequent festival of Kuningan, dedicated to the ancestors. *Wayang wong* is of special interest as it is the main theatrical genre to perpetuate the Ramayana epic. Usually a performance is devoted to a single episode from the epic. The dialogue, however, is limited and much simpler than in the shadow theatre. The large masks worn by the four servants, who are the counterparts of those in the latter genre, impede their speech, and while the servants translate into Balinese the Old Javanese spoken by their masters, they entertain the audience largely through their burlesque, slapstick humour. The narrative primarily provides a loose framework for the dances.

The most immediate source of *wayang wong* is the shadow theatre, as a prototype for the dramatization of stories. The music too is derived from the shadow theatre. The ensemble, *gamelan batel*, consists of the *gender* quartet with in addition percussion instruments, drums, small gongs and cymbals. The music accompanies the narrative sung by the dancers in accordance with the flowing vocal line provided by the lead singer in the ensemble.

The dramatic *gambuh* dance has also left its imprint on *wayang wong*, as is evident in the repertoire of movements and the splendid decorated costumes.

Only refined characters wear no mask, although their make-up and headdresses follow the iconographic principles of the *wayang* puppets. The masks of the monkeys, who follow noble Prince Rama, kindle the playful imagination of the people. The monkeys are an intriguing hybrid of mythical creatures, resulting from the intermarriage of a monkey with, for example, a bird or tiger. All demonic characters have reddish masks with bulbous eyes. A magnificent set of masks are known to be kept in the village of Kamasan and in the Pura Panataran, the principal temple for the Pulasari Clan, a family especially prominent in the courtly sphere in the nineteenth century.[32]

Wayang wong is a stately form of dance-drama. Yet the didactic and poetic content of the stories flowing from this genre tends to be negligible. Performances primarily stimulate and entertain the villagers who attend.

The Masked Dance: *Topeng*

It is probable that a form of *topeng*, the Chronicle Play of Bali, was, as previously mentioned, performed for the king in the eleventh century. In fact this dance-drama genre more than any other extols the prestige and authority of the *satria*. The stories dramatized are derived from chronicles (*babad*), most of which were composed by court scribes between the seventeenth and nineteenth centuries. The *babad* recount and celebrate the genealogical histories of extant high-caste families who trace their descent from nobles in Majapahit. Hence it is unsurprising that even today the courts are the main centres of *topeng* productions and performances, and that performances appeal to important men in general and high castes in particular.

A standard *topeng* is enacted by a troupe of between six and ten male actors. The form in which it is known today seems to have developed at the court of the King of Badung at the end of the nineteenth century out of the ritual *topeng*,[33] in which a single dancer (*topeng pajegan*) tells a story by portraying a succession of masked characters.[34] This dance is generally said to belong to the sacred *wali* category and is given as an integral part of either a temple festival or domestic celebration.

The members of a *topeng* troupe usually come from the same area (*koban*). The training of the actors is extensive, for strict conventions govern the dignified spectacle which has martial overtones and comic interludes. Political intrigue and war too are intrinsic to every story.

It is striking that the aristocrats remain silent throughout the play. It is left to the servants (called *panasar* and *kartala* in this genre), who know both Old Javanese and Balinese, to interpret their pantomime in expressive words and gestures. A sample of dialogue follows to illustrate the somewhat stark and direct language used in *topeng* which is appropriate to the power politics of the stories:

Panasar [adressing the prince] Your servant waits humbly upon his lord. Rise up! Rise up! the God of Day has mounted his chariot. At the second hour he had put on his raiment, the lord of a thousand prime ministers. Raiment of purple silk, and cloth-of-gold all glittering. His *keris*-hilt is ivory, curiously wrought; it sparkles with gold and jewels. [laughing] Behold the coming of our lord. In stature he is like Semara, the God of Love.

Kartala There is really something in what you say, for in this corner of his kingdom there is certainly no one in heaven or earth to match him [aside] except myself, of course.

Panasar Will you never stop chattering? . . . Princes and priests bow down and do obeisance. I also do obeisance [to the lord].[35]

As indicated by the above dialogue, aristocrats in *topeng* are attired in magnificent draperies of coloured brocade and woven materials decorated in glittering gold leaf. The aristocrats also don elaborate headdresses and golden collars encircle their necks.

All the characters wear masks. These distinguish nobles and prime ministers of the refined and 'sweet' type from their rough counterparts in accordance with the iconographic rules determining puppet form. The senior refined king, for instance, wears an oval-shaped, cream-coloured mask (*tapel dalem*) with a slight enigmatic smile showing small nautilus-shell teeth and elongated eyes. Masks of superlative quality that are lively in the dance are said to possess *taksu*, mystic power.

The servants, as befits their station, are more simply clad and wear half-masks or hinged masks. There are other masks, comic in intent, which represent the common people (*bebondresan*). These have such physical defects as hare-lips, superfluous teeth or a crooked mouth.

The dancing is particulary evocative in the first part of the performance, when the characters introduce themselves. Although essentially abstract, the dance suggests their rank, status, age and main characteristics. A striking character unique to *topeng*, and whom the audience awaits expectantly, is a frail, senile, yet dignified old man (*topeng tua*) who dances with tremulous steps while recalling his past.

The basis of any dance are the statue-like poses or postures, *agem*, that are precisely linked to the emotive content of the play. In the basic posture the thighs and knees are turned out, while the shoulders are pulled up so that the head sinks into the torso. The poses follow one another in flowing, controlled movements, *tandang*, whereby the dance, as well as the masks, become animated.

All structural elements of the dance – the poses, movements and choreography – accord with the music to form an intricate architectural unit. Formerly a large orchestra of up to forty

Plate 28 Dalem, *kingly type from the* topeng *mask play*

Plate 29   Village orchestra, gong kebya, *in Sidemen, Karangasem*

men, *gamelan gong gede*, accompanied shows, but now the smaller *gong kebya*, with about twenty-five men, has taken its place. This orchestra includes metallophones (*gangsa gantung*) that either produce the melody or ornament it, horizontal and vertical gongs for punctuation, accentuating cymbals (*ceng-ceng, rincik*), and a pair of drums (*kendang*) leading the orchestra. The rhythmic patterns of the drums also co-ordinate the dance with the music, while the dancers' supple finger movements paraphrase the figurations of the metallophones; the metrical accents of the gongs harmonize with the movements of the feet, head and eyes and indicate abrupt changes of direction or pace. Musicians often seem to select compositions called *gangsaran* out of the *topeng* musical repertoire. These are popular as they are played with élan and the motives and melodies are associated with specific *topeng* character types. *Topeng* emerges as a majestic dance through which the heroic past is entwined with the present. Consequently this genre is significant in preserving and renewing cultural continuity, particularly for high castes.

The Dance-dramas: Gambuh and Arja

Gambuh is an ancient and conventionalized dance form that originated in east Javanese courts when these were at the height of their splendour in the fourteenth century. Subsequently it was performed in Balinese courts and was often sponsored by nobles. This illustrious heritage is still evident in the titles of some of the characters[36] and in the costumes and gestures that mirror court behaviour during the great Majapahit era. *Gambuh* was in danger of becoming extinct, but it has been revived in recent decades by groups from Batuan and Pedulungan, as well as by the Dance Academy (ASTI) in Denpasar. Its significance relies in part on the influence it has exerted on the choreography, costumes and musical techniques, especially the drumming patterns, used in more modern genres such as *topeng*, *wayang wong*, the *legong* dance and, above all, *arja*, operetta.

The stories in *gambuh* are mainly derived from the romantic poem Malat (called Panji in Java), which recounts the adven-

Plate 30 Gambuh *theatre in Batuan*

tures of the handsome Prince Panji and his beautiful bride Princess Candra Kirana.

Numerous characters may enter the long, drawn-out plays. Apart from senior aristocrats of the refined and rough types, as in other dance-dramas, each rank is accorded its particular heralds and attendants. As stories involve conflict and conspiracy, armies too may be represented, generally by groups of four men. The hero Panji stands out clearly from other characters. He wears a downward-curving headdress and his splendid attire of brocade decorated with gold-leaf adds gravity to his dignified and restrained gestures and slow, sinuous dance movements.

The dialogue intensifies the ceremonial nature of this theatrical genre. Principal characters speak the archaic language Kawi and are translated into the vernacular by their servants. Throughout the speeches lengthy, flowery courtesies are exchanged which highlight a hierarchy of status and enable respect and obeisance to be shown to honoured personages.

The ritual aspects of *gambuh* come to the fore at the beginning of a performance. A village priest must first purify the space where it will take place by means of present-offerings to both gods and demons. He also consecrates the headdresses before use. These are venerated and passed down from generation to generation.

The music in *gambuh* deserves special attention for it is unique, the oldfashioned instruments invoking a legendary past for the spectators.[37] The ensemble includes long bamboo flutes (*suling gambuh*), a fiddle-like spiked lute played with a loose bow (*rebab*) a pair of drums, gongs of various types, cymbals, percussion instruments and bells. A lead singer (*juru tandak*) is also part of the ensemble. The drummers lead the orchestra. Their interplay is unusually, intricate and varied in *gambuh*. The melody is played by the large flutes which are blown with a difficult circular technique that produces a continuous sound. A fairly consistent unison is maintained by the flutes, contrasting to the relatively free interpretation of the melody by the *rebab*. It has a thin, rather acid tone, and a slight vibrato is sometimes used, while light, brief trills ornament the melody. The main punctuation is supplied by the

Plate 31 Gambuh ensemble in Batuan, Gianyar, with typical long end-blown ring flutes

gongs, and the other instruments create the background music.

It is of interest to note that the tonal qualities of the drums and the punctuating instruments can be replicated by onomatopoeic syllables which both musicians and dancers understand. For example, the sounds of the smaller 'male' drum (*lanang*) are called *tut, pèg, pèng, pung, ké*; the larger 'female' drum (*wadon*) produces the sounds *dag, pèg, pèng, ké*. A beating pattern can thus be transposed into onomatopoeic language such as: *dag, dag, pèg, dagekepègdag, tut, dag, tut, tutut, dag, tut, pègtutdag.*[38] Irrespective of the dance-drama genre, an instructor teaches young dancers by singing this language while standing behind the pupil and guiding his or her body into specific postures (*agem*) (plate 30).

This brings us to operetta, *arja*, which is clearly influenced by *gambuh*, although it has a unique poetic quality of its own. While its style, half acted and half danced, is derived from the latter genre, its tempo is much faster. The stories, too, are based on the Malat romances, which tell of Panji (called

Plate 32 *Player of the spike fiddle* (rebab)

Plate 33   I Gusti Gede Raka from Saba giving lessons in the
legong *dance*

various names in shows) and his gentle Princess Galuh. Galuh's counterpart is the ugly, 'mad' Princess Liku, who, usually through the use of a magical tool (*guna*), tries to usurp Galuh's place in the prince's affection.

The first *arja* performance was given in 1825 at the cremation of the King of Klungkung.[39] A striking feature of *arja* is the singing which largely accounts for its reputation throughout the island. These days it is broadcast regularly on radio every week, and even in the most isolated hamlets middle-aged woman in particular, but also men, enjoy listening to the songs.

The singing is co-ordinated with spoken lines, humorous interludes, dance and music during a show. In line with the lyrical, graceful quality of *arja*, the songs are romantic and sentimental, distinguished by their pathos. They are sung nowadays by both young women and men in thin, vibrant voices, the phrases being long, drawn-out and often adorned with elegant embellishments. In the past plays were accompanied by a small instrumental ensemble which included a special one-string bamboo zither (*guntang*). However, for some years now the full-scale orchestra *gamelan gong* has been used, with additional bamboo flutes (*suling*). The *suling* are more flexible than the large flutes played in *gambuh*. They produce swift, ornamental figurations in clear, slightly reedy tones, which mainly fill vocal or melodic pauses, during which a dancer may dance on the stage.

The actors in present-day troupes usually come from various areas of Bali. Formerly, burly men played coarse or masculine characters, such as Liku. However, apart from the male servants, actors nowadays are chosen for their attractive looks and pleasing voices. The training for *arja* is more demanding than for any other dance-drama form, even *topeng*. The performers must learn to interrelate their postures and gestures, or accents, not only with the music, but also with the melodic patterns sung and the phrasing of the vocal lines.

Costumes in *arja* are noteworthy. During a performance all the characters, even the servants, wear sumptuous clothes. The aristocracy are resplendent in variegated, dazzling shades of blue, green, orange, rose, purple and gold. Royalty also wear gilded headdresses decorated with frangipani and red hibiscus flowers.

As in other theatre genres, conflicts between contending parties are played out on the stage. In *arja* this takes place in the intimate family circle and revolves around ugly Liku and demure, refined Galuh. A short extract from an *arja* play witnessed in Tegallalang in Gianyar is included as it gives an idea of the lyrical tone of this genre.[40] The lines sung by Galuh are translated by her female servant, the *condong* (lady-in-waiting). The language used is mainly Balinese, with a few words of Old Javanese sprinkled throughout the songs and speeches.

Galuh   [My] actions express sorrow.

Condong   Yes, princess, it is true what you say. You are sad and acting in a distressed manner.

Galuh   Sang Hyang Widi [the supreme god] is not granting what I request.

Condong   Yes, princess, perhaps Sang Hyang Widi is not granting to you what you request.

Galuh   Why live? I would prefer to die.

Condong   Yes, may Sang Hyang Widi give you a quick release from your suffering.

The dancing of the princesses matches their looks and singing and intensifies the opposition between them. Galuh, a delicate, slender girl with a pale, white face, winds leisurely and gracefully about the stage. Her movements are slow and balanced. At times she drops in lament, bewailing her fate. Liku, on the other hand, is enacted these days by a robust girl whose face is tinted pink. In line with her haughty, uncouth character, she dances in a gawky, uncontrolled manner.

In *arja* performance, which continues from the evening until the early hours of the morning, contains an unusual analogy to the emotional life. Although there is conflict, it is muted, for this dance-drama seeks above all to generate an aesthetic perception in the beholders, which is referred to as *ulangun*, a lingering sense of enchantment.

Traditional Painting

The shadow theatre has profoundly influenced traditional painting in *wayang* (puppet) style. Its former place in society

Plate 34 *Sutasoma attacked by a tiger: painted ceiling in the former royal reception pavilion in Klungkung*

is unclear. However, it seems that royal courts up to the beginning of the twentieth century patronized *sudra* artists, the so-called *sangging*, who painted in *wayang* style and covertly guarded their skills. The *sangging* formed hamlets of intermarrying families. The hamlet of Sangging in Kamasan, near Klungkung, is one such. It is here that the artist Nyoman Mandera set up the Kamasan School of Art in 1974, where he teaches mostly *sudra* youngsters how to paint in the traditional style; the creative works produced are often of a high standard.

In the past traditional paintings served communal needs. They were hung under the eaves of pavilions or temples, or were used as curtains or adorned shrines. It was the *sangging*[41] who also painted the magnificent wooden panels that line the ceiling of the seventeenth-century law court Kerta Gosa and the adjacent pavilion Taman Gili (plate 34) at Klungkung.

The mythical themes of the paintings are drawn from classical literature. The figures are flat and linear, and their iconographic features and body colours are based on the puppets of the shadow play, although the postures of the characters are often more freely conceived.

Nowadays traditional paintings are produced for the growing tourist market, as are other modern paintings in tempera, acrylic and oil.[42] But the latter do not enjoy the same high regard as traditional paintings, which are appreciated by indigenous people and outsiders alike.

The Dramatic Experience

It is clear from the preceding discussion that opposition between two sides, one relatively noble, upright and refined and the other relatively ignoble and coarse, is pervasive in every play that is acted, irrespective of the dance-drama genre from which it flows. The ensuing conflict or war may be violent and long drawn-out, as in the shadow theatre or sometimes the masked dance, *topeng*, or it may be muted, as in the human dance-dramas, *gambuh* or *arja*.

The subject of warfare and contradiction is complex in Bali and can merely be touched on here. It is noteworthy, though, that the villagers understand and validate it by analogy with the production of rice. Analogies are a basic way of widening comprehension, and the significance of the reference to rice relates to its importance in the community. It is the staple food of the people. Moreover, cleansed white rice that is pure (*suci*) is used in all offerings. After the rice is harvested it is threshed and dehusked in order to sift the finer grains from the coarser ones. This is dramatically illustrated at the stage when a woman shakes the grains in a large, wide, round basket in order to remove the husks and dirt. In the same way, the villagers explain, opposition on the stage sets up a dynamic energy field which gives impetus to the conflict of ideas. Further, that which is morally good, pure and beautiful can only emerge in confrontation with greed, coarseness and pollution.[43]

It is against this background that the sanctity of the shadow theatre in Balinese life again emerges. As we have seen, more than any other dance-drama genre, it seeks to present to the spectators a vision of a higher reality where moral truth is conjoined with refinement, beauty and purity – even if only temporarily.

Yet a degree of idiosyncracy and indeterminancy is intrinsic to any artistic work. This is epitomized by the servants on the stage, who, with a measure of generosity, humility and humour, create a reflexive dialogue by exploring, commenting on and sometimes questioning the customary norms, values and behaviour patterns articulated during a performance.

7

The Persuasive Artistry of the Healer

Indigenous medical practices have remained remarkably stable over the years and traditional healers of repute continue to enjoy a large clientele, irrespective of modernization, the ever-increasing number of 'scientifically' trained specialists throughout the island and villagers' growing awareness of biomedical concepts.[1] Some healers, moreover, are not only esteemed but are also feared for their power and knowledge, which extends into the world of supernatural beings. Clearly, the power attributed to healers cannot simply be viewed in Weberian terms as 'rational' and secularly based, for it relates to an intricate cosmological system. As such, the power is a feature of an essentially opaque world of cultural symbols, ambiguous status, expressive performance and arcane knowledge, which impart meaning to experience. This also implies that indigenous medicine is one of the most private subjects on the island, all aspects of it being veiled, as is vividly expressed by the metaphor: '*sekadi makta toya matatakan daun candung*' (like carrying water in a container made of the leaves of a taro plant). In other words, a healer should carefully safeguard his knowledge and not allow it to spill or flow to others, for otherwise it will wane. This applies above all, as we shall see, to the literate healer.

After introducing the health-care system, the discussion in this chapter will focus on folk healers, with particular reference to the literate healer and the spirit medium. They are generally considered the most important traditional healers in the society and can in some ways be compared to psychotherapists in the west, as their treatment relies largely on their creative skill to mobilize healing forces in the client by psychological means. We shall then briefly touch on the importance of myth in relation to healing rituals, with a view to gaining an understanding of their place in Balinese culture and society, for definitions of healing and disease/illness are cultural concepts and, in Obeyeskere's words, 'are intricately locked into larger cultural and philosophical issues and problems of meaning'.[2]

The Health-care System

In order to gain an overview of the health-care system, it is essential to understand how the Balinese classify illness, as illness beliefs, behaviour and health-care activities are interrelated.

Like the Ndembu, whom Turner[3] eloquently described, the people do not rigidly distinguish between the causes of physical sickness, misfortune or emotional and mental difficulties. The latter is a broad, popular category which embraces a wide range of issues such as domestic conflict, inheritance problems, and disorder within the village. The category also includes personal distress arising out of uncertainty or unfulfilled wishes in almost any sphere – political, economic, romantic or artistic – and may lead to the quest for love potions, magic or charms, usually obtainable from a traditional healer.

The villagers themselves stress the prevalence of witches (*leak*) in the society. Witchcraft is a complicated subject which can only be alluded to here. It is apparently practised primarily by women, and only to a lesser degree by men. Their malign intentions are often initiated by envy in situations of love and commerce. Hence men may point out that many women who sell merchandise at local markets use witchcraft, and markets are predominantly run by women.

Witchcraft may be inherited down the female line or may be learnt. However, any person seeking to activate this knowledge must above all surrender her/himself to Durga, the goddess of the death temple. Supplications are made to receive the

Plate 35 Black magic: at a hidden place an old witch-teacher and her two pupils pray in front of a shrine dedicated to Batari Bucari, a manifestation of the goddess of Death

gift of negative mystical power, or left-hand (black) magic, *pangiwa* (from *kiwa*, left). The main feature of this power is the ability to transform oneself at night into a wide range of creatures or objects, such as monkeys, birds, chickens, pigs, goats, lights, and these days even trucks or motor bikes. The form assumed depends on one's level of power. Thus a person of great power can become the Supreme Witch Rangda, the mythic creature Barong or the lofty bird Garuda, Prince Kres-

Plate 36 Black magic: a witch-teacher whispering the last and most powerful magic formula into the fontanel of the leak *candidate*

na's vehicle. Witches may instil fear or even terror into others. A noise, a smell, an object out of place, any sensory evidence of witches, may arouse anxiety. More actively, witches may bring sickness or death to intended victims, initiate strife within the family or such troubles as crop failure.

In passing, it is of interest that obsessive behaviour, or what we would refer to as depression, tends not to be classified as illness, although it is conceded that it may cause an imbalance (leading to a state of 'darkness') and as a result to illness, 'madness'[4] (*kebudahan*) or suicide. A number of scholars[5] have already indicated that the depressive experience makes sense only in the context of the Euro-American cultural system. A person who is seen to be excessively sad and hopeless should, according to villagers interviewed, be continually in the company of others, in particular the family, who should strive to cheer him up with jokes, banter and conversation. They also give advice, but this should be done gently to avoid upsetting the person even more. Yet such a person does not require a medical specialist, although it might be useful to go to a folk healer in order to be ritually purified with holy water.

It is to these states of illness, misfortune or distress that the health system, as a social and cultural system, reacts. Kleinman[6] has argued that most health-care systems contain three distinct social arenas: professional, folk and popular. However, as figure 7.1 shows, in Bali these are not as separate as Kleinman's model suggests. The figure is based on the district of Tegallalang in Gianyar.[7] It is evident that folk healers use professionalized indigenous healing traditions. It is also noteworthy that, in contrast to many other parts of the world, including Java, the folk and professional sectors seem to intersect relatively harmoniously.[8]

Most villagers have specific views on sickness which determine which specialist they will consult. If the sickness is seen as arising from natural or obvious causes, that is, from the manifest world (*sekala*), a scientifically trained specialist is consulted – that is, if one can afford it. For example, if an elderly man suffers from rheumatism or failing eye-sight, this is probably because of his age.[9] Folk healers charge no fixed fee. Clients bring them offerings and a gift of money (*sesari*), depending on their means. If a person cannot afford to go a western-trained specialist, but above all if he or she suspects that the cause of sickness lies in supernatural causes, that is, from the unmanifest world (*niskala*), he/she will go to a folk healer. This category includes the invisible actions of gods or ancestors, who may punish descendants for misdeeds, and spirits, demons and witches, or *karma pala* (the law of cause and *effect*).

Professional sphere

This consists of 'scientifically' (western) trained specialists who for the most part work in health clinics that are now found in all districts of Bali. A health clinic includes:

- 1–2 doctors
- Dentist
- Midwife
- Nurses
- Assistants

Folk sphere

This consists of traditional healers, *balian*. They cannot be rigidly separated from the professional sector, according to Kleinman's model (see p.178), as they may combine Ayurvedic or Chinese traditions with indigenous ones. These are the main types of traditional healers:

- *balian usada*: who bases his knowledge on palm-leaf manuscripts, *usada*
- *balian tetakson*: a spirit medium who becomes the mouthpiece of either the gods, ancestors or spirits
- *balian paica*: who bases his healing on a divinely bestowed gift (*paica*), e.g. a piece of cloth, jewel, *keris*
- balian tenung: who specializes in divining
- *balian manak*: midwife
- *balian apun nulungang beling*: specialist in abortion (which is illegal nowadays)
- *balian apun*: masseur
- *balian tulung*: who sets broken bones
- *balian bangke*: who specializes in preparing corpses for cremation rites
- *balian uig* (from *wig*, to bring disturbance): specializes in spells and charms that may bring harm to others while helping a client whose intentions are often based on greed (*kemomoan*) or envy (*irihati*)

Figure 7.1 The health-care system in the district of Tegallalang in the regency of Gianyar

Traditional Healers

Background

Historical data on folk healers go back to the nineteenth century.[10] Chronicles and dynastic genealogies found in texts tell of scholarly healers who served royalty at the courts and were granted land in exchange. They were generally high castes and well-versed in the classical literature. However, as the nobles were patrons of the arts and the classics, they were not concerned with documenting the practices of the many healers who must have been distributed throughout the rural areas and who were not tied to the courts. They were for the most part of humble social status and illiterate; and, as today, it is probable that many were women. These healers transmitted their medical knowledge orally to trusted adepts. Moreover, as Balinese society is based on a type of patrilineal descent, men were ideally the perpetuators of cultural knowledge relating to philosophical, spiritual and medical matters. The texts tend to depict female healers as witchlike in appearance and conduct, resorting to illicit forms of magic.

Evidence from the classics further indicates that in times of political and social unrest the nobility consulted high priests (*padanda, bagawanta, purohita*), who were renowned for their learning and spiritual power, rather than healers.[11]

References to healers are also found in the arts, myths and poems. A number of the better-known mythical tales, such as that of the widow-witch Calon Arang (see pp. 197–9) and Sudamala ('Freed from Stain and Impurity'), were composed in Java between the fourteenth and sixteenth centuries and then transmitted to Bali. The tale of Sudamala is also the subject-matter of a series of reliefs on the walls of the fourteenth-century monument of Candi Tigawangi in east Java. Balinese *dalang* (puppeteers) still narrate this story today during special Wayang Sudamala performances (see chapter 6, p. 146), that are purificatory and exorcistic in intent. *Dalang* explain that the story is appropriate on these occasions because it tells of Prince Sahadewa, the youngest Pandawa brother, a powerful healer who neutralizes evil.

These mythical tales and works of art are expressions of the religious life of the period. Tantric conceptions that aimed at deliverance through magic-religious means flourished during the ascendancy of the east Javanese kingdoms and intermingled with Siwaist and Buddhist cults. Scholars such as de Kat[12] and Stutterheim[13] have pointed out that this tantric element is still evident in Balinese religion today, with its inherent belief in mystical forces and witchcraft.

However, neither the historical data nor myths give explicit information on the practices and techniques used by healers. In order to appreciate how they actually struggle with sickness, misfortune and suffering it is best to observe them in daily life. It is estimated that there are about 2,500 different types of folk healers on the island (see figure 7.1). Of these diverse practitioners, the literate healer and the spirit medium are especially important as they deal with a wide range of physical, emotional or mental issues; hence the discussion will focus on them. It is, however, relevant to point out that distress often seems to be presented in somatic form. Yet our distinction between illness (the experience of disease or the perceived disease) and disease (an underlying biological change) are inappropriate in examining the Balinese system of non-biomedical healing. This approach would ignore the rich symbolic (body, mind, spirit and society) forms of the indigenous system, and fail to account for the healer's power to mediate between spheres and to create and recreate 'truth'.

The literate healer: balian usada

Of the diverse array of folk healers, the literate healer, *balian usada*, is in general the most venerated by the villagers. He is so called because his knowledge is derived primarily from the palm-leaf manuscripts, *usada*. The manuscripts in question are medical treatises in Old Javanese that have such graphic titles as Kanda Mpat Buta (Treatise of the Four Demons), or Kali-Maha-Usada (The Great Medicine Granted by the Goddess Kali, i.e. Durga).[14] The manuscripts deal with both theoretical and practical issues, taking into account metaphysics, cosmology, mysticism, plant life and rituals. Unsurprisingly, most *balian usada* are literate scholars. However, knowledge

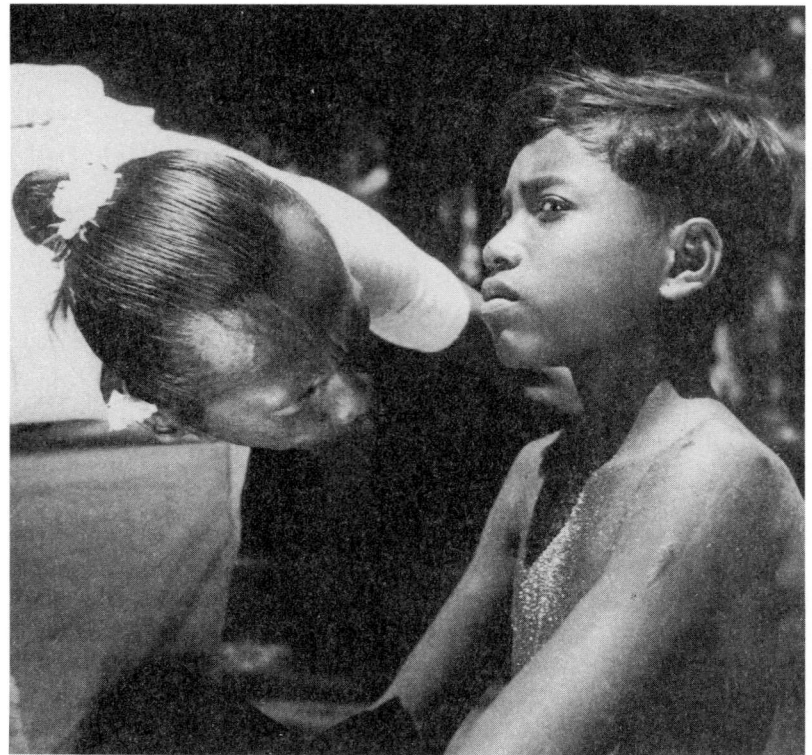

*Plate 37   Traditional healer (*balian usada*)*

itself is considered insufficient, for the gods must support the healer (*wisada duluran widi*). Only then can he form an opinion as to the cause of a patient's illness or trouble in order to cure him or her.

It is noteworthy, moreover, that the manuscripts are not only valued for their content, but are deemed to be objects in themselves as receptacles of mystic power, *kesaktian*. This energy can be conferred upon others by suitable incantations, offerings and holy water that has been in contact with the manuscripts.[15]

Balian usada are males and high castes, and the role is passed down the male line. But it depends on the inclination of a person, whether he wishes to take up the art of healing.

Successful *balian usada* may achieve close relations with clients, referred to as *paguruwang* (from *guru*, master or teacher). Their superior status and learning are then acknowledged, largely because the 'truth' of their statements has been demonstrated and their remedies and prescriptions have worked over time.[16]

Balian usada are often also respected and held in awe for the mystical power associated with them. As in other parts of the world, mystical power is ambivalent and amoral, easily convertible into different ends, good as well as evil. Villagers point out that healers, even benevolent ones, require knowledge of negative power as well as positive, right-hand (white) magic, *kesaktian panengen*. How otherwise could they control or neutralize the negative energy? Healers may also engage in fierce mystical battles at night with other healers or witches in order to counteract their harmful energy, which may be directed at bewitching victims.

The main medical paraphernalia of a healer are medicine, for the most part made from plant substances, so-called *sarana*, likened to mystical 'weapons', and holy water. It is worth drawing attention to these 'weapons'[17] as they are unique mystico-magical devices that pertain to the mythical, religious and social life of the people. These 'weapons' are primarily amulets or charms charged with magic by drawings (*rerajahan*) and sacred syllables. There are hundreds of such drawings with multiple, sometimes conflicting, aims.[18] Some, as the scholar Lovric argued, seem to be inspired by gross human pathology, with a view to containing the specific ailment involved.[19] There are also a large number of drawings that provide protection from enemies (witches) who seek to harm or bring illness to their intended victims (see figure 7.2).

As the drawings and syllables are found in medical treatises, it is the *balian usada* in particular who has knowledge of them. In the course of treatment he may adapt and recreate a specific drawing on one of a variety of materials, ranging from palm-leaf, sheaths of bamboo, bits of cloth, wood or hammered metal. It is then carefully wrapped up, usually in cloth, secured with string and handed to the client, together with offerings. The client takes this weapon home and hides it. It may be buried or placed surreptitiously in a crack in the wall

*Figure 7.2   The gods with their customary retainers; (left) the god
Wisnu with the demon* buta Ngadu-Nagada; *(right) the god*

of the house compound or shrine. A *sarana may also be
carried in a garment. It is essential to stress that the client is
not allowed to examine the 'weapon' and see the drawing for
then it would lose its power.*

A playful and humorous note may also be evident in the case
of some 'weapons'. For example, there is a 'weapon', known as
sarana tumbal joged, which is hidden in the home of a rich
family in order to prevent burglary. Owing to this weapon, a
thief on leaving the home suddenly encounters a seductive girl
who beckons him to dance the *joged* dance with her. He
succumbs to her beauty and drops the stolen goods in order to
dance. Unaware of other villagers approaching him, the thief is
easily caught and the girl disappears into the unmanifest world.
In reality, *joged* is a seductive dance in which young, unmarried
girls select partners from the audience to dance with.

Drawings may also be used as medicine. They are then
reproduced on paper which the healer quietly and solemnly

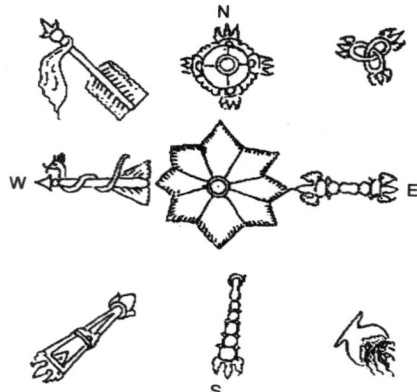

E	Iswara	thunder-hammer, *bajra*
SE	Mahésora	frankincense, *dupa*
S	Brahma	stick, *danda*
SW	Rudra	sword, *kadga*
W	Mahadéwa	snake-snare, *naga-pasa*
NW	Sangkara	banner, *dwaja*
N	Wisnu	mace or club, *gada*
NE	Sambu	trident, *trisula*
C	Siwa	lotus, *padma*

Figure 7.3   Magical drawings which provide protection against such enemies as witches

tears into small pieces, throws into a glass of holy water and gives to the patient to drink.

Balian usada emphasize that the medicine or weapons must first be ritually consecrated (*mapasupati*) by reciting incantations so that they become animated (*mangda urip*) and effective (*wiakti*). This is followed by other incantations indicating their purpose. One of these is included as an example; its aim is to protect the client:

May the gods Brahma, Wisnu and Iswara unite,
May the prince Sang Bima dwell in the left hand,
The monkey-god Sang Hanuman in the right hand,
The noble monkey Sang Sugriwa in the chest.
May the gods bestow strength so that the muscles become like wire, and the bones like steel.
No poison will then be effective.
And spirits who may wish to harm will be too frightened to approach.

Kummmmur . . . [imitating monkey sounds]
May the gods Brahma and Wisnu animate this 'weapon' [specified
  as a small precious stone, *mirah*, which the client swallows].

In order that the incantations retain their mystical energy,
the healer recites them softly so that they are inaudible to
others. In combination with the medicine, holy water and
weapons, they often seem to be efficacious. Is this based on
deception? Healers, clients and other villager draw attention
to the importance of 'believing strongly'. As one villager explained:

It is essential to 'believe', *pracaya*, first in the healer, and then in the
effectiveness of his incantations. It is further important to believe
that the medicine and 'weapons' will work.

Rodney Needham[20] has ably deconstructed the concept of
belief by pointing out that it refers to private states, which are
shifting and opaque. Indeed, he points out that *pracaya*, or
some Indonesian variant of it, can be rendered as: to trust, to
believe, to have confidence in, to have faith in, among other
meanings.

There are, of course, limits to our understanding of healing
methods, even in the west. We need only to think of the
acknowledged placebo effect of certain remedies or drugs that
physicians, though not patients, realize are pharmacologically
inert. Freud himself wrote: 'expectation coloured by hope
and faith is an effective force with which we have to reckon . . .
in all our attempts at treatment and cure'.[21] This point is also
taken up by Jerome Frank,[22] who, in discussing the universal
features of psychotherapy, stresses the importance of the
healer's ability to instil hope and trust in the patient.

Attention at this stage should be drawn to the performative
and liminal nature of healing rituals carried out by *balian
usada*. In line with Turner and Kapferer, it can be suggested
that this characteristic further contributes to the efficacy of
the rituals and their potential to achieve a transformation in
the experience and personality of the clients and relevant
participants. Moreover, as Kapferer put it, such rites often
have 'transcendental aspects, i.e. involve the construction of a
context and related identities at a higher level, subsuming and
resolving contractions and oppositions apparent at lower le-

vels of organization'.[23] This is best illustrated by a case study of an actual patient.

The *balian usada* involved was Cokorda Gede Ngurah from Payangan, Gianyar. He is elderly, highly respected and descended from a long line of healers. Patients come to him from early in the morning until late in the evening. He sometimes also visits patients in their homes when they are too ill to come to his place, *puri*. Villagers questioned say that this particular healer follows the path of *darma*, virtue and order, described as: '*Yadniyan kasampar antuk tai, yening meresidayang ngewalerang nyampur antuk sekar*' If faeces are thrown, flowers should, if possible, be thrown back. This implies that this healer does not seek vengeance, as many healers do, when destructive magic has been used on a client.

Case study 1 The patient is the son of I Mutu, also from Gianyar. The episode took place several years ago, when the boy was three years old. He became very ill. His symptoms were: continually shivering, although very hot (*kebus dingin*), and frequently waking up at night in a state of fear (*kesiap-kesiap wungi*). In consternation the father, I Mutu, first brought the boy and his two eldest sons (see figure 7.4) to a diviner.

The diviner asked the eldest boy to gaze into a bowl of water and tell him whom he saw reflected there. Apparently the boy discerned his maternal grandmother in the water. As a consequence the diviner pointed out that the grandmother was the cause of the illness. At night she became a witch and sought to harm the child. When the family heard this diagnosis they were understandably greatly perturbed. The youngest son of the grandmother, then twenty-two years old, even tried to stab her with a kitchen knife, and the other family members could only restrain him with difficulty.

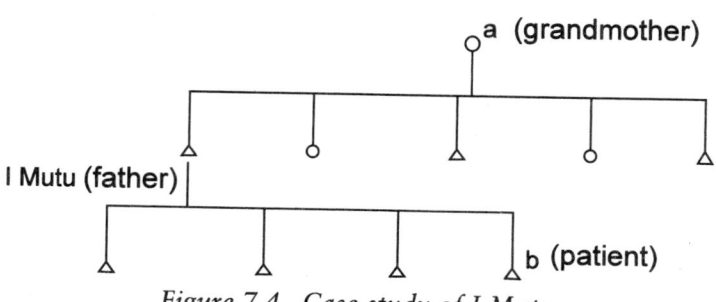

Figure 7.4 Case study of I Mutu

The father then decided to consult the healer, Cokorda Gede Ngurah, whom he respected highly. The healer requested him to bring the grandmother and other family members to his home. After contemplation and tests, he solemnly announced to them that the grandmother was indeed a witch, but unwittingly so; she was also not using a magic weapon, *sarana*. The reason that she was transformed at night was due to the fact that she had been born on an unpropititious day. Hence she was in effect blameless for her malign night-time actions.

Elaborate rituals were subsequently carried out in the healer's palace and in a special temple, Pura Yeh Ceruk in Sukawati, over a period of weeks, whereby the old woman was purified (*nglukat*) with purificatory water (*toya panglukatan*). These rituals were costly and time-consuming, for they involved making numerous, complicated offerings. The child in fact became well and to this day it appears that the grandmother has harmed no one again through witchcraft.

It is worth commenting on the aesthetic and reflexive setting of healing rituals, with particular reference to the healer, Cokorda Gede Ngurah. Patients literally sit for hours in the northern pavilion, waiting for the healer to appear. Suspended from normal life, they are surrounded by a strange and incongruous assortment of objects from the animal, plant, mineral and human world, and from different periods and cultures – Chinese, Indian, Dutch and Indonesian. A large television set in an ornately carved gilded frame is immediately evident. Like the small table in front of which the healer sits cross-legged, it is placed on a higher level than the clients, indicative of his status and scholarship. Programmes are broadcast softly during much of the day. Florid carvings, Dutch and Chinese porcelain plates, paintings of the Balinese mythical world, and a mounted deer head with antlers adorn the walls. A conspicuous cupboard with glass doors, in which hundreds of manuscripts are visible, stands to one side of the pavilion, highlighting again the learning of the healer. Throughout the palace are cages with birds that sing sweetly; these are gifts from grateful patients who have been cured. As Turner once wrote, these objects can be viewed as exemplifying a 'fructile chaos, a fertile nothingness, a storehouse of possibilities'.[24] The homes, and concomitantly the setting, of healing rituals carried out by other *balian usada* vary, of course. Yet they all seek in some way to provide a stage that initiates in the clients and participants, as well as the lookers-on, a contemplative and aesthetic mode of consciousness that presumably contributes further to the transformative potential of healing rituals.

In reviewing the case of I Mutu's son, it is evident that the curative performance embracing the grandmother, as it unfolded, was a process involving different contexts separated by time and space. As it progressed the subjective motives and affects of the participants were objectified and transformed into publicly accepted sets of meaning. However, only a *balian usada* of great repute in the community, such as Cokorda Gede Ngurah of Payangan, could neutralize the essentially destructive diagnosis of the first healer, the diviner, without discrediting him. Through the subsequent purificatory rites the ultimate cause of the boy's affliction was then addressed and resolved in a satisfactory way.

Spirit mediums: balian tetakson

Spirit mediums are often referred to as *balian tetakson*. This appellation is appropriate as Taksu is a special sacred spirit who empowers mediums to communicate with agents from the unseen world.[25] This spirit also inspires other healers, puppeteers and performers, enabling them to enchant humans with their performances. Mediums may also be called *balian tapakan* (from *tapak*, to enter). As in the case of the literate healer, the medium seeks through creative artistry to elicit confidence in clients in order to facilitate an attitude change.

This entails, as Jerome Frank put it: 'supplying the patient with a conceptual framework for organizing his chaotic, mysterious, and vague distress and give him a plan of action, helping him to regain a sense of direction and mastery to resolve his inner conflicts'.[26] In relation to the spirit medium this framework, as will become apparent, alludes not only to supernatural beings but also to mythical images and episodes of cosmic drama.

There are both men and women mediums. The women who successfully take on this role tend to be unmarried, childless or older widows, who are not bound by the traditional demands of childrearing and housework. Although mediums are usually low castes and illiterate, they may enjoy considerable influence and status. This, however, is considered tenuous, for their reputation depends on continued public approval of their therapy as well as divine approbation. Villagers in fact stress that mediums, like other humans, are fallible and their ritual purity can easily wane; the supernatural beings would then not wish to speak through them.

The incentive to become a medium is not financial. The income a medium earns is in any case usually negligible, although mediums of repute may nowadays obtain irregular donations of cash as a return for their services. Spirit mediums come to their calling through divine inspiration. Many seem to have gone through a mentally disturbed period before taking on their role. Generally only after this process of initiation are they able to go into a trance for the benefit of the community. Ritual possession or trance is highly institutionalized in Bali and found in various cultural areas. Temple priests may become vehicles for deities when they impart information to the congregation. Trance also occurs in specific dance-drama performances, a well-known one being Sang Hyang Dedari (the dance of celestial nymphs) with young girl dancers. There is no generic term for trance. It is often called *nadi* (from *dadi*, to become or exist, implying a higher level of reality). Trance is a state of disassociation which may be experienced from very mild to more extreme forms, and in mediums may last from ten seconds to about fifteen minutes.[27]

During trance, mediums may be entered by deities, ancestors, demons or spirits. However, the supreme gods, such as Siwa, Wisnu or Brahma, are too sublime to speak through humans. Humans approach and worship them through offerings and prayers.

The main reason for clients seeking to consult these agents of the supernatural, referred to as *nunas baos batara* ('requesting the gods to speak'), is illness. Sometimes patients have already been to another healer, or these days a western-trained practitioner, but to no avail. Clients also consult mediums about the reasons for a wide range of other troubles, such as a fire breaking out in the home or shrine; livestock dying; crop failure; theft; ignorance of one's temple of origin (*pura kawitan*); conflict or tension at home; premature death or suicide; how to carry out important rites correctly, in particular rites of cremation; bad dreams, and so forth.

Clients usually visit mediums in groups of three to five, which include both sexes. Often they are patrilineally related. Most clients hear of a medium by word of mouth from a friend or relative. It is, moreover, usual to consult a medium whom the client does not know personally and who lives some distance away. A medium may be consulted only once or more often, but usually not more than three times. If clients are dissatisfied with the advice obtained, they have no hesitation in going to another medium.

Rarely do clients give a medium explicit reasons for why they are visiting him or her. Skilled mediums, through shrewdly posed questions and intimate knowledge of village affairs obtained over time, gain some idea of the problem. In fact mediums often seem to be sensitive observers of human nature with insight into the spectrum of kin relations, who can help clients to express grief, affection, anger, deference, fear or contrition.

In order to gain a deeper understanding of the therapeutic artistry of a medium, two case studies of clients are briefly described below. The first involves a female medium from north Bali who had married into a household in Tegallalang in Gianyar. Figure 7.5 shows the layout of the house compound and family temple. She is unusual in that after a mentally disturbed period, when in several dreams the gods requested her to act on their behalf in the service of the community, she now works with her husband; he prepares the medicines for the patients.

Case study 2 The patient was Ni Jani, who was about two years old. She was brought by her mother and her paternal grandmother. They wished to consult the gods about why the little girl was ill. They were from Keliki in Gianyar. The girl's symptoms were: shivering, though hot (*panas dingin*), and a sick, swollen stomach (*basang beseh*). They had come six month previously as there was strife (*buwut*) in the home; people were often quarrelling.

The session began with a short preliminary talk between the medium, mother and grandmother. The medium then went to her shrine, *pangawangan*, in order to consult the gods. The family sat down on the bottom step of the shrine. The medium in her elevated position presented offerings to the gods and murmured an incantation, requesting the gods to descend. The medium moaned slightly as the god entered her, then slumped. The god's visitation was brief and undramatic. Some of the words were indistinct. Essentially the god said the following:

'Your child is ill as witches are seeking to harm her. These are none other than *layak gigi* [literally 'tongue and teeth', implying members of the innermost family circle]. Your family is also punished by the ancestors (*batara hyang guru*) as insufficient offerings have been prepared for rites (*yadnya*).

'Once you are home you must prepare medicine for the child. [Here detailed instructions followed of how to make the medicine]'.

The medium came out of trance. She gave the family holy water to drink and her husband gave them the ingredients for

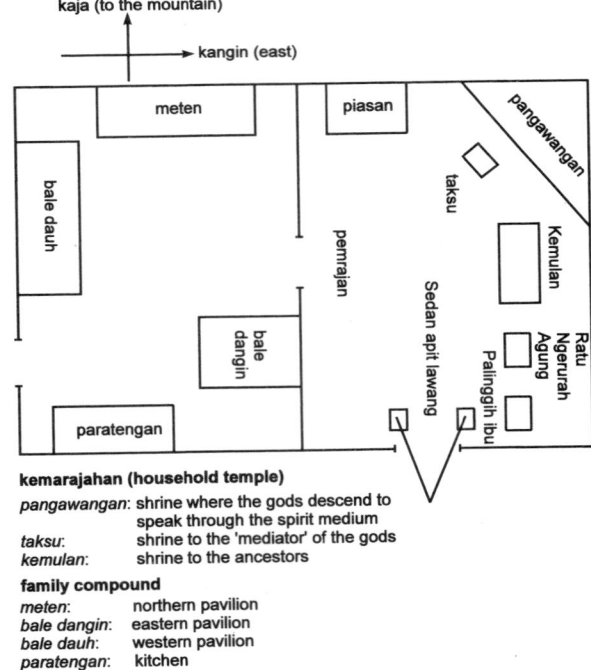

Figure 7.5 Plan of the house compound of the spirit medium and her husband in Tegallalang, Gianyar

the medicine. During the ensuing conversation it emerged that there was less tension in the household now. The family group then gratefully left the medium and returned home.

As in the case of Ni Jani, witchcraft, together with offending the ancestors, is the most frequent cause of illness diagnosed by this particular medium.

A number of gods enter her. A striking characteristic of most of them is that they also manifest themselves as magnificent masked figures in ceremonial performances. As these are frequent in south Bali, the villagers are well acquainted with their powerful presences, which carry authority whenever they appear. On the above occasion the medium proclaimed after the séance that the god Ratu Gede Landung had spoken through her. Ratu Gede Landung and his wife, Ratu Gede Isteri, manifest themselves in life as tall masked figures classified as *barong* (see next section). Other deities who may enter the medium, apart from this couple, are Batara Mas, the god of the majestic mythic creature Barong Keket, or Batara Sakti, alias Durga, who also reveals herself as Rangda, the Supreme Witch.

When in a trance the medium, moreover, talks and moves in a manner befitting the god who has entered her, thus echoing his or her speech and dance in the performing arts. For example, in the above case Ratu Gede Landung, being elderly, speaks somewhat tremulously, in a low voice; his movements are slow and ponderous and his gait shuffling. In passing, it is of interest to note that this particular medium had had a stroke about one year previously and had been in hospital for several weeks. The stroke had left her infirm and weak, and Ratu Gede Landung would be one of the easiest gods for her to impersonate.

It is evident that the medium evokes powerful, expressive symbols of gods during seances which, in Jacques Maquest's[28] sense, participate in the nature of what they stand for. This intensifies the dramatic, as well as the contemplative quality of the séance, which in turn helps to validate the status and authority of the spirit medium in her diagnosis and recommended cure. As such, the conceptual scheme presented to clients and their accompaniment is an important contributory factor to the efficacy of the 'symbolic healing'[29] carried out by the medium.

Healing rituals, however, as indicated earlier, must be seen as performative and dynamic processes during which a transformation of experience is initiated whereby therapeutic forces are channelled into the lives of the clients and participants. This comes to the fore in the following case study of a family in distress; it involves another female medium, from Sukawati. This case is of special interest as it illustrates the interchange which can occur between clients and supernatural agents of the cosmos.

Case study 3 The reason for distress related to the death of I Made Alon from central Bali. The boy, who was thirteen years old at the time, suddenly became unconscious while doing exercises with his schoolmates on the sportsfield and died almost immediately. His family was devastated for he was young and was the sole heir. They have a younger daughter.

The parents and paternal grandfather went to a medium in Sukawati the same evening to consult the gods about why the boy had died. The grandfather was the main petitioner and spokesman. At the medium's home a brief conversation ensued between her and the family. The medium then went to her shrine. After reciting an incantation she was entered by the spirit of the boy, *pitra*,[30] who had just died. In order to give a glimpse of the cosmic world created and expressive quality of the séance, a short excerpt of the dialogue between the spirit and the family of the deceased follows:[31]

Medium/*pitra* The *pitra* [spirit of the ancestor] is now descending and granting me speech. Mother, father, grandfather, you are sad for your child, suddenly dead. Do not grieve for I am content where I am now resting at the shrine of Rajapati [dedicated to the goddess Durga]. My death was not caused by any mistake you committed *vis-à-vis* the gods or ancestors. No human caused death [through witchcraft]. You made no mistake in the perceptible world of humans [*sekala*] or in the imperceptible world [*niskala*]. Although I was still young, my appointed time had come to leave this world [*puniki wantah pekaetan tiang*]. Return home in harmony with one another. There take care of my younger sister who is now alone.

Grandfather I am content to hear your words, but talk to your mother who feels sorrow and pity for you. It would have been easier if you had been ill for at least three days (for then we would have had time to adjust to your death). You passed away so suddenly.

Plate 38   Medium in a trance

Medium [*coming out of trance*] What did the gods say?

Grandfather The spirit of our grandson told us he was now resting at the shrine of Rajapati and that we should not grieve for him for his time had come to leave this world. We should also take care of his sister.

Medium You should not now, mother, be so distressed that your son passed away.

Mother Yes.

Medium It was ordained that he should be on earth for only a short time. Return home and carry out your chores as usual and take care of his sister. Request that the gods take care of him, as well as protecting you on earth.

Parents Yes.

Grandfather Yes.

The session ends. It is interesting that a number of villagers came to the family's home the next day and encouraged the wife to have another child as she was still young. In due course the family will go again to this or another medium to ask the spirit whether they carried out all the cremation rites satisfactorily and to ensure that he is content.

This séance gives an idea of how public symbols pertaining to the imperceptible world of supernatural beings serve private needs. Yet the symbols are used flexibly for specific ends, in this case to bring consolation to a family suddenly bereaved of their only son and heir.[32] In part this was achieved by removing any misgivings they might have that they had been in some way responsible for his death in a morally and culturally elaborate universe, underpinned by numerous rites and regulations.

Lévi-Strauss,[33] in his poetic work on the shamanic healing of a woman in difficult labour in a Central American Indian community, argues that the shaman séance is the counterpart of the psychoanalytic session, but with all the elements reversed. So the shaman is an active agent organizing the experiences of the essentially passive patient by presenting her with a social myth. However, a séance with a spirit medium is clearly a creative process, during which a personal problem is acted out in a highly structured setting. Although the idiom of the séance is controlled and takes place in a cosmological and mythological frame-work, clients and deities or spirits sometimes interact with one another, enabling the former to reorganize their assumptive worlds. Indeed, the people point out that one must not simply believe what the medium says. It is even sensible, especially if the problem is grave, to take along to a medium someone who is articulate and knows some Old Javanese. Not only can he understand the sayings of the deities, which at times are obscure and interspersed with Old Javanese words, but he can dispute with them. Moreover, as we have already seen in the discussion of dance-drama performances, villagers explain that often one can only discover what is correct and virtuous through confrontation and disputation.

Myth and the Persuasive Power of the Unseen

A number of scholars[34] have stressed the importance of cultu-rally shared, meaningful schemata called myths in symbolic healing. From the preceding discussion it emerges that both healers and clients draw on symbols particularized as the case demands from general myths to communicate distress and care. So, for example, humans with great mystical power may be perceived by villagers as bringing affliction to others through witchcraft when they transform themselves into such mythical beings as the magnificent, shaggy creature Barong or the Supreme Witch Rangda. Healers, in the area of Tegalla-lang, may also be entered by the gods associated with these same figures, as well as by other deities or the ancestors. Numerous myths are in fact perpetuated that tell of the realm of the dead, where the ancestral spirits dwell. However, in this context it is worth drawing special attention to the well-known myth of the widow (*rangda*) Calon Arang,[35] for it provides a potent area of discourse concerned with human suffering and distress, and the attempted resolution of these through other humans or spiritual beings.

The myth can be briefly summarized as follows:
Calon Arang, the widow-witch of Girah, lived during the reign of the great East Javanese King Airlangga. Out of fear of Calon Arang's demonic powers, no suitor dared approach her beautiful

daughter. In revenge, Calon Arang goes to the graveyard with her apprentices; she dances, makes offerings and appeals to Durga to be permitted to bring devastation to the land. The goddess grants the request and terrible epidemics break out. The god Siwa then advises King Airlangga to enlist the help of the powerful sage Mpu Baradah. Through his mystic power Mpu Baradah averts the calamity. He purifies Calon Arang with holy water and manages to convert her to good.

For the Balinese, Calon Arang is above all Rangda,[36] the Supreme Witch, who appears as a wild-eyed, demonic figure in theatrical performances. There she is confronted, but never defeated, by the sage Baradah, who may take on the form of the

Plate 39   Mask of Rangda, queen of black magic

protective-benign mythical creature Barong Ket, referred to as Banaspati Raja, 'Lord of the Jungle', or Batara Gede, 'Great God' (plate 40). As the emphasis in the present chapter is on healers, this is not the place to consider these masked theatrical performances, except to point out that myth, art, ritual and theatre are intimately connected in Bali. The drama of Rangda and Barong may also have therapeutic value, according to the villagers. Indeed, the scholar Lovric[37] argued that, in the case of Rangda and Barong, we are dealing with a Tantric-orientated 'cult of demonic deities' who are both protective and destructive, in the sense that they can act either as agents who create epidemics or, on the other hand, contain them.

There are a variety of other animal *barong*,[38] such as the wild boar, cow or tiger *barong*. Barong Ratu Gede Landung and Ratu Gede Isteri, mentioned earlier in relation to mediums, are included in the category of *barong*. These tall, majestic figures portray an old, ugly couple. All these *barong* wander from village to village during Balinese religious festival

Plate 40 *Batara Gede, the powerful tutelary spirit and supernatural healer of Sidemen*

Galungan, when they have a protective function, warding off harmful influences in the forms of demonic beings (*kala* or *buta*).

All these impressive masked figures have been consecrated and are deemed to possess great supernatural power.[39] Hence they are treated with considerable respect and their presence in drama or in ritual or ceremonial processions carries with it the authority derived from the supernatural world.

The seen and the unseen, *sekala* and *niskala*, are spheres that have been alluded to several times in discussing illness and healing rituals. The latter is generally rated as superior to the former. Spirits and deities dwell in the invisible world and are equipped with greater perception and comprehension than humans. However, to the indigenous people these spheres are revealed in a relationship of complementary opposition.[40] As such, they are intrinsic to the cosmological and aesthetic principle of binary opposites, *rwa bhineda*:[41] day–night, right–left, sadness–happiness, sickness–health, life–death, and so forth. Yet there is no radical distinction between opposites: one flows into the other. This is vividly illustrated, as we have seen, by the shadow theatre. During the performance the shadows act as the bridge between the seen and the unseen, or the higher reality that hovers on the edge of actualization. Thus the shadows indicate to the beholders the illusory and transformatory nature of all categories of manifestation.

It is the unseen sphere, with its inherent mystical powers, that healers seek to penetrate when confronted by villagers experiencing illness or disorder. Consequently, mediums in structured séances allow clients to defy momentarily the separation between this world and the next by enabling them to interact with cosmic agents of the dark.

Literate healers, on the other hand, keep their knowledge secret and shroud their techniques and paraphernalia, in particular the incantations and 'weapons', in silence and mystery. This, too, has to be seen in relation to the power of the unseen. This type of healer, more than any other on the island, is said to probe the invisible realm. The fact that his knowledge is not disclosed, it can be suggested, emphasizes to clients that it partakes of the spirit world and intensifies his persuasive artistry, enabling him on occasion symbolically to heal persons in distress in the community.

8

The Process of Modernization

As explained in chapter 3, Balinese society and its economy have been subject to the interplay of internal and external influences or constraints since early times. The inclusion of Bali in the Dutch colonial empire had especially far-reaching consequences. This occurred despite lower economic potential (and therefore less colonial exploitation) than on many other islands and also despite the fact that a number of Dutch officials residing in Bali enjoyed the reputation of being scholars of Balinese culture. In the subsequent discussion, the changes in the political-administrative area which occurred as a result of the subjugation of Bali to the colonial regime will be shown. Subsequently, the effects of the Japanese occupation (1942–5) and the path to decolonization will be sketched. Finally, attention will be focused on the inclusion of Bali in the Republic of Indonesia and the consequences of statewide modernization measures, which are formulated and implemented by the central government in Jakarta.

Bali's Inclusion in the Dutch Colonial Empire

The various Balinese kingdoms were not incorporated simultaneously into the colonial empire as was the case in the Dutch conquest of the neighbouring island of Lombok in 1894. As a result of the Dutch military expeditions of 1846, 1848 and 1849, the colonial government achieved direct control over north Bali. Buleleng was the first kingdom to come under colonial rule (1854) and Jembrana the second (1855). A Dutch officer (*controleur*) officiating as subordinate of the Resident of Banyuwangi (east Java) and stationed in Buleleng was promoted to the rank of Assistant Resident in 1860. It was his duty to oversee both kingdoms and to administer them according to directives from Batavia. Moreover, he had to investigate developments in other regions of Bali and on Lombok and report these events to his superiors.[1] It took several decades before the final aim of control over the remaining kingdoms on Bali and Lombok was achieved. It was not until 1894 that the Balinese kingdom of Lombok and its vassal state of Karangasem in east Bali was incorporated, after battles with many casualties on both sides. The south Balinese kingdoms of Gianyar, followed by Badung, Tabanan, Bangli and Klungkung, were only brought under colonial rule between 1900 and 1908.

The conquest of Badung (1906), above all, attracted worldwide attention. Dutch war reporters and press photographers who accompanied the expedition army witnessed what was to western observers an incomprehensible event. Five warships dropped anchor at Sanur and the ship's artillery fired for days on end at the centre of the city of Badung (today's Denpasar) six kilometres away and left it in ruins. Then about 3,000 troops of the Dutch colonial army, armed with cannons and repeaters, marched into the capital of the kingdom of Badung on 20 September 1906. The advancing soldiers were faced by thousands of festively dressed men, women and children, armed simply with a *keris* or spear, who streamed unflinchingly out of the two palaces, rank on rank, into the fire from the Dutch cannons and guns and onto the bayonets of the expedition army; others stabbed each other or died by their own hands. Such heroic and distressing ritual mass suicide is known as *puputan* in Bali.[2]

H. H. van Kol, who was a member of the upper house of the Dutch parliament, sought to unravel the 'truth' behind this event:

This investigation was embarrassing for someone who valued the observation of international law. But as I wandered alone in the quiet night in Dèn Pasar and Pametjoetan, along the paths where crowds of men, women, the elderly and children (people like ourselves), had faced death with heads held high, and where corpses had been stacked in layers – as I saw in my mind's eye 'this dreadful mess of smashed bones and limbs torn to pieces, dragged through the dirt': at that moment I decided – whatever may happen – to do my duty in the name of Christianity and Humanity.[3]

Contrary to the official Dutch version, van Kol tried to show that the captain had purposely allowed the Chinese-owned ship *Sri Koemali* to run aground on a reef on 26 May 1904, so that he could claim compensation for the alleged theft of a fictitious sum of money and goods on board. Likewise, it was established that the Prince of Badung was not himself involved in the 'piracy'. Therefore the legitimacy of the punitive expedition against the ruler, alleging infringement of the prohibition on pillage of stranded ships, was essentially a deliberately invented *casus belli*. Years earlier, the Dutch had made surveys of everything that would be relevant in a war, drafting maps and sending out spies. For example, in 1903, a field officer undertook 'a reconnaissance voyage in the event of a potential conflict'. Van Kol branded such activities by the colonial regime as imperialistic, and the various *puputan* which it provoked as the 'extermination of an heroic race'.

Dutch Colonial Administration

In connection with the reorganization of the Dutch colonial administration, the government in Batavia aimed to unify the political-administrative structures even beyond Java and to guarantee the Pax Neerlandica within its sphere of influence. In Bali, the effect of the new regulations of the administrative structure introduced in 1906 was that the administrative section (*residentie*) of Bali and Lombok, managed by a Resident, was divided up into three divisions (*afdelingen*) – north Bali, south Bali and Lombok – which were each administered by an Assistant Resident. The *afdelingen* were further divided into subdivisions (*onderafdelingen*), which on Bali corresponded more or less with the former kingdoms. In order to acknowledge their voluntary subjugation to colonial rule, the three south Balinese subdivisions of Karangasem, Gianyar and Bangli were granted indirect Dutch rule (*indirect bestuur*) and their own sovereign dynasties were left intact. By contrast, the three rebel kingdoms of Tabanan, Badung and Klungkung, like the older Dutch dependencies of Buleleng and Jembrana (in north Bali), were initially subject to direct colonial government (*direct* or *rechstreeks bestuur*).

Because the few European officials of the Ministry for the Interior (Binnenlands Bestuur) were overworked due to their many assignments, such as the development of the material infrastructure, the modernization of agriculture, jurisdiction and numerous administrative duties, the co-operation of the indigenous nobility was essential to the success of Dutch rule. Local civil servants were recruited from this group. In the case of indirectly ruled areas, the Governor General in Batavia (contemporary Jakarta) appointed Balinese princes as viceroys (*wakil*), who exercised mainly administrative functions in their areas. The self-determination of such local 'rulers' was less comprehensive than earlier, because even in these areas European officials had ultimate control.[4] Foreign interference was even more evident within the subdivisions under direct Dutch rule. These were governed directly by European *controleurs*, that is, without the participation of Balinese princes. Moreover, in areas under direct rule, royal landed property

Plate 41　Drinking Dutchmen: bas relief

was confiscated and declared government property. The justification for placing the former kingdoms of Badung and Tabanan in this unfavourable position was the conviction that among the progeny of former rulers who had survived the various *puputan* there were no trustworthy personalities to whom government duties could be transferred.[5] The consequence of this was that in the conquered kingdoms administrative posts were awarded mainly to members of the next-lower stratum of gentry.[6]

Subdivisions were divided into districts, which were sometimes even divided into subdistricts. All of them were officiated over primarily by Balinese nobles who had previously acted as viceroys for their *raja*. In subdivisions under direct rule, the head of the district was directly subordinate to the Dutch *controleur*; on the other hand, territorial units under indirect rule continued to be administered by their former rulers. Heads of districts received the title of *punggawa* and heads of subdistricts were awarded that of a *manca*. In addition to the segmentation into subdivisions, districts and subdistricts and the setting up of corresponding government bodies, the colonial authorities also endeavoured to bring the villages into the system of government. In the first decade of the twentieth century, the decision had been made to integrate all *banjar* and other settlements having a mutual *bale agung* to form the village (*desa*).[7] Each *desa* was to have two leaders: on the one hand, the *bandesa*, the 'spiritual' leader,[8] and on the other hand, the *perbekel*, the new 'secular' leader. *Perbekel* were to be directly subordinate to salaried civil servants, that is, to the district and subdistrict heads, whilst religious village matters such as temple ceremonies and celebrations of sacrifice continued to fall within the realm of the *bandesa* and the *pamangku*. Through this reorganization the colonial power hoped not only for a well-regulated government structure and stricter order but also for a strengthening of the position of the village without changing its *de facto* inner order.[9] This endeavour was expressed in the fact that, according to the structure of government organization, the head of the *banjar* (*klian banjar*) was subordinate to the *perbekel*. For subdivisions that had their own native government, the civil servants next in line could be appointed by the Balinese viceroy –

provided the European Resident approved. In the subdivisions that were directly ruled by the colonial regime, even the nomination of the *perbekel* was dependent upon the consent of the Resident.

The idea behind the colonial concept of village reorganization rests on the Dutch interpretation of the *desa* (or of the *banjar*) as the basic element of Balinese society, which is democratically organized within these units and displays a primarily religious character. The *desa* was hence perceived as being the 'original democratic village republic'. Under the guise of wanting to protect the egalitarian village community from princely despotic rule, or at least to counterbalance the power of the princes, the Dutch government body often built completely new territorial units (*perbekelan*, later called *desa dinas*) which were referred to as villages. Thus, the villages enabled the colonial authorities to control the *perbekelan* administratively. However, in this way a previously non-existent dichotomy was created between religion and *adat*, on the one hand, and between secular and administrative life, on the other. This dichotomy still exists today (see chapter 4, p. 93) and is reflected in the contrast between the political municipality and the village defined according to the *adat*, which often do not cover the same territory. Despite this, many Dutch civil servants were convinced, at least initially, that these measures originated from traditional village administration.[10]

In conjunction with the formation of political municipalities, the village reorganization completed in 1920 led not only to multiple meanings of the word 'village' but also to confusion in its subunits, the *banjar*. Initially, the *banjar* fulfilled a double function: they were part of the newly created 'government village'; further, they were subunits of the original *desa adat*, which implied that the *klian banjar* had to perform duties according to the *adat* as well as 'modern' administrative functions for the colonial government. Only years later, by analogy to the *desa*, were its subunits split into the institutions of *banjar adat* and *banjar buku*[11] (the latter being called *banjar dinas* later on), with specific officials responsible for the respective functional area: on the one hand, the *klian banjar adat*, who worked closely with the *bandesa* in the *desa adat*, and on the other, the *klian banjar buku* (the future *klian banjar dinas*), who was subordinate to the *perbekel*.

No matter how Dutch colonial rule was practised, it revealed a characteristic feature of western law, that is, the principle of clearly demarcated administrative-political territories, which had not existed in this form under Balinese kings (cf. the discussion about the ambiguous Balinese term '*druwe*' = 'possession' in chapter 3, pp. 49f). This meant that the *adat* legal concept of *matilas*[12] was explicitly ended, thanks 'to the fact that sometimes ten different *punggawa* had subjects in the one village'.[13] The colonial government fostered more rigorous leadership by reducing the number of indigenous heads of districts, who previously had not ruled a specific area but a 'personal' circle of commoners. Furthermore, these new bearers of authority were now obliged to take up residence within their district.

How does the socialist parliamentarian van Kol estimate the 'blessings of Dutch colonial rule', according to his report published in 1914?[14] His judgement turns out to be conflicting. As positive factors, he noted among other things the prohibition of the immolation of widows, the abolition of the princely right to confiscate widows and female children and their possessions upon the death of the head of the family without male heirs (the so-called *hak camput*, see chapter 3, p. 53) and the less bloodthirsty (even though more frequent) punishment of offenders. But more oppressive under Balinese rule than before were the level of cash taxation and above all the so-called 'service to the master', that is, compulsory labour to be performed by physically able heads of families, especially in road- and bridge-building and the construction of public buildings. For example, before the turn of the century in the kingdom of Bangli, commoners had had to work a total of one day per month for the palace, the village and the irrigation community, but now thirty to fifty days of compulsory labour per annum had to be put in for the Dutch government. Sometimes even children were recruited.

The liberation of the *triwangsa* from hard compulsory labour and the inclusion of the nobility in matters of colonial government produced two closely related results. The first was that many Balinese from the upper class of commoners tried to raise their status by decree and applied to the court to recognize them as members of the gentry. The second was that the fluid transition between the aristocracy and non-aristocracy yielded to a more rigorous division. Whilst in pre-colonial times, castes mainly enjoyed ideological significance, they were branded as facts by the Dutch colonial administration and organized as a closed system.[15] In this way, the *sudra* title groups such as Bandesa, Pasek, Pande and Sengguhu lost their former privileges and their members were included among the undifferentiated mass of fourth-caste Balinese. Van Kol also doubted the justification expressed by supporters of colonial rule in 1906, according to which Dutch armed intervention would quickly create conditions very different from those already existing. Henceforth internal Balinese wars would be out of the question; agriculture, the trades and industry would flourish and the common people could count on the fair administration of justice.

Initially only parliamentarians from the opposition were critical. Yet uncertainty also emerged later among officials about the smoothness of the prospective operation of their administrative system. In a government paper of 1920,[16] village reorganization was reported to be encountering serious difficulties. Criticism was expressed because *perbekel* and *klian banjar* were only rarely selected by open elections (as was considered to be in keeping, from the Dutch viewpoint, with the postulated 'village republics'), but were instead chosen by indigenous aristocratic civil servants. The reason for this was obvious: the reduction in the number of administrative units ushered in by the Dutch robbed many nobles of their hereditary official positions (which they had held at the time of the independent kingdoms) and their associated incomes. However, according to traditional law, they felt authorized and called upon to act in future as government office-holders. Often related to the former ruling family or its governor, they thought it quite natural to be nominated by their Balinese overlords. Duties still available to them comprised at best official power over a series of territorially defined *banjar*, which were united to form a *perbekelan*, or – less sought after – the office of *klian banjar*. In both cases the successful person was remunerated with the right of usufruct over an 'office field'. It is important that it was the Balinese nobility who assumed the tasks of civil administration from the subdistrict to the *banjar*, that is from the highest to the lowest administrative level. As it was often impossible or appeared to be unacceptable to the newly appointed aristocratic official to take up residence in his newly allotted official area, a further principle was disregarded which required the office-holder to live in his administrative area. One could not speak of strict control of the political-administrative apparatus because, as mentioned in the government report, when vacancies occurred it often happened that neither the European *controleur* nor the Balinese *punggawa* were informed about the appointment of the *klian banjar*. This was carried out arbitrarily by their *perbekel* and therefore not registered.

To suppress the influence of incipient nationalist movements and also to help contain expenses, the colonial administration became increasingly indigenized in the third and fourth decades of the twentieth century. In Bali, this implied that the nobility further consolidated their social position. Areas which had been directly ruled by the Dutch were now again in the hands of traditional rulers – the ancient nobility. Linguistically, this change was expressed by the *onderafdelingen* being renamed *negara* and their Balinese heads *negara* regents (*negarabestuurders*). This changed nothing, in fact, for the eight *negarabestuurders* remained formally subordinate to the Dutch Resident and Assistant Resident.[17]

Shortly after the end of the world economic crisis, in 1938 the colonial power reorganized the governmental and administrative structure of the areas beyond Java. The Residency of Bali and Lombok became part of a newly created administrative unit – 'Greater East' ('*de Groote Oost*'). Its capital city was Macassar on Celebes. The self-government of the Balinese *negara* by the nobility was recognized (but not the self-government of the subdivisions on Lombok), despite partial opposition by the western-educated intelligentsia and many Balinese from the *sudra* caste. After they had signed the document recognizing the overarching sovereignty of the Netherlands, the eight 'newly crowned' *raja* were ceremoniously raised to the position of 'self-governors', the event taking place in the mother temple of Besakih on the Balinese Galungan holiday.

This of course illustrated that the Dutch rulers were acting in contradiction to democratic principles and were strengthening their position by reappointing princes as regents and recognizing the princely status of the former *negara* heads. This decision was justified by arguing that Balinese culture was unique; its continuity could best be guaranteed by maintaining 'traditional' princely rule. However, that a new feudal structure had thereby been created was entirely disregarded.[18] The formerly rather flexible caste structure became more pronounced and hierarchical positions more defined. As only the native dynasties received the hereditary appointments, they were concerned with maintaining law and order to the point at which they crushed developing attempts at independence – a stance compatible with the interests of the colonial power.[19] The eight *negara* were tied into collective Balinese (and thus colonial) matters by the newly created Bali Council (Paruman Agung), in which all the eight *raja* and the Dutch Resident – the latter as chairman – were represented. On the next-lower level (that is, within the self-governed kingdoms), *negara* councils were established, with noble heads of districts participating.

Japanese Conquest

In the course of the conquest of South-East Asia, Japanese troops landed on the coast of Sanur in February 1942. The few soldiers of the colonial army to be stationed on Bali soon capitulated, enabling the invaders, after merely a few weeks, to exercise strict control over the island. The Japanese navy (*kaigan*) ruled the Lesser Sunda Islands for over three years. On Bali, the government and administrative structures installed in 1938 were retained, together with the indigenous civil servants (in their respective functions). Yet the authority of the *raja* was diminished as the Japanese *controleurs* (*kanrikan*) were granted greater authority than that conceded to their Dutch precursors during the short period of Balinese self-government.

Two of the changes introduced by the Japanese produced results that had consequences for the second Dutch colonial phase (that is, the period from the Japanese capitulation until the Indonesian declaration of independence). The first change concerned the abolition of the previously segregated school system. It was replaced by educational establishments open to children of all ethnic groups. In these Japanese-controlled schools, the spirit of Greater Asia (Asia Raya) was evoked; moreover, at the beginning of every school day the Indonesian national anthem ('Indonesia Raya') was sung. As a result, the idea of a united, self-reliant Indonesia stretching from Sumatra to former New Guinea was born in the younger generation for the first time. The Japanese Prime Minister Koiso's promise (19 September 1944) to lead Indonesia to independence paved the way for Indonesian nationalism. The second change consisted in the creation of military or paramilitary organizations. Here, Balinese were initiated into military matters. This also entailed the formation of Indonesian 'fatherland defenders' (Pembela Tanah Air: PETA). For example, the three regiments from the *negara* of Klungkung, Tabanan and Negara comprised over 5,000 young soldiers. Together with Java and certain regions of Celebes, Bali belonged to those areas where strong resistance developed against the reinstallation of Dutch colonial rule. Resistance fighters were recruited from members of nationalist groups already formed before the Second World War, as well as from members of the group of 'fatherland defenders' drilled by the Japanese.[20]

Striving for Independence

In March 1946, the Dutch Indies Civil Administration gained a hold on Bali once more. Previously appointed members of the government were relieved of their positions and arrested.[21] Internal Balinese conflicts were initiated because, on the one hand, nationalistically inclined natives resisted the reinstallation of the colonial regime and, on the other hand, nobles safeguarding their own interests supported the Dutch returnees. The latter reactivated the Paruman Agung in its earlier form as the council of nobles from Bali.

Because of the pressure exerted by Indonesians striving for independence, the Dutch relaxed their regime by endeavouring to transform the former centrally administered colony into a confederation (Negara Indonesia Serikat). This meant that each partial state possessed its own parliament, while the United States of Indonesia as an entity was to remain under the Dutch crown. The creation of the Negara Indonesia Serikat arose out of tactical calculations, for with the creation of a plurality of states the Dutch hoped to counterbalance the Republic of Java.[22] Bali, as one of the thirteen political administrative subunits (*daerah*), belonged to the State of East Indonesia. Bali was in fact again transformed into a federation of self-governments, which implied that the authority of the former Assistant Resident and his *controleurs* was reduced to the function of a consultant for native self-governors. The executive power of the *daerah* in Bali was transferred to the newly created Council of Raja (Dewan Raja-Raja) and the legislative power exercised by a Paruman Agung was altered. Henceforth, the latter was to comprise forty members: thirty-four were to be elected by the people, while the other six seats represented the ethnic minorities. As the next-lower parliamentary level (that is, in the eight principalities), *negara* councils (Paruman Agung) were created, their members to be chosen by free elections at the village level. The parliamentary system of government, reminiscent of the western model, was soon called into question one month later, when the elections to the parliament of the *daerah* Bali where annulled. In the eyes of the pro-Dutch Council of Raja, the voters had decided for too many 'extremists' (that is, nationalists).

During the impending process of decolonization, the authority of the colonial regimes was substantially reduced. On the one hand, the United Nations expressed disapproval of the Dutch desire to reconquer Indonesia; on the other hand, the resistance of the indigenous inhabitants was aroused. For example, the parliamentary election had to be repeated on Bali and the Paruman Agung reconvened. With the inauguration of this democratically legitimated parliament, the resistance movement felt that a good part of its demands were fulfilled and ceased its activities. In March 1946, the Dutch dissolved their residency of Bali and Lombok and ceded their powers to the Council of Raja. At the Round Table Conference which met in The Hague from 23 August until 2 November 1949, the form and conditions of the transfer of sovereignty to the government of the Republic of Indonesia were negotiated, and finally, on 27 December 1949, the Netherlands recognized Indonesia as an independent state.[23]

The newly won freedom was used, amongst other things, to dismantle any remaining colonial institutions and to replace them with indigenous ones. Thus the Council of Raja was forced to relinquish its powers to an elected parliament. Just before its dissolution, the state of East Indonesia issued a law in June 1950 which granted legislative power to the People's Parliament (Dewan Perwakilan Rakyat: DPR). This laid the cornerstone for what was to be a short period of democratic development.

Bali's Integration into the Republic of Indonesia

Within the framework of the unification of regional governing bodies, East Indonesia lost its privileged position in 1957, when it was fully integrated into the Republic of Indonesia. The totality of state territory was divided into 'autonomous' hierarchical levels. Up to the present day, the provinces (*propinsi*) continue to constitute the highest political-administrative level (*tingkat* I). Provinces were, in turn, divided into administrative entities on a second level (*tingkat* II: *kabupaten*) (see chapter 1, pp. 8f).

In Bali, the eight *kabupaten* are identical with the earlier self-governed subdivisions. What changed decisively after 1957 was the degree of authority of the various administrative levels. Until the proclamation of the state of emergency by the Indonesian State President Soekarno in 1959, the members of the executive of a *daerah* (on the next lowest level of a *kabupaten*) were elected by a parliament (the legislature and their vertical integration into the central government was guaranteed by a civil servant appointed by Jakarta, namely the governor). The governor's duty comprised above all the management of various provincial ministeries, for example, the Departments of Works, Health, Education and Culture, and so on. After the withdrawal of parliamentary democracy and its replacement by a 'guided' democracy, a presidential decree was issued whereby the former two highest office-holders of a *daerah* were to be replaced by a single public servant installed by the central government to which he was responsible. A further dismantling of direct democracy resulted from the withdrawal of power from the regional parliaments, which were now no longer composed of elected people's representatives but of representatives of interest groups. From this time on, parliamentary majority decisions were no longer made by ballot. Balloting was replaced by the principle of consent (*musyawarah untuk mufakat*). Should a discussion not end in agreement, the decision was left to the head of the *daerah* who represented the central government.[24] Shortly before Soekarno's fall from power (1965) and the replacement of the 'Old Order' (Orde Lama) by the 'New Order' (Orde Baru), the judicially sanctioned strengthening of central power was reinforced by a presidential decree. Hence for the furtherance of the unity and entirety of the Indonesian State took precedence.

The failed *coup d'état* of 30 September 1965 (GESTAPU), initiated by progressive revolutionaries, led to bloody disputes between 'powers maintaining the state' and 'atheists and enemies of the New Order'. In Java and Bali, the arguments degenerated into a massacre, the frenzied killings bringing unimaginable grief to the inhabitants.[25] Thousands and thousands designated as communists were murdered – amongst them many agricultural labourers and share-croppers who had been encouraged by the Indonesian Communist Party (PKI) to assert their rights under the Agrarian Basic Law of 1960 (Unsur-Unsur Pokok Agraria: UUPA) and occupy land belonging to their landlords. With the situation running out of control, the opportunity was taken to settle old scores within and between village communities with a *keris* or lance. According to Balinese informants, armed groups – the leader carrying a *barong*-mask recharged with magic power – invaded 'hostile' *banjar* at night, massacring their inhabitants: women, children, the young and old. Less than three years earlier, a natural catastrophe in the form of a volcanic eruption had brought suffering and distress to the Island of the Gods (see chapter 1, p. 13). This time it was emotional outbreaks that brought Bali to the edge of anarchy. Hunger, grief and despair marked the situation there, as the first hotel of international standard, the Hotel Bali Beach in Sanur (financed with the help of Japanese war indemnity), opened its doors in 1966.

Tourism and the Process of Modernization

In 1890, on the occasion of the Paris World Exhibition, performances by dancers and musicians from Java brought the art and culture of the contemporary Dutch Indies to visitors' attention. They inspired musicians such as Claude Debussy to write impressionistic compositions. Although it lies on the southern edge of the South China Sea, Bali soon became the embodiment of a South Sea island, an island of cosmologically anchored culture where the graceful Balinese danced to the exotic sounds of the *gamelan* against a backdrop of temples, the very antithesis of the industrial prototype of the western world. In the 1920s, Bali was visited by a few hundred tourists a year; in the 1930s by a few thousand. They used to stay either on a cruise ship, anchored in Padang Bay, aboard the weekly KPM steamship that called at the port of Buleleng, or in resthouses for Dutch officials. The first hotel – the famous 'Bali Hotel' in Denpasar – was ready to accommodate guests from 1928. Sightseeing was limited to a few standard excursions by car. After two or three days the tourists left Bali for their next destination. Globetrotters, artists and anthropologists settled in Bali for shorter or longer periods. Their paintings,[26] photographic albums and books[27] tended to confirm the image of a paradisiacal dream island. So it was only logical that in the course of the economic liberalization of Indonesia after General Suharto's official seizure of power (1968), the smallest province became the blueprint for the opening up of the Republic of Indonesia for tourism.

The first Indonesian Five-Year Development Plan (1969–74) stressed the importance of international tourism as a factor in Indonesian economic development. On behalf of the government, the French consultancy firm SCETO drafted a concept for the development of tourism in Bali, the main idea being to minimize the negative results of tourist activities on Balinese culture, while at the same time not endangering the profitability of the tourist industry.[28] This idea is remarkable for three reasons. First, the master plan provided for new first-class hotels to be concentrated in the 425-hectare tourist resort of Nusa Dua, close to Ngurah Rai international airport, so that possible negative effects on Balinese culture would be spatially confined. Secondly, the majority of publications in Bali relevant to tourism caught on to this key idea. Thirdly, the consideration within planning of the negative effects of tourism preceded the worldwide debate on the issue. The inference that the economic results of tourism are mainly advantageous but the socio-cultural effects are undesirable represents the quintessence of the debate on tourism during the last three decades. This dichotomy is based on the assumption that tourism impinges upon a static, receptive, closed society and culture, and is the most important trigger (although not the only reason) for change, which is judged to be negative, above all in the cultural sphere. An oversimplification of this kind leads directly to an overestimation of the effects of tourism. In fact, in regional and national contexts, tourism is only one of several reasons for economic and social change. In contrast to tourism, which originally appeared only

Plate 42   Weaving weft ikat *(endek) on a treadle loom*

in certain places, the consequences of integration into the market economy and the state affect the whole island.

One of the symptoms of Indonesian economic growth and the increasing integration of the population is the growing number of domestic tourists. Urbanization processes and the development of a middle class have awakened new ambitions and needs, such as to travel and spend holidays abroad. But heavy taxes on leaving the country[29] have prompted many Indonesians to take holidays in their home country. Popularized by foreign tourists, Bali has been granted special favours. It looks as if the region of Denpasar–Nusa Dua will develop into a kind of 'home' resort for those members of the Javanese upper class living in large cities. Weekend flights from Jakarta to Bali are usually fully booked. Direct contacts facilitate decision-making when it comes to investing or building a second home on Bali.

Development trends since the opening of the international airport (1969), the number of tourists and the Gross Regional Domestic Product (GRDP) of the province of Bali give some

Plate 43 *Mimpi sedih – Miserable Dream . . .*

idea of the meaning of tourism for the Balinese regional economy. Whilst in 1970 only 46,200 foreign tourists visited the

Table 8.1 Distribution of Gross Regional Domestic Product (GRDP) by industrial origin, 1969, 1984 and 1990 (at current market prices)(%)

Industry	1969		1984		1990	
1 Agriculture (including fishery and forestry)	59.4		42.4		34.7	
2 Quarrying	0.6		0.7		0.3	
3 Manufacturing	1.7		4.4		5.3	
4 Electricity and water supply	0.1		0.8		1.2	
5 Construction	5.2		6.3		4.9	
6 Trade, hotels and restaurants:	12.2		15.9		21.4	
Trade		10.6		11.15		13.6
Hotels, guest-houses and restaurants		1.6		4.76		7.8
7 Transportation and communication	3.2		9.2		11.4	
8 Banking and other financial intermediaries	1.9		2.2		3.6	
9 Ownership of dwellings	2.1		0.9		0.7	
10 General government and defence	4.1		8.1		7.3	
11 Services	9.5		9.2		9.2	
Total	100		100		100	
Rupiah, at current market prices	32 billion		1,092 billion		3,018 billion	

Sources: Kantor Statistik Propinsi Bali, *Statistik Bali: Statistical Yearbook of Bali: 1989* (Denpasar, 1990: 308f); *1990* (Denpasar, 1991: 308f); *1991* (Denpasar, 1992: 360f)

Island of the Gods, there were 334,600 foreign and an estimated 300,000 Indonesian guests in 1984. In 1992, a total of 2.5 million tourists spent their holidays on Bali. Adjusted to the price level of 1975, the GRDP of Bali amounted to 99 billion rupiah in 1969 and to 425 billion rupiah in 1984 – a fourfold increase within fifteen years.[30] The Balinese economy expanded at 9.8 per cent real growth per annum between 1971 and 1980, that is, more vigorously than Indonesia as a whole (7.5 per cent per annum). Table 8.1 shows the structure of the Balinese GRDP at current prices for the years 1969, 1984 and 1990.

The transportation and communication sector grew by 360 per cent between 1969 and 1990, and the general government and defence sector nearly doubled. In the same way, the area of trade, hotels and restaurants enjoyed average growth. The increase in mobility discernible in the development of the GRDP, the increasing importance of manufacturing and the phenomenon of administrative expansion are all indicators of an increasing integration into the totality of the Indonesian and international economic circuit. This can be verified by the value of exported Balinese goods (amongst other things), which has increased from US$15 million in 1979 to US$42 million in 1985 and (up to) US$225 million in 1991. At the same time, the absolute export value of agricultural products (excluding fish and sea products) has fallen slightly, from US$16.9 million in 1985 to US$15.9 million in 1991, while the percentage declined from 40.2 per cent to 7.0 per cent during this period. The export of handicraftgoods and garments has increased by leaps and bounds. Whilst the export value of the former increased from US$5.7 million in 1985 to US$42.9 million in 1991, the increased importance of garment exports, which rose from US$15.8 million in 1985 to 8.7 times that figure in 1991 (i.e. to US$ 138.1 million) is even more obvious. The clothing industry contributed 61.3 per cent to the total export value of the province of Bali in 1990.[31] Profiting from direct tourist contact, it superseded coffee in 1981 as the most profitable export product. In today's Bali, fashion is created and produced not only for Indonesia's large cities but also for overseas markets. The design is created by collaboration between foreigners and Indonesians and often has little to do with traditional patterns. Production, however, exhibits a typically Balinese component: it could only have originated in the touristically accessible south Bali. Only there, attracted by Balinese culture (and by tropical beaches), could Euro-American creativity and know-how interact with Balinese creative energy and manual dexterity, enabling contemporary trends to emerge. The international airport guarantees connections with foreign countries and jobs are welcome, though poorly paid.

The total contribution of tourism to the Balinese economy can only be estimated approximately, for its share extends beyond the official figure of 7.8 per cent for 1990. This percentage refers only to the operative phase of the tourist trade, but there are important additional backward and forward linkages. For example, the amount of garments and arts and handicraft goods sold is not the only factor that depends on the number of visitors; the same applies to proceeds from the delivery of vegetables, fruit, flowers, meat, fish and other seafood to the tourist establishments. There is hardly a branch of the economy which is not associated with the booming tourist trade. Estimates of the tourism-related contribution to the GDRP give figures of 20–30 per cent while the direct and indirect effects on employment is assessed as one-eleventh of the employed population.[32]

Conspicuous is the fact that in the last ten years the concept of the spatial concentration of tourists has ceased to be observed. What had not been anticipated by the planners was that not only would the number of high-spending 'package-tour'-type tourists rise but that there would also be more low-budget individual tourists, the so-called 'hippies'. The latter were not unwelcome to some Balinese who had voiced criticism that 'the development of high-class "star" hotels does not guarantee equality if it turns out that the larger the hotel the greater the tendency to import its daily necessities. Equalization doesn't mean building four-star hotels in every regency in Bali.'[33]

That the Balinese take both these customer categories into account is evident from the way both new hotels in the higher price categories and simple guest houses are being built within and beyond the original planning zones. Wherever a potential for tourism is suspected, speculators (mostly non-Balinese known as Orang Jakarta ('Jakarta people'), appear on scene. This happens in the agriculturally disadvantaged zones of the coastal region from Karangasem to the beaches of north and west Bali, but also in the pass regions of Kintamani and Bedugul. Poor peasants gladly sell or lease their land when the net proceeds lie far above its agricultural value. A process is thus introduced which has consequences for the price of land in the agriculturally favoured zones. For only in this way can those who have come into money fulfil their wish to become rice-growers, especially when they can outbid the customary local price for *sawah* plots. Taking into account both the rapid expansion of tourist demand and the threatened danger of a shortage of land (and the associated escalation of land prices), the government of the province has decided to open up fifteen regions for tourism, but to give over not more than 0.7 per cent of the total area of Bali to touristic infrastructure.[34]

Cheap tourist accomodation can be found in villages such as Candi Dasa, Lovina, Ubud, Kuta and Legian, which have developed into secondary tourist centres. Guest lodging can also be found in family compounds or – especially popular – in the huge palaces of noble families, where parts of the buildings have been transformed into bungalows. For example, there is the Puri Sukawati in Ubud, whose owner – like many European nobleman – finances the costly upkeep of his castle by accepting paying guests. A further possibility for creating tourist accomodation consists in the construction of proper guest houses. In this case, a landowner builds some 'home stays' furnished with minor conveniences such as a lavatory. Higher standards are usually offered in holiday homes financed by foreigners and built on the property of a Balinese. When the foreign homeowner is absent (which is true for most of the year), the landowner asks for the right to rent out these houses. The construction and maintenance of these bungalows and catering for guests is in any case entrusted to Balinese people.

The question of social and cultural costs connected with tourism arises first of all in villages which have developed into popular destinations for low-budget mass tourism, for example Kuta and Legian. Until 1967 they were sleepy fishing and peasant villages on one of the most beautiful beaches of the island. In the eyes of many cultured Balinese, they have now acquired a reputation as an 'ugly part of Bali', with hundreds of places for accommodation, blaring discos, bars that hold beer-drinking competitions, nude swimming, and sometimes even drug-dealing and -consumption, prostitution and crime. 'How many more Kutas?' is a standard question posed by Balinese critics of further tourist promotion. But it is remarkable that the core of Kuta village, located one to two kilometres from the shore, has suffered less from cultural breakdown than might be imagined. On account of the higher income, not only have many temples been restored, but extensive religious ceremonies have been reactivated. What has, in fact, suffered severely is the image of foreign visitors, who the Balinese initially considered to be some kind of superior beings, but who are now clearly differentiated by their behaviour. Hence they sometimes become objects of ridicule, as this short extract from a contemporary drama performance in the 1980s (*drama gong*) illustrates. The dialogue is between the servant I Apel and the Prime Minister:

I Apel There is no country as beautiful as ours. The prime ministers, though, are old and incapable. I would make a better prime minister!

Prime Minister How sweetly you talk. [*Sarcastically*] You are clever!

I Apel Indeed I am! I have even acted as a guide to tourists. I have talked to them for an hour without stumbling.

Prime Minister What language did you speak?

I Apel I know English. I asked them: 'Where are you going?' I then told them that I was going to Kuta beach to watch the tourists *maleging* [swimming].

I Apel mispronounces the word 'swimming' and uses the Balinese word *maleging*, which means 'nude behinds'. The audience breaks into laughter, for in fact there are tourists who swim in the nude – and the villagers think they are very strange.

Even in the pre-war years visitors to Bali were worried about the influence of tourism on the island. Would it endanger the indigenous culture? For example, K. Helbig, a participant in an expedition arranged by the International Geographical Congress to the Dutch Indies in 1937, wrote: 'Serious dangers for the future lie most probably in tourism. May the Dutch administration be successful in educating and guiding the streams of tourists in such a manner, that tourism contributes as much as possible to the maintenance and as little as possible to the destruction of this reservation' (that is, Bali).[35] A much-discussed theme was and is the tourism-related commercialization of culture. That Balinese dances are performed for tourists, sacred symbols used to decorate hotels and restaurants, wood-carvings and paintings made by sometimes hurried mass-production, and religious ceremonies impaired by the presence of obtrusive strangers contributes to the negative aspects of tourism and is stigmatized by W.A. Hanna, in allusion to Hawaii, as the 'Waikikianization' of Bali.[36] Authors who reject tourism completely overlook the fact that the tourist trade can also contribute to the selective reinforcement of local traditions. The traditional roles of the Balinese as stonemasons, woodcarvers, musicians and dancers have been – at least partially – revived. They provide individuals, groups or *banjar* communities with additional income. At the same time the Balinese know very well how to differentiate between divine and secular addressees. In collaboration with Balinese who respect their *adat*, tourist authorities have divided the dances into three categories of decreasingly sacred and increasingly profane character. Dances of the third category are allowed to be performed in hotels. In the same way, the originally free access to sacred functions is being managed more selectively than before.

The prognosis that Bali's future economic prosperity will depend upon cultural production for tourism and that a post-industrial, service-orientated society will be established, with tourism rewarding the Balinese for what they do so well, namely arts and craftwork or the celebration of religious festivals and ceremonies,[37] is not quite correct and needs to be revised. As already mentioned, industrial production and the trades have developed decisively, while the revitalization of

Balinese dance and theatre arts has not been become a tourist priority. The annual cultural festivals held in Denpasar since 1979, presenting new creations of the conservatory and performances by dance and music groups from all over Bali, are not frequented by tourists, as was originally anticipated. They are mainly attended by local people, who completely fill the cultural centre every evening. Holidaymakers prefer the standardized, shorter version of dances which have been offered for many years and differ little from the folklore evenings in western tourist spots. Requests from tourists did in fact stimulate Balinese artists in the beginning, but music and dance (not so much painting and woodwork) are renewed and revived out of their own traditions, and new creations are measured against the reactions and judgement of the indigenous population. Such creations as the now extremely popular *drama gong*, with its modern elements, underline the dynamic quality of Balinese culture and show clearly that cultural influence is a many-tiered process which can be explained neither mono-causally nor as running exclusively in one direction.

Similar ideas to those regarding the 'erosion of indigenous culture' are advanced by critics of tourism in connection with changes in the Balinese social structure. Western authors think they can distinguish serious effects, such as 'a gradual loss of concern for mutual aid activities . . . within the village or ward';[38] 'old customs such as *goto-royong*[39] . . . dying out';[40] or even 'transmitted forms of solidarity of the autochthonous society such as *goto-royong* [*sic*], a form of collective work, [being] destroyed'.[41] Where these statements can be substantiated at all, it is only with reference to the fact that members of the *banjar* fulfil their obligations by way of monetary contributions rather than by means of their own work, as was formerly the case. This statement is at least partially correct. Immigrants to the rapidly growing capital city of Denpasar (1991: 328, 150 inhabitants) often exhibit only minimal achievements because they still feel attached to their native village and fulfil their obligations there. Where *banjar* are ethnically mixed, they seem in time to resemble ward associations, organizations upon which the administration leans to carry out its duties. The dissipation of formerly duty-bound neighbourly assistance (*tolong-menolong*) and community work for the benefit of the *banjar* and village community (*gotong royong*) is a result of urbanization processes, which have led amongst other things to a separation of native village, place of residence and work place.

In Balinese cities it can be observed that the daily offerings to appease demons and venerate the gods, normally carefully prepared by women and girls, are often bought hastily at the market before going to work. Nevertheless, social time has still not given way entirely to material interests. Not only is there more money available (above all in the tourist centres) for matters concerning the temple and religious ceremonies, but many Balinese still do time-consuming work for the community, sometimes to the frustration of modernization-hungry officials and entrepreneurs. H. Tjandrasari, in his article about social and cultural influences on small businesses in the clothing industry, praises the enormous dexterity of the Balinese, but also points out that

the social, cultural and religious rituals in Bali seriously affect the small garment industries in Bali in a negative manner. The influence

Plate 44   *Learning different systems of values: the Siddha Mahan School in Sidemen, Karangasem*

of norms, of tradition and religion is much stronger than those of laws and regulations in local industries. By disobeying the work rules, workers decrease productivity. It is difficult to make production planning because of weak working discipline among workers in industry[42]

Even though the Balinese debate over the conflict between tourism and culture has lost much of the explosive power it had in the 1970s, its importance should not be underestimated. It has contributed substantially to a reconsideration of cultural and religious values and strengthened the Balinese image of themselves within the multi-ethnic Indonesian society. Since the middle of the 1980s, Balinese anthropologists have named the general socio-economic processes of modernization, and not tourism alone, as the crucial change-inducing factor.[43] They allude to the fact that the measures taken towards unity ('*indonesianisasi*'), as ordained by the central government, refer to geographical space and not to the presence of tourists. Similarly, aspirations to assert 'the overall Balinese individuality' ('*balisasi*') within the framework of Indonesian nation-building can also be found on the next-lower level of government. *Balisasi*, introduced by the government of the province, takes effect in such areas as the reform of the Hindu belief (through to the purified Agama Hindu) as well as in the revision and reformulation of previously divergent village statutes (*awig-awig*), which are being made compatible with the constitution of the Republic of Indonesia and the government's ideas on modernization. Irrespective of tourism, transformation is continuing, and the members of the once strongly ritualized, communal society are being guided more and more by individual, profit-orientated thinking.[44]

But even though the earlier *adat* diversity has been curtailed, the will to fulfil common sacred duties is still firmly rooted in the people. Visitors to Bali at the turn of the millenium will find neither an exotic reservation nor a paradise. They will find an active society with a culture that is not simply aligned to the desires of foreigners. It is a society that is continually seeking its own identity within changing frames of reference.

Notes

Chapter 1: The Land and its People

1 The literal translation of Indonesia would be thus 'the Indian's island area'. See Jones (1973: 93–118).
2 See Röll (1979: 7–10).
3 Embassy of the Republic of Indonesia, Berne (1992: III. 12).
4 Uhlig (1988: 487f).
5 Geertz (1963: 12–15).
6 Nothofer and Pampus (1988: XIIIf).
7 Ramseyer (1983: 6).
8 Nothofer and Pampus (1988: XIIIf).
9 The second administrative level (*Kabupaten*) in urban areas is called *Kotamadya* and is headed by a *walikota*.
10 Putut Tri Husodo, 'Fatwa untuk Sebuah Pura Tua', *Tempo*, 9 (1990), 85.
11 See P. N. Virama Karya, 'Masterplan', Jakarta, 1971 (unpublished).
12 Kantor Statistik Propinsi Bali (1988: 5f).
13 Leemann (1979: 34–9).

Chapter 2: Pre-colonial Bali

1 Stuart-Fox (1987: 300–3).
2 Heine-Geldern (1932: 543–619).
3 Bellwood (1985: 16).
4 Ibid.: 43–68.
5 Soejono (1979). The excavations done in 1963, 1964 and 1973 were supervised by R. P. Soejono, then head of the Archaeological Service Bali Branch. The excavation site was 137.5 m², at a depth of 1.75–3.25 m.
6 R. P. Soejono, 'A late prehistoric burial system in Indonesia: additional notes on Gilimanuk, Bali', in *Conference Papers on Archaeology in Southeast Asia* (Hong Kong: University Museum and Art Gallery, University of Hong Kong, 1995), pp. 181–9.

7   The earliest evidence of cultivated rice comes from the mid-Yangtze valley, where presumed non-Sinitic peoples were the first systematically to cultivate this inconspicuous meadow-grass some 8,000 years ago. As now, there were probably two predominant cultivation systems in Taiwan, the Philippines and western Indonesia: wet-rice cultivation and shifting cultivation of dry rice.

8   Bellwood (1985: 98).

9   Radiocarbon dating suggests settlement between 3000 and 2500BC.

10 Soejono (1979: 195–7).

11 Bernet Kempers (1991: 13–15).

12 Heger (1902).

13 Bellwood (1985: 292).

14 For the finds of Sembiran, see Ardika and Bellwood (1991).

15 The 'Moon of Pejeng' can be viewed *in situ* in the innermost district of the old imperial temple of Pura Penataran Sasih (Intaran, Pejeng). For a detailed description, see Bernet Kempers (1991: 16–31). Pictures, including details, can be found in Ramseyer (1977: figs 6, 22, 23).

16 Ardika and Bellwood (1991: 229–30).

17 Goris (1954).

18 However, the Han Chinese form an exception. They made North Vietnam a province of their empire in 111BC, and were subsequently very active in early Metal Age trade.

19 Glover (1979: 167–8). For maritime trade and state development in South-East Asia, see Hall (1985).

20 Goris (1954: Bundle A, Old Balinese documents).

21 The Indian *saka* year is 78 years behind the Gregorian calendar. The Old Balinese edicts are thus dated *saka* 804–836.

22 Danandjaja (1985: 20–1).

23 The use of masked and shadow plays for the ideological indoctrination of villagers was thus not invented by the Majapahit regime and its Javano-Balinese vassals in Bali; it was a far older instrument of East Javanese policy.

24 Calon Arang, a drama with an exorcistic purpose, tells the story of exorcist priest Mpu Baradah's battle against the mighty Calon Arang, a witch and protégée of the goddess Durga. During the dramatic finale of the exorcism, Mpu Bharada and Calon Arang often turn into Barong and Rangda, the embodiments of white and black magic.

25 Mpu Kuturan is regarded as a religious reformer. The Kahyangan Tiga temple system still operative today is, for example, traced back to him. According to this system, every Adat village must possess at least three temples – Pura Desa with Bale Agung, the village temple with assembly pavilion for the village council; Pura Puseh, the temple for worshipping the heavenly deities and deified ancestors; and Pura Dalem, the temple of the dead (cf. chapter 4, pp. 90–1).

26 Guermonprez (1987: vol. 142).

27 The ancestors of the inhabitants of Tenganan Pegeringsingan, for example, are often associated with human sacrifice and cannibalism. Despite concrete, scientific proof to the contrary, the rumour that human blood is used

to dye the renowned double-*ikat* textiles produced in this village evidently cannot be eradicated. Cf. Urs Ramseyer, 'Clothing, ritual and society in Tenganan Pegeringsingan (Bali)', *Verhandlungen Naturforschende Gesellschaft in Basel*, 95 (1984), 191–241.

28 *Nagarakretagama*, Canto 49, verses 4a–d and Canto 79, verse 3. The conquest of Bali occurred during the reign of the queen regent Tribhuvana. Her son Hayam Wuruk succeeded to the throne as Rajasanagara in AD1350.

29 In contrast to the higher-ranking Satria Dalem, the descendants of the Arya clans are called Satria Jawa and can be recognized by the titles I Gusti, I Gusti Ayu or Anak Agung (cf. chapter 4, pp. 76–8).

30 The male descendants of the Satria Dalem bear the title I Dewa or Cokorda, the female ones I Dewa Ayu.

31 See Putra (1991). Putra provides the first account of the 'History of the Dalem' in the Indonesian language, from a palm-leaf manuscript belonging to Jero Kanginan, Sidemen. I should like to thank I Dewa Gede Catra, who viewed five different versions of the Babad Dalem, compared them in terms of both content and textual criticism, and was kind enough to share his knowledge with me in the course of many conversations.

32 Urs Ramseyer, 'Songkèt, golden threads, caste and privilege', in Hauser-Schäublin et al. (1991: 33–40).

33 Vickers (1989: 11–20).

34 See Geertz (1980).

35 Vickers (1989: 77–130).

Chapter 3: Agriculture, Crafts and Spheres of Exchange

1 Raffles (1817: vol. II, appendix IX, p. ccxxxiii).

2 Zollinger (1845: 11f). It can be concluded that over a thousand years before this, rice from Bali was already well known, as the Chinese used to call at the island of 'Paali' as early as the seventh century and referred to it as the 'rice island' (cf. Agung, 1991: xi).

3 Zollinger (1845: 45; transl. A. Leemann).

4 Citation F. A. Liefrinck, in Goris (1984: 82).

5 Sang Amawa Bumi (Kawi language): a prince who possesses unrestricted power over his land. Even if this abstract claim is mostly understood in a figurative sense, it could, in the case of the subjection of a foreign area, have drastic consequences for those concerned (as, for example, following the Balinese conquest of Lombok in the seventeenth and eighteenth centuries) (cf. Röll and Leemann, 1987: 99–108).

6 Land owned by the village: *tanah desa*; in *banjar* possession: *tanah banjar*; land possessed by a temple: *laba pura*; land owned by certain groups of people: *tanah pauman*, etc.

7 Geertz (1980: 127f).

8 According to customary law, the mortgaging of land follows principles different from those in western countries in that the mortgager has to cede his plot to the mortgagee. The latter enjoys unrestricted usufruct over the mortgaged land until the mortgager has paid off his debts. Thus, the yields

produced by the mortgagee on the piece of land comply with the mortgage rate (i.e. the rate of interest charged by the creditor).

9   Raffles (1817: vol. II, appendix IX, p. ccxxxiv).

10 Kraan (1983: 320). In this connection, the question arises whether *subak* plots were ever in communal possession at all. Were not perhaps only uncultivated plots of land, allotments planted with trees (*kebun*), some fields under dry cultivation (*tegalan*) and fields supplied by dammed-up rainwater (*sawah tadah hujan*) subject to communal right of disposal? For example, in only the last two cases was it possible to grant usufructuaries, approximately equally sized allotments, on an annual rotation basis.

11 Even though serfdom is no longer tolerated in the constitution of the Republic of Indonesia, reminders of it can still be encountered today. When the author asked a servant at the palace of a nobleman his name, he explained that he was nameless because he 'belonged' to the Cokorda ('*punya Cokorda*').

12 Geertz (1980: 64f).

13 *Camput* = to be without successors. In societies with patrilineal filiation this has the same meaning as the absence of *male* successors. Land without any inheritors returned to the possession of the village in the case where the latter had the right of disposal over land within its boundaries.

14 Geertz (1980: 67).

15 Indonesian *adat* legal scholars stress the fact that share-cropping contracts are not to be considered as tenancy agreements, but must be interpreted as working contracts only, containing regulations concerning the ratio of distribution of harvested crops and work obligations. Consequently, *panyakap* are listed according to the portion of the harvests that they have to deliver (e.g. *panandu* = a share-cropper who is pledged to deliver one-half of the harvest). On *sawah*, which can be watered during the rainy season only, the assignment of part of the harvest is valid only for wet-rice, but not for other useful plants (*palawija*) cultivated by the share-cropper between two rice cycles. According to customary law, the landowner is entitled to withdraw the right to cultivation of his *panyakap* at the end of each vegetation cycle.

16 Geertz (1980: 175).

17 *Pauman* land is entered in the land register today. As the areas are mostly modest (usually less than one hectare), there is no friction with the land reform regulations of 1960. All members of the group are entitled to shares, even those not resident in that place. If land is awarded to a clan (*dadia*), then in many cases a part of the harvest will be donated to the clan temple (*pura dadia*).

18 Similar to the *laba pura* of the Balinese Hindu, lands associated with endowments of Muslims (*waqf*) are not subject either to the area limitations of the modern Indonesian agrarian law or to any state tax. Strict specifications apply only in respect of the registration of such properties, their alienation and above all, in the case of *waqf* land, the use of the profits.

19 Those obliged to provide royal service are called *pangayah dalem*. They were in a certain sense like *pauman* members, obliged to *ngayahang ka*

puri (i.e. to work without pay for the palace). On the other hand, the king felt bound to invite the *pangayah dalem* and *pauman* members to royal ceremonies and to entertain them. Those holding *bukti* lands (*bukti* = proof) were designated for village service (*ngayahang ka desa*). Cf. Schaareman (1986: 88f).

20 Korn (1932: 228).
21 Geertz (1980: 176).
22 Reported by Indonesian television TV RI, 15 September 1982.
23 Boon (1977: 18, 40, 94).
24 Geertz (1980: 213).
25 Wage-labour was looked down upon by many *adat*-conscious Balinese right up until the twentieth century. If work during the most labour-intensive time of the agricultural cycle, such as the rice harvest, could not be mastered by mutual assistance alone, it was transferred to 'harvest-clubs' or individuals who were paid for their effort with 1/11 (*nyolasin*) of the cut sheaves.
26 It is striking that, with the exception of the cattle-trade, the market has remained mainly women's domain up to the present day. Whether this phenomenon rests on the fact that women are subject to less-rigid social control than men would be worth examination. The fact is that such activities, which would be concomitant with a loss of face for men, are willingly devolved upon women and children.
27 Zollinger (1845: 4, 15, 16; transl. A. Leemann).
28 Raffles (1817: II. ccxxxi, appendix K).
29 According to Balinese *adat* law, those living in coastal areas were entitled to appropriate the cargo of stranded vessels and clear away wrecks (*hak tawan karang*), an old legal conception which led to numerous conflicts with the colonial government, providing the pretext for the Dutch conquest of south Bali at the beginning of the twentieth century.
30 Ardika and Bellwood (1991: 221–32).
31 Wälty (1995).
32 Münster (1628: 1604).
33 Kraan (1983: 329–34).
34 Zollinger (1845: 7f; transl. A. Leemann).
35 Geertz (1980: 88f).
36 Ibid.: 202–4.
37 Hanna (1976: 50–9); Geertz (1980: 92–4, 204–10).

Chapter 4: Social Organization

1 Korn (1932).
2 Geertz (1959: 991).
3 Guermonprez (1980: 37; transl. A. Leemann).
4 Schaareman (1986: 141).
5 Howe (1989).
6 Alisjahbana (1966: 3–5).
7 The first known Balinese royal edict, dated 882, mentions the king's order to build a Buddhist monastery together with a hospice for travelling

traders near today's village of Kintamani. It was only after the beginning of the eleventh century that Siwaitic priests took the place of Buddhist monks as royal advisers. Cf. Wälty (1995b).

8 In the pre-Majapahit period, Balinese kings – to whom Mountain Balinese had to pay tribute and to render services – resided in villages on the slope, as at Pejeng, for example.

9 In the pre-Majapahit period, the involvement of the Kintamani region in interregional and interinsular trade is supported by documentary evidence. Products like onions, garlic, dye and cotton were conveyed to the fortified harbour village of Julah on the north coast whilst imported goods were sold at busy market places in the highlands. As taxes levied by the king had to be paid in money, and in some villages plots of land have been tradeable goods, this is evidence of an early monetarization of the economy in the Batur region. Thus, the assumption that at this time the Mountain Balinese in the Batur region lived on the basis of subsistence has to be rejected (cf. Wälty, 1995b).

It is to be supposed that due to the shift of the new political and economic power centres to the southern lowlands and for reasons of rivalry between power-hungry rulers, the Kintamani trade route and in with this the market places in the Batur region lost of their earlier importance from the fifteenth until the nineteenth century. This process of marginalization may have stimulated farmers to tend in their agricultural activities towards a more subsistence-orientated production. Salt, produced at the north coast and carried from Tianyar over steep tracks to market places in the Kintamani region, continued to be exchanged for highland products.

10 Howe (1989: 56f).

11 See also the process of the development of *adat* law from the usufruct of peasants on land in communal ownership to private ownership of land in Sudiyat (1981: 1–5).

12 It is however possible that members of mountain villages occasionally claim to be members of several descent groups.

13 Guermonprez (1984: 95, 393f, 396).

14 Leemann (1989: 9f).

15 Cf. Leemann (1976: 27–65).

16 Cf. the analagous misinterpretation through 'folk etymology' of the word *boda* by 'advanced' Sasak, who derive *boda* from the Indonesian word *bodoh* (dumb) or even from the Sasak word *buduh* (crazy). Discrimination is similar in the identification of the Sasak Boda as 'wild man of the woods' or 'mountain man'.

17 *Bedaulu (syn. beda muka)* = 'different head'. Descendants of the Dalem Bedaulu still carry the name *Muka* (= face) today.

18 The section concerning Bali's early history and the Bali Aga follows the argumentation of Samuel Wälty's PhD thesis (1995b) and his paper (1995a).

19 Transcriptions and Dutch translations of royal edicts issued between 882 and 1025 are contained in Goris (1954).

20 Cf. Giddens (1984: 33, 180ff). Social integration implies reciprocity of practices between actors in circumstances of co-presence, understood as continuities in and disjunctions of encounters (ibid.: 376). System integration implies reciprocity between actors or collectivities across extended time-space, outside conditions of co-presence (ibid.: 377).

21 Ibid.: 183. Giddens's term 'symbolic order' corresponds with the meaning of *adat* (pp. 74–5).

22 Wälty (1995a: 9ff).

23 Reference to the Majapahahit civilization is to be found in *Nagarakretagama*, a work written in verse form by the Javanese poet and historiographer Mpu Prapanca in the second half of the fifteenth century. A further source is the *Pararaton* (Slametmulyana, *Nagarakretagama dan tafsir sejarahnya*, bhratara, Jakarta, 1979), which was written later, in prose, probably between 1478 and 1486.

24 Hanna (1976: 3).

25 Jan Lodewijk Swellengrebel, 'Introduction', in Swellengrebel (1984: 22).

26 *Wau rauh* (Balinese) = 'just arrived'. In Lombok, Danghyang Nirartha is known under the name Danghyang Sangupati, in Sumbawa under the name Pangeran Semeru.

27 The names and numbers of Danghyang Nirartha's daughters and sons vary according to the source consulted. Differences in the names can occur, for example, because persons can take on new names on the occasion of the ordination ceremony for a priest (*resi yadnya*).

28 Sugriwa (1990: 59–68).

29 '*Disengguh padanda*' (Balinese) = 'mistaken for a priest'. Therefore the title group *sengguhu* expresses this mistaken identity.

30 The version of the Balinese Research Team on the history of Ida Hyang Nirartha on the formation of the title group *sengguhu* differs in time and place, but not in the basic idea of the mixing up of a *sudra* with a Javanese Brahman priest as beneficiary and the acknowledgement of the title group for the conducting of ceremonies to appease chthonic powers (*upacara percaruan*). According to the interpretation of the above-mentioned research team, the Javanese priest Danghyang Nirartha was supposed to have made a stop in the village of Kapal on his missionary travels through Bali, Lombok and Sumbawa (fifteenth and sixteenth centuries). Here he learned from its *bandesa* that I Guto used to be in charge of *pujawali* ceremonies in the Pura Sada. As a result, Danghyang Nirartha strictly forbade the conducting of divine rituals (*dewa yadnya*) but allowed I Guto and his descendants (as *sengguhu*) to lead the ceremonies to exorcize demons.

31 The principal of the Kantor Agama Hindu in Denpasar substantiates the chicken meat taboo for *padanda* in that the transference of the bad character of clucking, quarrelsome hens must be avoided by the priest. Ducks, which are considered by the Balinese to be peaceful and clever birds, are classified more positively.

32 Schulte Nordholt (1986: 12f.).

33 *Buk padan* (Balinese) = 'dust of the feet'. The same meaning is inherent in

the rule of address for important personalities: Paduka – literally translated as 'shoe' – originates from the Kawi language. Cf. during President Soekarno's presidency: 'Paduka Yang Mulia Presiden' or during the colonial period, 'Paduka Kanjeng Tuan Besar Residen' for Dutch officials.

34 A Balinese who is aware of his *adat* responsibilities has to pay his respects to the 'three teachers of wisdom' (*triguru wisesa*): his parents, teachers and ruler.

35 Geertz and Geertz (1975: 5ff).

36 Ibid.: 14ff).

37 Schaareman (1986: 45f).

38 When a commoner dies, the whole village falls into a condition of impurity (*sebel*). When a nobleman dies, this extends to a whole region. This period of impurity lasts about 25 days in the east Balinese village of Jangu, during which a whole series of religious ritual events are taboo.

39 *Nyepi* = 'to remain quiet'. On Nyepi day no island inhabitant may leave his compound (nor a tourist his hotel). Nyepi, the day of physical inactivity, is the day for self-communion and contemplation and initiates a new year. As it is generally understood that passions and illnesses afflict humans in the form of heat, it is forbidden under threat of punishment to light fires on New Year's Day.

40 Geertz and Geertz (1975: 17f).

41 Schaareman (1986: 44).

42 Geertz and Geertz (1975: 16).

43 Hobart (1980: 85, 102); Guermonprez (1984: 384).

44 Schaareman (1986: 82).

45 Occasionally – as in the village Sempidi – the *Pura Puseh* and the *Pura Desa* are combined in one temple.

46 Tarnutzer (1993: 165–71).

47 Cf. chapter 1, p. 8: Administrative hierarchy of an Indonesian province.

48 Geertz and Geertz (1975: 20).

49 Schaareman (1986: 121).

50 Bundschu (1987: 41).

51 Ibid.: 43f).

52 Schaareman (1986: 121).

Chapter 5: Religion and Beliefs in Practice

1 Boon (1976: 192).

2 Geertz and Geertz (1975: 94–102). Old Balinese outside the 'three-caste' system (*triwangsa*) are known as *anak jaba* (*jaba* = outside).

3 The most comprehensive information about older and more recent legal views can be found in: Pudja (1963), and *Pengantar tentang perkawinan menurut hukum Hindu* (Jakarta: Maya Sari 1975).

4 Hooykaas (1974: 93–128).

5 For the role of the Kanda Mpat and Panca Mahabuta in the classification systems of Hindu-Balinese medicine, see Weck (1937).

6 Putra (n.d.: 29–33).
7 Hooykaas (1960).
8 Hauser-Schäublin et al. (1991: 68–9).
9 Ibid.: 72, figs 5.13 and 5.14.
10 Leeman (1992: 164). This article includes descriptions and analyses of various *rites de passage*. For southern Bali, particularly Sanur, see the monograph Mershon (1971).
11 See Wirz (1928: 3–8). David J. Stuart-Fox (1987) writes about the special conditions in Besakih; for information on burials among various Pande groups, see Guermonprez (1987).
12 See chapter 4, pp. 87–90.
13 Wikarman (1993).
14 See the comprehensive monograph Stuart-Fox (1987).
15 Maquet (1986: 51–5).
16 For a detailed description of *bebangkit*, see Stuart- Fox (1974: 7–34).
17 Brinkgreve (1987: esp. 149).
18 Bandem and deBoer (1981: 1).
19 Zoete and Spiess (1973: 56).
20 A daytime puppet show may also be associated with the *sudamala* rite, when purifactory water is made; see the next chapter when the shadow play is discussed (p. 146).

Chapter 6: Myth and the Artistic Tradition

1 Hinzler (1981: 29).
2 Zoetmulder (1974: 68).
3 The prince and his beloved may also represent tribal moieties that belong to a pristine indigenous organization; see Pigeaud (1967: I. 207).
4 See Stutterheim (1935: 7).
5 Geertz (1973: 380–4).
6 Hobart (1987: 41–2).
7 Zoetmulder (1974: 77–8).
8 Zoetmulder (1965: 269).
9 Ramseyer (1977: 59).
10 Zurbuchen (1987: 92).
11 Ibid.: 13.
12 Geertz (1970: 103).
13 Scholars may classify these genres somewhat differently, cf. Bandem and deBoer (1981: 75–96).
14 For a summary of the shadow theatre's origin and historical background, see Holt (1967: 128–31).
15 See Chinkah (1969).
16 Sukawati in the regency of Gianyar is particularly well known for its *dalang*. This is also the regency where the author did research on the shadow play.
17 Hooykaas (1973: 160).
18 Ibid.

19 The area focused on here is south Bali. In the north of Bali there seems to be a variant form of the shadow play, see Hinzler (1975).

20 Javanese shadow-play puppets are more stylized than their Balinese counterparts. This may be as a result of the Islamic prescription of image-making, see Holt (1967: 135).

21 For a more detailed discussion of the symbolism of puppet iconography, see Hobart (1987: 82–122).

22 McPhee (1970: 146); on the *gender* music, see also McPhee (1966: 201–33).

23 A percussion group, *batel*, is added to the *gender* quartet for plays based on the *Ramayana*, ibid.: 201.

24 This was sung by the *dalang* Ida Bagus Gede from Bonkasa; ibid.: 229.

25 Cf. Hooykaas (1973: 25).

26 Ibid.: 51.

27 On the artist as 'worldmaker', parallel to the scientist, see Goodman (1985: 102).

28 As dialogues are highly idiomatic and repetitive, they are paraphrased.

29 Steiner (1975: 142).

30 See Zoetmulder (1974: 210).

31 Bandem and deBoer (1981: 49).

32 Ibid.: 65.

33 Ibid.: 95.

34 The last mask that appears in *topeng pajegan* is known as Sida Karya. It is a comic-demonic mask which is said to bring good fortune.

35 Zoete and Spies (1938: 191).

36 The precursors of the king are called *arya*, a title still used in Java by princes (ibid.: 138).

37 For a detailed discussion of *gambuh* music, see McPhee (1966: 113–39).

38 Ramseyer (1986: 229).

39 Bandem and deBoer (1981: 90).

40 The verse form of Galuh is *semarandana*.

41 On the *sangging*, see Forge (1987: 7).

42 On Balinese contemporary painting, see Djelantik (1986) and Ramseyer (1995).

43 Vickers points out that those who 'win' in the Balinese cockfight do so because they are right. The same can be said of the more virtuous group in any dance-drama performance. See Vickers (1991).

Chapter 7: The Persuasive Artistry of the Healer

1 Additional information for this chapter was obtained during Angela Hobart's research year in Bali in 1993. This was supported by grants from the British Academy and Social Science Nuffield Foundation, which are here gratefully acknowledged.

2 Obeyesekere (1985).

3 Turner (1964).

4 'Madness' is not dealt with here. It implies to the people weird, uncontrolled, even dangerous, behaviour and garbled or crude speech. 'Mad'

people may be accompanied to a healer, or a healer may visit them at home. There are also two mental hospitals in Bali.

5 Obeyesekere (1985); Lutz (1985).

6 Kleinmann (1980: 35–60).

7 Although the ensuing discussion is largely based on research in Gianyar, folk healers do not form homogeneous body and considerable variation exists in their knowledge and practices across the island. Throughout, clients' names have been changed.

8 Luh Ketut Suryani, 'Psychiatrist, Traditional Healer and Culture Integrated in Clinical Practice in Bali' (unpublished paper, 1990), p. 6.

9 It is interesting that with modernization and people's growing awareness of bacteria and viruses and x-rays, this category of natural or evident causes (i.e. *sekala*) is expanding.

10 Connor et al. (1986: 22).

11 Ibid.: 23.

12 Kat (1921).

13 Stutterheim (1956: esp. 117–21).

14 Hooykaas (1973: 16).

15 For more information on the contents of the medical manuscripts, see Weck (1976).

16 Cf. Parkin (1985: 59).

17 *Sarana* can be very expensive. The villagers with whom I worked pointed out that they were sure that President Suharto wore a ring with a protective 'weapon' which must have cost him at least one billion rupiah (about £30,000). After all, he had many enemies and so required protection.

18 Hooykaas (1980: 11).

19 Lovric (1990: 162).

20 Needham (1972: 35–6).

21 Quoted in Frank (1961: 137).

22 Ibid.: 325–30.

23 Kapferer (1979: 11).

24 Turner (1985: 295).

25 See Connor (1989: 261).

26 Frank (1961: 62).

27 For a detailed discussion of various types of trance or possession in Bali, see Belo (1960).

28 Maquet (1986).

29 See Dow (1986).

30 *Pitra* is the name given to the spirit of a person immediately after death, when still impure. Numerous rites are subsequently carried out. Once the spirit is purified, it is called *pitara*. Only after completion of the cremation rites does the spirit become a deified ancestor, *sang dewa hyang*, of his descent group and worshipped in the ancestor shrine.

31 The dialogue here is summarized and paraphrased. Such dialogues are often repetitive and at times obscure. It is based on the account of a relative of the bereaved family who is known for the keenness of his observations and who participated in the whole event.

32 For an eloquent narration and annotated translation of a complete trance séance in relation to a young boy's death in south Bali, see Connor et al. (1986: 88–172).

33 Lévi-Strauss (1968).

34 Ibid.; see also Dow (1986).

35 A number of versions of the myth exist in Java and Bali, written during the fifteenth and sixteenth centuries. For the oldest version, see Poerbatjaraka (1926).

36 For an interesting account of the identity of Rangda and Barong, see Belo (1949).

37 Lovric (1987: 300–17).

38 Essentially, *barong* is simply a generic term, usually followed by the name of an animal.

39 On these masked figures, their consecration and making, see Ramseyer (1977: 179–91).

40 For an evocative comparable description of the interrelationship of the unseen and seen among the Kakuli people of Papua Guinea, see Schieffelin (1976: 94–116).

41 On *rwa bhineda*, see Weck (1976: 94–116).

Chapter 8: The Process of Modernization

1 Hanna (1976: 60f).

2 *Puputan* (Balinese): 'until the last'; 'until the bitter end'. Despite the fact that several mass suicides are recorded in Balinese history, many Balinese connect the notion of *puputan* above all with the battle of the kingdom of Badung and the self-sacrifice of the lords and their subjects. The tragedy has been made known to a wider reading public through the novels by Baum (1937) and Vanvugt (1987).

3 Kol (1914: 385; transl. A. Leemann). On the subject of the *puputan* of Denpasar and Pamecutan and the background events, see ibid.: 385–413.

4 Adatrechtbundel XXXVII (1934: 478).

5 Feuilletau de Bruijn (1925: 68).

6 Geertz (1980: 254f).

7 Adatrechtbundel XXXVII (1934: 475).

8 Cf. chapter 4, p. 91, for the sphere of duty of a *bandesa* in pre-colonial times.

9 Adatrechtbundel XXXVII (1934: 475).

10 Schulte Nordholt (1986b: 27–34).

11 *Buku* (Indonesian): book; *banjar buku*: officially registered *banjar*.

12 *Matilas*: the right of commoners to choose or to change the rulers to whom they owed tribute and obedience (cf. chapter 4, p. 85).

13 Kol (1914: 427).

14 Ibid.: 417f, 424, 429ff.

15 Schulte Nordholt (1986a: 20).

16 Adatrechtbundel XXXVII (1934: 482–9).

17 Tarnutzer (1993: 64).

18 Geertz (1980: 256).

19 Schulte Nordholt (1988: 290–5).

20 For a detailed account of the political situation at the time of the Japanese occupation and the post-war period, see Tarnutzer (1993: 102–4).

21 Indonesian Independence was first declared in Jakarta on 17 August 1945. On Bali this was made public about a month later.

22 Dahm (1979: esp. 101).

23 Ibid.: 103.

24 Tarnutzer (1993: 114).

25 Dahm (1979: 206ff).

26 Such artists as Walter Spies, Adrien Le Mayeur de Merpres, Rudolf Bonnet and Theo Meyer.

27 Krause (1920); Yates (1933); Katz (1935); Covarrubias (1937); Baum (1937); Zoete and Spies (1938); Bateson and Mead (1942); McPhee (1947); Cartier-Bresson (1954); for further references see Vickers (1989).

28 Wälty (1990: esp. 127–30).

29 Travel abroad is taxed by the Indonesian government; for example, 1992: 250,000 rupiah (US$125) per person and per exit.

30 Leemann, Andreas Tarnutzer, Samuel Wälty, 'Bali: Tourismus und Entwicklung, in *Wirtschaft, Kultur und Entwicklung*, Materialien zum Internationalen Kulturaustausch, Nr. 28 (Institut für Auslandbeziehungen, Stuttgart, 1987), pp. 179–196, esp. pp. 182–184.

31 Kantor Statistik Propinsi Bali, *Statistik Bali: Statistical Yearbook of Bali* (Denpasar, 1991), pp. 360f.

32 Hakim and Wedja (1991: 81f).

33 Picard (1990: esp. 8).

34 Hidayat et al. (1991: esp. 74f). Of the total of 79 officially registered Balinese hotels (1991), only 16 were located in regencies other than Badung.

35 Helbig (1939: esp. 378; transl. A. Leemann). Like Helbig, many authors proceed on the assumption that Bali is a cultural enclave which is able to keep its fascinating peculiarity only in isolation. This premise is a construct which neglects the involvement of Bali in far-reaching historical processes (cf. chapter 4).

36 Hanna (1976: xi–xiii, esp. xiii).

37 McKean (1978: esp. 10).

38 Francillon (1975: 68).

39 Correct spelling: *gotong royong*. The concept includes mutual-aid activities to the advantage of the village or the *banjar* community.

40 O'Grady (1982: 26).

41 Scherrer (1986: 239; transl. A. Leemann).

42 Tjandrasari (1989: esp. 72).

43 Wälty (1990: 148).

44 I Gusti Ngurah Bagus, *Tempo*, 45 (1991), 77.

References

Adatrechtbundel XXXVII (1934) *Bali en Lombok*, Koninklijk Instituut voor de Taal-, Land- en Volkenkunde van Nederlandsch-Indië, Martinus Nijhoff.

Agung, I. A. A. Gde (1991) *Bali in the 19th Century*, Jakarta: Yayasan Obor Indonesia.

Alisjahbana, S. T. (1966) *Indonesia: Social and Cultural Revolution*, Kuala Lumpur, Singapore, London, Melbourne: Oxford University Press.

Ardika, W. and Bellwood, P. S. (1991) 'Sembiran: the beginnings of Indian contact with Bali', *Antiquity*, **65**: 221–32.

Backhaus, N. (1995) *Globalisierung, Entwicklung und traditionelle Gesellschaft. Chancen und Einschränkungen bei der Nutzung von Meeresressourcen auf Bali/Indonesien*, Inaugural-Dissertation, Geographisches Institut der Universität Zürich, Zürich.

Bandem, I. M. and deBoer, F. E. (1981) *Kaja and Kelod: Balinese Dance in Transition*, Oxford: Oxford University Press.

Bateson, G. and Mead, M. (1942) *Balinese Character: A Photographic Analysis*, New York: Academy of Science.

Baum, V. (1937) *A Tale from Bali* (English version of 'Liebe und Tod auf Bali'), London: Geoffrey, Bles.

Baum, V. (1946) *Liebe und Tod auf Bali*, reprinted Zürich: Büchergilde Gutenberg.

Bellwood, P. S. (1985) *Prehistory of the Indo-Malaysian Archipelago*, Sydney: Academic Press Australia.

Belo, J. (1949) *Bali: Rangda and Barong*, Monographs of the American Ethnological Society, no. 16, Seattle: University of Washington Press.

Belo, J. (1960) *Trance in Bali*, New York: Columbia University Press.

Bernet Kempers, A. J. (1991) *Monumental Bali: Introduction to Balinese Archaeology and Guide to the Monuments*, Berkeley, Cal. and Singapore: Periplus Editions.

Boon, J. A. (1976) 'The Balinese marriage predicament, individual, strategical, cultural', *American Ethnologist*, 3(2): 191–214.

Boon, J. A. (1977) *The Anthropological Romance of Bali, 1597–1972*, Cambridge, London, New York, Melbourne: Cambridge University Press.

Brinkgreve, F. (1987) 'The Cili and other female images', in E. Locher-Scholten and A. Niehof (eds), *Indonesian Women in Focus*, Dordrecht, Holland: Foris Publications, pp. 135–51.

Bundschu, I. (1985) *Probleme der agraren Grundbesitzverfassung auf Bali/Indonesien*, Mitteilungen des Instituts für Asienkunde, Nr. 143, Hamburg.

Bundschu, I. (1987) *Kooperation und landwirtschaftliche Entwicklung*, Mitteilungen des Instituts für Asienkunde, Nr. 165, Hamburg.

Cartier-Bresson, H. (1954) *Bali*, Paris: Robert Delpire.

Chinkah (1969) 'Statement of Chinkah on Bali', in *Indonesia*, Ithaca, N.Y.: Cornell University Press, vol. 7, pp. 83–122.

Connor, L. (1989) 'The unbounded self: Balinese therapy in theory and practice', in A. Marsella A. and G. White (eds), *Cultural Conceptions of Mental Health and Therapy*, Dordrecht: Reidel, pp. 251–67.

Connor, L., Asch, P. and Asch, T. (1986) *Jero Tapakan: Balinese Healer. An Ethnographic Film Monograph*, Cambridge: Cambridge University Press.

Covarrubias, M. (1937) *Island of Bali*, New York; Alfred A. Knopf; reprinted Kuala Lumpur, Singapore, Djakarta: Oxford University Press/P. T. Indira, 1972.

Dahm, B. (1979) 'Indonesien – ein historischer Rückblick', in H. Kötter, K. H. Junghans and R. O. G. Roeder (eds), *Indonesien*, Tübingen and Basel: Horst Erdmann Verlag, pp. 65–115.

Danandjaja, J. (1985) *Upacara-upacara lingkaran hidup di Trunyan, Bali/Life Cycle Ceremonies in Trunyan, Bali*, Jakarta: PN Balai Pustaka.

Departemen Pendidikan dan Kebudayan (1977) *Sejarah Nasional Indonesia*, jilid 1, Jakarta: PN Balai Pustaka, pp. 85–98.

Djelantik, A. A. M. (1986) *Balinese Painting*, Oxford: Oxford University Press.

Dow, J. (1986) 'Universal aspects of symbolic healing: a theoretical synthesis', *American Anthropology*, 88: 56–69.

Embassy of the Republic of Indonesia, Berne, Switzerland (1990–5) *Indonesia Information Bulletin*, Berne: Information Section.

Feuilletau de Bruijn, A. A. G. (1925) *Oost-Indische Krijgsgeschiedenis XI: De expeditie naar Bali in 1906*, Breda: Koninklijke Militaire Academie.

Forge, A. (1987) *Balinese Traditional Painting*, Sydney: Australian Museum.

Francillon, G. (1975) *Bali: Tourism, Culture, Environment*, Paris: UNESCO, mimeo.

Frank, J. (1961) *Persuasion and Healing: A Comparative Study of Psychotherapy*, New York: Schoken.

Geertz, C. (1959) 'Form and variation in Balinese village structure', *American Anthropologist*, **61**: 991–1012.

Geertz, C. (1963) *Agricultural Involution: The Processes of Ecological Change in Indonesia*, Berkeley, Los Angeles and London: University of California Press.

Geertz, C. (1970) *Peddlers and Princes*, Chicago: University of Chicago Press.

Geertz, C. (1973) 'Person, time, and conduct in Bali', in *The Interpretation of Cultures*, New York: Basic Books, pp. 360–411.

Geertz, C. (1980) *Negara: The Theatre State in Nineteenth-century Bali*, Princeton, N.J.: Princeton University Press.

Geertz, H. and Geertz, C. (1975) *Kinship in Bali*, Chicago and London: University of Chicago Press.

Gerdin, I. (1981) 'The Balinese Sidikara: ancestors, kinship and rank', in *Bijdragen tot de Taal-, Land- en Volkenkunde*, deel 137, le aflevering, 's-Gravenhage, pp. 17–34.

Ghaussy, A. Ghanie (1986) *Das Wirtschaftsdenken im Islam. Von der orthodoxen Lehre bis zu den heutigen Ordnungsvorstellungen*, Bern and Stuttgart: Verlag Paul Haupt.

Giddens, A. (1984) *The Constitution of Society*, Cambridge: Polity Press, in association with Oxford: Basil Blackwell.

Glover, I. C. (1979) 'The late prehistoric period in Indonesia', in R.B. Smith and W. Watson (eds), *Early South East Asia: Essays in Archeology, History and Historical Geography*, New York and Kuala Lumpur: Oxford University Press, pp. 167–84.

Goodman, N. (1985) *Ways of Worldmaking*, Indianapolis: Hackett; 14th edn, first edition 1978.

Goris, R. (1935) 'Het Godsdienstig Karakter der Balische Dorpsgemeenschappen', *Djawa*, **15**: 1–16.

Goris, R. (1954) *Prasasti Bali: Inscripties voor Anak Wungsu*, 2 vols, ed. Lembaga Bahasa dan Budaya, Masa Baru, Bandung: Universitas Indonesia.

Goris, R. (1984) 'The religious character of the village community', in J. L. Swellengrebel (ed.), *Bali: Studies in Life, Thought and Ritual*,

Reprints on Indonesia series, Dordrecht, Holland and Cinnaminson, USA: Foris Publications, pp. 77–100.

Guermonprez, J.-F. (1980) 'L'organisation villageoise à Bali', in *Cheminements: Ecrits offert à Georges Condominas*, Paris: ASEMI, XI, 1–4; 37–54.

Guermonprez, J.-F. (1984) *Les Pandé de Bali: la formation d'une 'caste' et l'imaginaire d'un titre*, Paris: Ecole des Hautes Etudes en Sciences Sociales, mimeo.

Guermonprez, J.-F. (1987) *Les Pandé de Bali: la formation d'une 'caste' et la valeur d'un titre*, Paris: Ecole française d'Extrême-Orient.

Guermonprez, J.-F. (1990) 'On the elusive Balinese village: hierarchy and values versus models', *Review of Indonesian and Malaysian Affairs*, 24: 55–89.

Hakim, J. and Wedja, I. N. (1991) 'Ada yang Sukses, Banyak yang Prihatin', *Tempo*, 45(5): 81–3.

Hall, K. R. (1985) *Maritime Trade and State Development in Early Southeast Asia*, Honolulu: University of Hawaii Press.

Hanna, W. A. (1976) *Bali Profile: People, Events, Circumstances (1001–1976)*, New York: American Universities Field Staff.

Hauser-Schäublin, B., Nabholz-Kartaschoff, M.L. and Ramseyer, U. (1991) *Textiles in Bali*, Berkeley, Cal. and Singapore: Periplus Editions.

Heger, F. (1902) *Alte Metalltrommeln aus Südostasien*, Leipzig.

Heine-Geldern, R. (1932) 'Urheimat und früheste Wanderungen der Austronesier', *Anthropos*, 27: 543–619.

Helbig, K. (1939) 'Bali. Eine tropische Insel landschaftlicher Gegensätze', *Zeitschrift für Erdkunde*, 7. Jahrgang, Heft 9/10: 357–78.

Hidayat, Y., Hakim, J., Silawati, Wedja, I Nengah and Pudyastuti, S. (1991) 'Bukan Sekadar Membangun Hotel', *Tempo*, 45(5): 70–5.

Hinzler, H. I. R. (1975) *Wayang op Bali*, The Hague: Nederlandse Vereniging voor het Poppenspel.

Hinzler, H. I. R. (1981) *Bima Swarga in Balinese Wayang*, Leiden: Koninklijk Instituut voor Taal-, Land- en Volkenkunde, vol. 90.

Hobart, A. (1987) *Dancing Shadows of Bali: Theatre and Myth*, London: Kegan Paul International.

Hobart, M. (1979) *A Balinese Village and its Field of Social Relations*, PhD. thesis, School of Oriental and African Studies, University of London, mimeo.

Hobart, M. (1980) *Ideas of Identity: The Interpretation of Kinship in Bali*, Denpasar: Universitas Udayana.

Holt, C. (1967) *Art in Indonesia: Continuities and Change*, Ithaca, N.J.: Cornell University Press.

244 *References*

Hooykaas, C. (1973a) *Religion of Bali*, Leiden: Brill.

Hooykaas, C. (1973b) *Kama and Kala: Materials for the Study of the Shadow Theatre in Bali*, Amsterdam: Verhandelingen der Koninklijke Nederlandse Akademie van Wetenschappen, deel 79.

Hooykaas, C. (1974) *Cosmogony and Creation in Balinese Tradition*, The Hague: Martinus Nijhoff.

Hooykaas, C. (1980) *Drawings on Balinese Sorcery*, Leiden: Brill.

Hooykaas, J. (1960) 'The changeling in Balinese folklore and religion', *Bijdraagen tot de Taal-, Land- en Volkenkunde*, 116(4): 424–36.

Howe, L. E. A. (1980) *Pujung: An Investigation into the Foundation of Balinese Culture*, PhD thesis, University of Edinburgh.

Howe, L. E. A. (1989) 'Hierarchy and equality: variations in Balinese social organization', in *Bijdragen tot de Taal-, Land- en Volkenkunde*, deel 145, le aflevering, 's-Gravenhage, pp. 47–71.

Jacques, M. (1986) *The Aesthetic Experience: An Anthropologist Looks at the Visual Arts*, London: Yale University Press.

Jones, R. (1973) 'Earl, Logan and "Indonesia" ', *archipel*, 6: 93–118.

Kantor Statistik Propinsi Bali (1988) *Statistik Bali / Statistical Year Book of Bali 1987*, Denpasar.

Kantor Statistik Propinsi Bali (1989) *Buku Saku, Statistik Bali / Statistical Pocketbook of Bali 1988*, Denpasar.

Kantor Statistik Propinsi Bali (1990) *Statistik Bali / Statistical Year Book of Bali 1989*, Denpasar.

Kantor Statistik Propinsi Bali (1991) *Statistik Bali / Statistical Year Book of Bali 1990*, Denpasar.

Kapferer, B. (1979) 'Introduction, ritual process and transformation of context', *Social Analysis* (University of Adelaide), no. 1: 3–19.

Kat, A. de (1921) 'De Leak op Bali', *Koninklijk Bataviaasch Genootschap*, no. 60: 1–43.

Katz, R. (1935) *Heitere Tage mit braunen Menschen*, Erlenbach: Eugen Rentsch.

Kleinman, A. (1980) *Patients and Healers in the Context of Culture*, Berkeley, Cal.: University of California Press.

Kol, H. H. van (1914) *Driemaal dwars door Sumatra en zwerftochten door Bali*, Rotterdam: W.L. & J. Brusse's Uitgeversmaatschappij.

Korn, V. E. (1932) *Het Adatrecht van Bali*, tweede herziene druk, 's-Gravenhage: G. Naeff.

Kraan, A. van der (1983) 'Bali: slavery and slave trade', in A. Reid, (ed.), *Slavery, Bondage and Dependency in Southeast Asia*, St Lucia: University of Queensland Press, pp. 315–40.

Krause, G. (1920) *Bali: Volk, Land, Tänze, Feste, Tempel*, 2 vols, Hagen: Folkwang.

Leemann, A. (1976) 'Bali, Auswirkungen des balinesischen Weltbildes auf verschiedene Aspekte der Kulturlandschaft und auf die Wertung des Jahresablaufes', *Ethnologische Zeitschrift Zürich*, II: 27–65.

Leemann, A. (1978) 'Sozioökonomische Erhebungen zum Tourismus in Bali (Indonesien)', *Zeitschrift für Fremdenverkehr*, 3: 19–23.

Leemann, A. (1979) *Bali – Insel der Götter*, Innsbruck: Pinguin-Verlag, and Frankfurt a.M.: Umschau-Verlag.

Leemann, A. (1989) *Internal and External Factors of Socio-cultural and Socio-economic Dynamics in Lombok (Nusa Tenggara Barat)*, Schriftenreihe Anthropogeographie, vol. 8, Zürich: Geographisches Institut der Universität Zürich.

Leemann, A. (1992) 'Zeremonien im Lebensablauf der Balinesen', *Geographica Helvetica*, 4:155–66.

Leemann, A., Tarnutzer, A. and Wälty, S. (1987) 'Bali: Tourismus und Entwicklung', in *Wirtschaft, Kultur und Entwicklung, Materialien zum Internationalen Kulturaustausch*, 28, Stuttgart: Institut für Auslandbeziehungen, pp. 179–96.

Lévi-Strauss, C. (1968) 'The effectiveness of symbols', in *Structural Anthropology*, Harmondsworth, Middx: Penguin, pp. 186–205.

Lovric, B. (1987) 'Rhetoric and reality: the hidden nightmare, myth and magic as representations and reverberations of morbid realities', unpublished PhD dissertation, Sydney.

Lovric, B. (1990) 'Medical semiology and the semiotics of dance', *Review of Indonesian and Malaysian Affairs*, 24: 136–94.

Lutz, C. (1985) 'Depression and the translation of emotional worlds', in A. Kleinman and B. Good (eds), *Culture and Depression: Studies in the Anthropology and Cross-culture Psychiatry of Affect and Disorder*, Berkeley, Cal.: University of California Press, pp. 35–62.

Maquet, Jacques (1986) *The Aesthetic Experience*, New Haven, Conn.: Yale University Press, pp. 103–17.

Marr, D. G. and Milner, A. C. (1986) *Southeast Asia in the 9th to 14th Centuries*, Canberra: Institute of Southeast Asian Studies/Research School of Pacific Studies, Australian National University.

McKean, P. F. (1978) 'Towards a theoretical analysis of tourism: economic dualism and cultural involution in Bali', in V. L. Smith (ed.), *Hosts and Guests: The Anthropology of Tourism*, Oxford: Basil Blackwell.

McPhee, C. (1947) *A House in Bali*, London: Victor Gollancz.

McPhee, C. (1966) *Music in Bali*, New Haven, Conn.: Yale University Press.

McPhee, C. (1970) 'The Balinese Wayang Kulit and its music', in J. Belo (ed.), *Traditional Balinese Culture*, New York: Columbia University Press, pp. 146–97; first published 1936.

Mershon, K. E. (1971) *Seven Plus Seven: Mysterious Life Ritual in Bali*, New York, Washington and Hollywood: Vantage Press.

Münster, S. (1628) *Cosmographia, Das ist: Beschreibung der gantzen Welt*, Basel; reprinted Lindau: Antiqua-Verlag, 1984.

N. N. (1991) 'Kompromi Budaya, Wisata, dan Bisnis', *Tempo*, 45(5): 76–80.

Needham, R. (1972) *Belief, Language and Experience*, Oxford: Basil Blackwell.

Nothofer, B. and Pampus, K.-H. (1988) *Bahasa Indonesia. Indonesisch für Deutsche*, Teil 1, 2. Aufl., Heidelberg: Julius Groos.

Obeyesekere, G. (1985) 'Depression, Buddhism, and the work of culture in Sri Lanka', in A. Kleinman and B. Good (eds), *Culture and Depression: Studies in the Anthropology and Cross-culture Psychiatry of Affect and Disorder*, Berkeley, Cal.: University of California Press, pp. 63–100.

O'Grady, R. (1982) *Third World Stopover: The Tourism Debate*, Geneva: World Council of Churches.

Parkin, D. (1985) 'Controlling the U-turn of knowledge', in R. Fardon (ed.), *Power and Knowledge*, Edinburgh; Scottish Academic Press, pp. 49–60.

Picard, M. (1990) 'Kebalian Orang Bali: tourism and the uses of "Balinese culture" in New Order Indonesia', *Review of Indonesian and Malaysian Affairs*, 24: 1–38.

Pigeaud, Th. G. (1960–3) *Java in the 14th Century: A Study in Cultural History*, 5 vols, The Hague: Martinus Nijhoff.

Pigeaud, Th.G. (1967) *The Literature of Java*, vol. 1, The Hague: Martinus Nijhoff.

Poerbatjaraka, R. M. Ng. (1926) 'De Calon Arang', *Bijdragen tot de Taal-, Land- en Volkenkunde*, 82: 110–80.

Poerwadarminta, W. J. S. (1976) *Kamus Umum Bahasa Indonesia*, Jakarta: PN Balai Pustaka.

Pudja, Gede (1963) *Sosiologi Hindu Darma*, Bali: Jajasan Pembangunan Pura Pita Maha.

Putra Agung, A. A. Gde (1976) *Silsilah Keluarga Raja Karangasem – Bali*, Denpasar: Fakultas Sastra Universitas Udayana, mimeo.

Putra, I. B. R. (1991) *Babad Dalem*, Denpasar: Upada Sastra.

Putra, I. G. A. (n.d.) *Upakara Yadnya*, Denpasar: Institut Hindu Darma.

Raffles, Th. S. (1817) *The History of Java*, 2 vols, London; reprinted Peting Jaya, Selangor, Malaysia: Oxford University Press, 1982.

Ramseyer, U. (1977) *The Art and Culture of Bali*, Oxford: Oxford University Press; reprinted 1986.

Ramseyer, U. (1983) *Bali, Insel der Götter*, Ausstellungsführer durch das Museum für Völkerkunde und das Schweizerische Museum für Volkskunde Basel; Basel: Museum für Völkerkunde.

Ramseyer, U. (1995) *Farewell to Paradise: New Views from Bali,* Basel: Museum für Völkerkunde.

Röll, W. (1979) *Indonesien. Entwicklungsprobleme einer tropischen Inselwelt,* 1. Aufl., Stuttgart: Ernst Klett.

Röll, W. and Leemann, A. (1987) *Agrarprobleme auf Lombok. Unter-suchungen zur Wirtschafts- und Sozialstruktur in Nusa Tenggara Barat, Indonesien,* Hamburg: Institut für Asienkunde.

Schaareman, D. (1986) *Tatulingga: Tradition and Continuity. An Investigation in Ritual and Social Organization in Bali,* Ethnologi-sches Seminar der Universität und Museum für Völkerkunde Basel, Basel: Wepf & Co. AG.

Scherrer, Ch. (1986) *Dritte-Welt-Tourismus. Entwicklungsstrategi-sche und kulturelle Zusammenhänge,* Berlin: Reimer.

Schieffelin, E. (1976) *The Sorrow of the Lonely and the Burning of the Dancers,* New York: St Martin's Press.

Schulte Nordholt, H. (1980) *Macht, Mensen en Middelen: Patronen van Dynamiek in de Balische Politiek, 1700–1840,* Doctoral thesis, Vrije Universiteit Amsterdam, mimeo.

Schulte Nordholt, H. (1986a) 'From contest state to "steady state" ', in *International Workshop on Indonesian Studies,* no. 1: *Balinese State and Society,* Leiden: Royal Institute of Linguistics and Anthro-pology, pp. 1–40.

Schulte Nordholt, H. (1986b) *Bali: Colonial Conceptions and Political Change, 1700–1940. From Shifting Hierarchies to 'Fixed Order',* in crasp 15, Rotterdam.

Schulte Nordholt, H. (1988) *Een Balische Dynastie; Hiërarchie en Conflict in de Negara Mengwi, 1700–1940,* Haarlem: Academisch Proefschrift, Vrije Universiteit te Amsterdam.

Setia, P. (1991) 'Rusak?', *Tempo,* 45(5): 69.

Slametmulyana, (1979) *Nagarakretagama dan tafsir sejarahnya,* Jakarta: bhratara.

Soejono, R. P. (1979) 'The significance of the excavations at Gilima-nuk (Bali)', in R. B. Smith and W. Watson (eds), *Early South East Asia: Essays in Archeology, History and Historical Geography,* New York and Kuala Lumpur: Oxford University Press, pp. 185–98.

Steiner, G. (1975) 'Linguistics and poets', in *Extraterritorial: Papers on Literature and the Language Revolution,* Harmondsworth, Middx: Penguin Books, pp. 135–62.

Stuart-Fox, D. J. (1974) *The Art of the Offering,* Penerbitan Yayasan Kanisius.

Stuart-Fox, D. J. (1987) 'Pura Besakih: a study of Balinese religion and society', unpublished dissertation, Australian National University.

Stutterheim, W. F. (1935) *Indian Influences in Old-Balinese Art*, London: The Indian Society.

Stutterheim, W. F. (1956) 'An ancient Bima cult', in *Studies in Indonesian Archaeology*, The Hague: Martinus Nijhoff, pp. 107–43.

Sudiyat, I. (1981) *Hukum Adat. Sketsa Asas*, Yogyakarta: Liberty.

Sugriwa, I G. B. (1990) *Babad Pasek*, Denpasar: Balimas.

Suryani, L. K. (1990) 'Psychiatrist, traditional healer and culture integrated in clinical practice in Bali', unpublished paper, Denpasar.

Swellengrebel, J. L. (ed.) (1984) *Bali: Studies in Life, Thought, and Ritual*, Reprints on Indonesia series, Dordrecht, Holland and Cinnaminson, USA: Foris Publications.

Tarnutzer, A. (1993) *Kota Adat Denpasar (Bali). Stadtentwicklung, staatliches Handeln und endogene Institutionen*, Schriftenreihe Anthropogeographie, vol. 12, Zürich: Geographisches Institut der Universität Zürich.

Tjandrasari, H. (1989) 'Social and cultural effects on the small-scale garment industry in Bali', in S. Soemardjan, K. Boender and P. Hesseling (eds), *Indonesian Design of Industrialism: Emerging Norms for Increasing Life Chances in the Nineties*, Indonesian-Dutch Symposium at the Roosevelt Study Center, Middelburg, part 1: pp. 60–73, mimeo.

Tri Husodo, P. (1990) 'Fatwa untuk Sebuah Pura Tua', *Tempo*, 9(28): 85.

Turner, V. (1964) 'An Ndembu doctor in practice', in A. Kiev (ed.), *Magic, Faith and Healing*, New York: Free Press, pp. 230–63.

Turner, V. (1985) *On the Edge of the Bush: Anthropology of Experience*, Tucson: University of Arizona Press.

Uhlig, H. (1988) *Südostasien*, 2. Aufl., Frankfurt a.M.: Fischer Taschenbuch Verlag.

Vanvugt, E. (1987) *De val van Bali*, Haarlem: In de Knipscheer.

Vickers, A. (1989) *Bali: A Paradise Created*, Ringwood: Penguin Books Australia.

Vickers, A. (1991) 'Cockfights and Anger in Bali: Representation in Action', unpublished paper, Princeton, N.J.

Virama Karya, P. N. (1971) *Masterplan*, Jakarta, mimeo.

Wälty, S. (1990) 'Weltbank und Weltenbummler im Paradies. Touristische Erschliessung und Regionalentwicklung in Bali', in S. Wälty, Th. Knecht and G. Seitz (eds), *Von nachholender zu nachhaltiger Entwicklung*, Schriftenreihe Anthropogeographie, vol. 10, Zürich: Geographisches Institut der Universität Zürich, pp. 127–50.

Wälty, S. (1995a) 'Origin and transformation of Bali Aga culture and society: an institutional analysis of communities in the early kingdoms', unpublished paper, prepared for the EUROSEAS conference, Leiden, 29 June–1 July.

Wälty, S. (1995b) *Kintamani: Dorf, Land und Rituale. Entwicklung und institutioneller Wandel in einer Bergregion auf Bali*, Inaugural Dissertation, Zürich: Geographisches Institut der Universität Zürich.

Weck, W. (1976) *Heilkunde und Volkstum auf Bali*, Jakarta: Bap Bali and Intermasa; first published 1937.

Wikarman, I Ny. (1993) *Ngodalin pada Sanggah Pemrajan*, Bangli: Yayasan Widya Shanti.

Wirz, P. (1928) *Der Totenkult auf Bali*, Stuttgart: Stecker & Schröder.

Wolters, O. W. (1982) *History, Culture and Region in Southeast Asian Perspectives*, Singapore: Institute for Southeast Asian Studies.

Yates, H. E. (1933) *Bali: Enchanted Isle. A Travel Book*, London: George Allen & Unwin.

Zoete, B. de, and Spies, W. (1938) *Dance and Drama in Bali*, London: Faber & Faber; reprinted Oxford: Oxford University Press, 1973.

Zoetmulder, P. (1965) 'Die Hochreligionen Indonesiens', in W. Stöhr and P. Zoetmulder (eds), *Die Religionen Indonesiens*, Stuttgart: Kohlhammer, pp. 231–79.

Zoetmulder, P. (1974) *Kalangwan: A Survey of Old Javanese Literature*, The Hague: Martinus Nijhoff.

Zollinger, H. (1845) 'Land-en Volkenkunde. Een uitstapje naar het eiland Balie', in *Tijdschrift voor Neerland's Indië*, zevende jaargang, vierde deel, pp. 1–56.

Zurbuchen, M. S. (1987) *The Language of Balinese Shadow Theatre*, Princeton, N.J.: Princeton University Press.

Index